oct 7
1953

20

Economic
Development

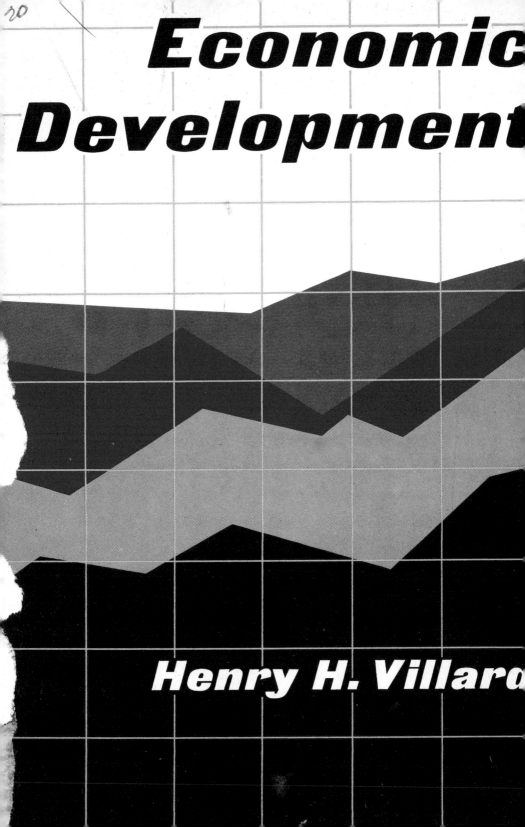

Henry H. Villard

ECONOMIC DEVELOPMENT

John Perry Miller, Consulting Editor

Other Rinehart Books Relating to Economic Development

Jack N. Behrman and Wilson E. Schmidt   *International Economics: Theory • Practice • Policy*

Ralph H. Blodgett   *Our Expanding Economy*

Michal Kalecki   *Theory of Economic Dynamics*

Alfred R. Oxenfeldt   *Economic Principles and Public Issues*

Alfred R. Oxenfeldt   *Economic Systems in Action*

Ellsworth Raymond   *Soviet Economic Progress*

E. Strauss   *Common Sense About the Common Market*

HENRY H. VILLARD

The City College of New York

ECONOMIC
DEVELOPMENT

RINEHART & COMPANY, INC., NEW YORK

HD
82
.V54E
1959

For the mate and the crew

PREFACE

The primary purpose of this book is to facilitate an extended consideration of economic development in the introductory economics course. The reasons why I believe such consideration desirable have been set forth in the Introduction and need not be repeated. Because much of the content of the volume is not readily available elsewhere, it may also be of use in advanced courses dealing with various aspects of development. The book does not, however, assume any previous training in economics, and will, I hope, be entirely comprehensible to the general reader. It is mainly for his benefit that the two chapters of Part I, dealing with measurement and differences in living levels, have been included.[1]

Most work in economic development has thus far been done in connection with the problems of underdeveloped areas. In contrast, half of this volume, comprising all of Part II, is concerned with the development of *developed* areas, especially Great Britain and the United States. Part III, constituting a quarter of the book, is devoted to the Soviet Union, because of its potential challenge and its importance as a case of unusually rapid development. Only the final quarter of the discussion, in Part IV, deals with underdeveloped areas. The individual sections are substantially independent, assuming no more than general familiarity with the national income concepts discussed in Part I.

I believe that the questions with which this book is concerned are of broad importance. Why has real income per man-hour over the last 75 years increased perhaps twice as rapidly in the United States as in Great Britain? Why has real income in the Soviet Union, in favorable periods at least, increased significantly faster than in the United States? What is the probable impact of increasingly rapid population growth in underdevel-

[1] Where students have had discussions of national income concepts so recently as to make review undesirable, deletion of some of the material covered in Part I may well be advisable.

oped areas on the prospects for rising living levels in such areas? While the discussion of these questions is designed primarily for students in introductory economics courses, I hope that it will prove to be of wider interest.

There is unfortunately little agreement among economists regarding the factors responsible for economic development. In the absence of agreement one alternative is to catalog all the factors that have ever been mentioned without attempting to indicate their relative importance. This definitely has not been done. For example, because there appears to me to be convincing evidence that changes in technology rather than in the quantity of capital have been mainly responsible for the improvement in our living level since the Civil War, I have presented the evidence that convinced me and have then devoted four chapters to research and innovation and one to capital formation. Again, because the prospects for underdeveloped areas seem to me to depend heavily on the rate of growth of their populations, I have devoted much attention to this aspect of the matter. Moreover, in the course of the discussion I have made it clear that I think our present research performance inadequate and continued population growth undesirable. In short, I have presented the factors which seem to me to be most important and have made no effort to conceal my appraisal of their significance. This is in the nature of a warning. The reasons for what I have done are set forth in the final section of the Introduction.

My debt to others is unusually large—and the need to disassociate those who helped from the errors and judgments of the volume unusually urgent. I have greatly benefited, undoubtedly in more ways than I am aware, from the comments of Lester V. Chandler, Albert G. Hart, John Kenneth Galbraith, Richard A. Musgrave, and Lloyd G. Reynolds. Special thanks are due to John Perry Miller, who read the entire manuscript in its final form. While Alfred R. Oxenfeldt has seen little of the final draft, it reflects discussions with him going back more than a decade. I am also greatly indebted to the Economics Department of City College, whose members have had my developing ideas inflicted on them in more ways and on more occasions than I can possibly remember. Singling out any member is undoubtedly unfair, but aid far beyond the call of duty requires special mention of Benjamin J. Klebaner, Robert B. McNee (in connection with Chapter 9), Edwin P. Reubens, and Elliot Zupnick. The suggestions of the editorial staff of the College Department of Rinehart & Company were most helpful.

In connection with the presentation of American achievements in Chapter 3, Simon Kuznets and the National Bureau of Economic Research were kind enough to allow me to make considerable use of the as yet unpublished revisions of Professor Kuznets' national income series. Ansley J. Coale and Edgar M. Hoover permitted me to see and utilize material from their unique study of interrelations of population growth and economic development in India, while that study was in galley proof. Adam Kaufman's help in preparing the statistical material used in Part III was invaluable, and the comments of Ellsworth Raymond most helpful. My ideas on underdeveloped areas profited from discussions with Hans Singer.

The contribution of my wife, no economist but a remarkable editor, has been immense. Were it not for her help and distraction, this volume would have appeared more rapidly and have been infinitely less comprehensible.

HENRY H. VILLARD

New York, N. Y.
January, 1959

CONTENTS

Introduction   *1*

Part I   **Measurement and Differences**
  1 Measurement of Living Levels   *15*
  2 Differences in Living Levels   *25*

Part II   **Developed Areas**
  3 What Has Been Accomplished   *35*
  4 The Role of Fundamental Research   *49*
  5 The Role of Practical Research   *61*
  6 The Role of Practical Research (Continued)   *71*
  7 The Role of Innovation   *82*
  8 The Role of Saving   *98*
  9 The Role of Natural Resources   *111*
 10 Other Factors Influencing Economic Development   *124*

Part III **Development Under Communism**
 11 The Russian Background   *137*
 12 What Russia Has Accomplished   *151*
 13 Factors Explaining Russian Development   *166*

Part IV   **Underdeveloped Areas**
 14 The Role of Population   *177*
 15 Population and Living Levels   *187*
 16 Production in Underdeveloped Areas   *197*
 17 Prospects for Underdeveloped Areas   *208*

Index   *219*

TABLES

1-1	National Income and Product in 1957	21
2-1	International Differences in Average National Income Per Person for the Period 1952-1954	26
2-2	Income Per Person by Continental Divisions	27
2-3	Gross National Product Per Person in Four European Countries as a Percentage of Gross National Product in the United States on Various Bases	28
2-4	Estimates of Relative Income Per Person	29
2-5	Comparisons of Income and Calories Consumed Per Person	31
2-6	Major Components of the American Diet in 1955	32
3-1	Physical Measures of American Economic Development	37
3-2	Income Measures of American Economic Development	40
3-3	Measures of British Economic Development	43
3-4	Tentative Estimates of Hours Worked and Hourly Income in Great Britain	44
3-5	Relative Economic Development	45
4-1	Research in the United States	54
4-2	Concentration of Research in Large Firms	55
6-1	Years Required to Offset Initial Income Declines	74
7-1	Automobile Profits Per Share	85
8-1	Sources and Uses of Saving in the United States	100
8-2	Distribution of New Saving Among Saver Groups	101
8-3	The Importance of Saving	104
8-4	Comparisons of Investment Rates	106
12-1	Production of Producers' Goods	153

12-2 Production of Consumers' Goods   154

12-3 Distribution of the Labor Force   155

12-4 Distribution of Nonagriculutral Employment in the USSR
      and USA   155

12-5 Uses of the National Income   156

12-6 Lag of Soviet Production behind American Production   158

12-7 Assumed Russian and American Development   159

14-1 Possible World Population   180

14-2 Resource Use with Various Populations   185

15-1 Income in 2000 Given Various Excesses of Income Increases
      Over Population Increases Starting with a 1950 Income of
      $50 Per Person   190

15-2 Income in 2000 under Various Conditions Starting with a
      1950 Income of $50 Per Person   190

15-3 Indian Income Growth with Different Rates of Population
      Growth   192

16-1 Agricultural Yields in 1947-1948   198

ECONOMIC DEVELOPMENT

INTRODUCTION

Interest in economic development is today greater than ever before. But systematic consideration of the factors responsible for economic development has not usually been a part of the subject matter of economics as reflected in the typical economics text. The purpose of this introduction is to consider, first, the relationship between economic development and the more usual content of economics and, second, the importance of economic development.

The subject matter of economics

Every economy starts with a certain quantity of factors—land, labor, and capital—that are needed to produce the goods and services which satisfy economic desires. The quantity of the productive factors is limited: there is an ultimate limit on the number of hours people *can* work and an even more immediate limit on the number of hours they are *willing* to work; the quantity of land, and particularly usable land, is limited; and the quantity of capital is limited, because capital goods are, in the last analysis, a combination of land and labor.[1] Thus, even in the richest country in the world, the scarcity of productive factors makes it impossible to produce all of the vast array of goods and services that people would

[1] The "capital" of a country includes those things—such as tools, locomotives, and factories—which help to produce additional goods and services. But a locomotive represents essentially iron ore (which an economist includes under the heading of "land") transformed by labor into a form that aids in further production.

1

like. A basic problem faced by all economies, therefore, is how to use scarce productive factors so as to produce those goods and services which will satisfy economic desires to the largest possible extent. This is sometimes called the problem of *resource allocation* or *economizing;* in a nutshell, it is the problem of how best *to allocate scarce means of production among alternative uses.*

Note that "economizing" in this technical sense involves deciding both *what* and *how much* to produce and ensuring that the desired production takes place with the *least* use of scarce resources. Under free enterprise the problem is solved—within certain restraints established by government—by having income recipients establish production objectives by the way in which they spend their income. These objectives are then met by entrepreneurs who undertake to combine the smallest possible quantities of scarce means of production to produce the most urgently desired goods —not in the fulfillment of any high social purpose but because this is the way to make the largest possible profit. *Provided* there is sufficient competition to keep profits to a reasonable level and *provided* one agrees that production objectives should be established by the way in which income recipients spend their income, it can be shown that, in striving to maximize their profits, entrepreneurs tend to bring about the allocation of resources which is socially most desirable.

Much of the analysis of economics has been developed in connection with the economizing process. This is the section which includes, for example, the determination of prices through the interaction of supply and demand, the establishment of the equilibrium of the firm through the interaction of marginal revenue and marginal cost, and the problems raised by imperfect competition and monopoly. As a result, it sometimes happens that the logic of resource allocation under free enterprise just outlined is not always successfully demonstrated in introductory courses; there have been students who failed to see the forest for the trees!

Closely related to what goods and services are to be produced is the question of how they are to be *distributed* to the land, labor, and capital responsible for their production. Broadly the answer is that income—and therefore the goods and services that income will buy—is distributed on the basis of the market price each factor receives when it sells its services. But, again broadly, the market price that a factor receives, when competition prevails, tends to correspond to its contribution to production. As a result, goods and services tend to be distributed among the productive factors in proportion to their contribution to production. It is necessary to use "broadly" in stating the matter because, while the general statement is certainly correct, factor payments in specific cases reflect the impact of such "imperfections" as ignorance, immobility, and lack of competition.

Economizing and distribution have historically constituted the most important part of the subject matter of economics. But more recently increasing attention has been paid to the factors responsible for determining the level of national income—and therefore the level of output of goods and services and the level of employment of the productive factors. The present interest in the level of income is the result of the severe fluctuation in income that occurred during the Great Depression which started in 1929. The study of economizing and distribution is sometimes called "microeconomics" because the emphasis is on the individual firm or the individual factor of production, while the study of the causes which determine the level of income is called "macroeconomics" because the emphasis is on output as a whole. In addition to these basic matters, the typical text in economics is likely to include an extended discussion of international trade and finance, a quick look at alternative economic systems and problems of war and defense, and—in recent volumes at least —a chapter or two on economic growth and development.

Economics and economic development

What is the relationship between economic development and the usual subject matter of economics which we have just outlined? One answer is that economics, especially microeconomics, has been interested in the behavior of an economy at an *instant* of time while economic development is interested in the behavior of an economy over a *period* of time. While the emphasis of this distinction is valid, its logic should not be pushed too far. For a period of time is nothing but the sum of a series of instants of time. This means that the matters with which this volume is concerned—research performance, the effectiveness of innovation, rates of capital formation, and the like—can all be conceived of as involving nothing except the effectiveness of resource allocation at an instant of time. But while they can be conceived of in this way, they are not subjects typically considered in the usual discussions of resource allocation; in fact, they are often specifically excluded from consideration. Nor are they matters on which much insight is provided by the tools that economics has thus far developed.

Actually, economic development is probably more closely related to macroeconomics than to microeconomics. Once the factors responsible for determining the level of income at a point of time had been formulated, it was logical to go on to consider what was involved in achieving a steady and stable growth of income over a period of time. This is a matter which has received considerable attention, especially of a theoretical nature, in recent years. But while it is in form similar to the subject of this volume, it is in substance rather different. Such work as has been done has concentrated mainly on discovering patterns of growth capable of explaining unemployment and depressions. This volume, on the other hand, is primarily concerned with *the reasons for differences in the rate of increase in the output of goods and services when the productive factors are fully employed.*

Economic performance vs. economic understanding

Is this rather unusual emphasis on economic development justified? Should development receive this much attention? If it is felt that a course in economics should deal with matters about which economists have an agreed body of *understanding* to convey, the present emphasis is *not* justified; we know extraordinarily little of what is involved in economic development. (Nor am I so vain as to believe that this volume will noticeably alter the situation!) But if we instead judge the importance of economic matters in terms of *potential improvement in economic performance,* we reach rather different conclusions. To understand what is involved, let us first consider the benefits likely to result from improved performance in the areas of economics discussed in the typical economics text and then consider the benefits likely to result from more rapid economic development.

Possible improvements in economic performance

Let us start with a word of warning: because economists have been more interested in understanding than evaluating, there is no general agreement regarding possible improvements in economic performance. But it is fairly obvious that improvements in the economizing process are likely to be quite limited in scope. Advertising, for example, is often accused of being economically wasteful. But the over-all cost amounts to about 3 per cent of the national income; my guess is that perhaps two thirds of this cost provides information and supports media (such as newspapers, magazines, and radio and television stations) that we should want in any event. Again I am convinced that the elimination of corporate monopoly profits would increase the consumption of those not owning monopolies by no more than 1 or 2 per cent.[2] Or, turning to distribution, suppose we were to agree that an income range of $2,000 to $25,000 would be socially desirable (to provide appropriate incentives and rewards). If the present distribution were altered by cutting everyone back to a maximum of $25,000, the consumption of those with incomes under $25,000 would be increased by no more than 3 or 4 per cent. Once more, there

[2] The reasoning leading me to this conclusion is presented in the *Political Science Quarterly,* September, 1957.

is no doubt that our present program of aid to farmers is wasteful; but agriculture as an industry today accounts for less than 5 per cent of the national income, so that it is obvious that the waste involved must be small on any over-all basis. For the same reason the impact of the tariff in reducing specialization (and therefore productivity)—in the case of the United States at least—cannot be of major quantitative significance, as commodity exports are currently rather less important than agriculture. (This, of course, is a reflection of the fact that the United States has within its own boundaries the most important free-trade area the world has ever known; the potential advantages from the reduction of tariffs within Europe are undoubtedly significantly higher.)

In short, I find it hard to believe that economic performance in the United States can be increased more than perhaps 20 per cent by improvements in the aspects of economizing and distribution discussed in the typical economics text. If improvements capable of bringing about a larger increase in performance are to be achieved, I believe that it will be necessary to go beyond the conventional criticisms into areas where economics, in its desire to be "scientific," has been quite reluctant to travel. Of course, if our scope is broad enough, many improvements in the microeconomic area are conceivable. To what extent, for example, can retailing costs be significantly reduced by relatively small expenditures on consumer education? To what degree are costs in general—and selling expenses in particular—socially necessary in an economy where competition is never— well hardly ever—perfect? Are large cities really economic or do they merely appear so because we count as "productive" much activity—such as expensive transportation systems—which merely serves to offset their disadvantages? How important is the economic waste involved in racial discrimination? Or in premature obsolescence due to unnecessary style changes?

Clearly, to repeat, there is no doubt much that can be done to improve performance in the microeconomic area. But quantitatively significant improvements are, I believe, likely to involve matters which have received little attention from economists (largely because nasty questions of relative values are involved) and even less from writers of our typical texts. Improvements in the areas covered in our usual texts are, I am convinced, likely to be of small importance. The student should, however, recall the warning regarding the tentativeness of these estimates—and the economist who disagrees should produce better estimates!

The waste that can occur in the macroeconomic area is of a different order of magnitude. Valued in the prices which prevailed in 1954 the gross national product—which measures at one and the same time the total production of goods and services of an economy and the total income that is generated in the process—amounted to $182 billions in 1929 and to $238 billions in 1941.[3] Between these years income increased by $56 billions, or an average of $4.5 billions a year.[4] Suppose steady growth at the average rate of $4.5 billions a year had taken place over the period. Then income would have been $186.5 billions in 1930, $191 billions in 1931, and $195.5 billions in 1932, continuing until $233.5 billions was reached in 1940 and $238 billions in 1941. On this basis income over the period would have averaged $210 billions. Actually, because of the Depression, income in 1930 was only $164.5 billions and in 1940 had reached only $206 billions, so that the actual average for the eleven years following 1929 was only $163 billions. This means that during the eleven years in question production was 10 per cent less than it had been in 1929 and over 22 per cent less than it would have been had growth continued without interruption. In the worst year—1933—output was 30 per cent below what it had been in 1929 and 37 per cent less than it would have been with uninterrupted growth. It is obvious that the waste involved in a severe depression is immense—and these estimates are without any of the difficulties and ambiguities raised by those presented in the previous paragraphs. It is small wonder that after 1929 the attention of economists was overwhelmingly concentrated on efforts to determine what was required to eliminate severe depressions.

On the other hand, gross national product in 1954 prices was $283 billions in 1946 and $402 billions in 1956. With uninterrupted growth it should have averaged $342 billions. Actually it averaged over $335 billions, so that measured in this way the loss of output in recent years was only in the order of 2 per cent. Not too much weight should be placed on this estimate; it is possible that changes—such as devices to speed up transfers between jobs—might permit us to do even better in the future than the best that we have thus far achieved in periods when labor was "fully employed." Even so it is obvious that, in the postwar period, waste in the macroeconomic area has not been serious.

The importance of economic development

Thus far our approach has been negative. We have suggested the importance of economic development by pointing out that, apart from severe depressions, improvements in economic performance in the areas covered in the usual economics course are likely to be relatively limited. They are, moreover, one-time improvements; once achieved they cannot be repeated. Now let us look at the positive side by examining some of the

[3] The concept of "gross national product" is discussed in Chapter 1. As unemployment had not been completely eliminated in 1941, the estimates are conservative. The income totals are from the *Survey of Current Business*, July, 1958, Table 7.

[4] To simplify, compounding has been disregarded.

benefits of rapid economic development. Let us start with some estimates of the quantity of goods and services that the American economy has produced, is producing, and is likely to produce in the future. As before, to make the quantity of such goods and services comparable, we shall value them in each period at the prices that prevailed in a particular year—in this case 1950. Thus, although we will be dealing with dollar totals, they are totals which summarize *actual quantities* of goods and services *unaffected by changes in prices.*

On this basis the United States in 1875 was a country of 46 million people with an annual income of $16 billions, which gave an average income per worker of about $1,050 and per person of about $350. To earn this income the average worker put in roughly 6 eleven-hour days and received 33¢ for each hour he worked. Seventy-five years later, in 1950, we were a nation of over 150 millions with a total income of $240 billions, which works out to an average per worker of almost $4,000 and an average per person of almost $1,600. Further, to earn this income the average worker put in 5 eight-hour days and received just under $2 for each hour he worked. In short, each hour that the average American chose to work in 1950 yielded him almost *six times* as large a quantity of goods and services as the hour put in by his forefather in 1875.[5]

Increases of this magnitude are neither universal nor automatic. Great Britain, for example, had a level of living in 1875 that was not greatly different from that of the United States. But a slower rate of economic development—partly for reasons beyond British control—has led to an average income level in 1950 that is roughly half that of the United States, a work week that is a day longer, and a threefold rather than a sixfold increase in income per hour of work.[6]

Let us look to the future. If the rate of development achieved from 1875 to 1950 continues until the year 2000, then in that year the average income per person—still measured in terms of the prices that prevailed in 1950—will be over $4,700, the average income per worker almost $9,500, and the average income per family (allowing for some further increase in the percentage of those working) perhaps $15,000. Moreover, all this will be achieved with a work week of not more than thirty hours.

It is important to realize that differences in rates of economic development which produce such spectacular differences over time may in any year appear trivial; it is the compounding which counts. Thus the difference between Great Britain and the United States in the behavior of income per man-hour—perhaps the most significant single measure of economic development—is the result of a 1½ per cent rather than a 3 per cent average annual increase in income per man-hour. In discussing pos-

5, 6 For details, see Chapter 3.

sible improvements in performance in the microeconomic area, we concluded that 20 per cent might well be as much as could be realized by eliminating the usual criticisms of economizing and distribution—and once achieved the improvement could not be repeated. Yet the difference that results from a 3 per cent rather than a 1½ per cent annual increase in income per man-hour, when compounding is taken into account, is 20 per cent in a *single decade*—and the difference can be repeated in each subsequent decade. When such small variations in any year can lead to such spectacular differences over time, the importance of understanding the factors responsible for rapid economic development appears rather obvious.

Affluence and economic development

Recently the opposite point of view has appeared. The argument has been put forth that America has been so affluent that, at least at the margin, production no longer satisfies *real* wants but only those which are "contrived" or "created." [7] If the wants are not real, why should we seek by rapid economic development to produce the goods to satisfy such wants? We may admit at once that increases in production do not guarantee that people will be "happier" or "better off" in any general sense; our desires can always increase faster than our ability to produce. [8] What, however, is meant by "wants being created"? As man is a social animal, his wants are obviously influenced by the society in which he lives; Robinson Crusoe's wants changed the day that Friday hove into sight! Determining pristine wants, uninfluenced by social pressures, is equivalent to determining what heredity would have made of a man if he had not been influenced by his environment. If this is the meaning of "created," it is undeniably true. It is also undeniably true that there is a sense in which "production creates the wants that it satisfies." For example, I would not today list the services of a fountain of youth among the things I presently want. But let some clever entrepreneur develop such a fountain—and have its merits attested to by the medical profession—and I would indeed add its services to my Christmas list. In fact, so long as a product is advertised—or, carrying the matter to its logical conclusion, so long as it is made by a specialized producer who stands to gain from my purchasing it—it is impossible to deny that, perhaps subtly or even subliminally, I may have had my "wants created." Hence the charge is at once both true and, for practical purposes, meaningless.

What one really wants to know is how many of the two thirds of all workers who received incomes below the national average of $4,000 in

[7] John Kenneth Galbraith, *The Affluent Society* (Boston: Houghton Mifflin, 1958).
[8] This point is elaborated in Chapter 1.

1950 felt themselves to be affluent, or felt that the wants they could not satisfy existed only because they had been "contrived" or "synthesized" by clever advertising. I rather suspect that affluence is a matter worried about almost exclusively by people whose income today equals or exceeds the income that rapid economic development may provide for the average person in 2000! There is, second, no reason why the increasing capacity to produce provided by economic development should be used entirely to increase production; it may be used equally well to increase leisure. In fact, since 1875 about one third of our enlarged capacity has gone into a reduction of hours. Perhaps the present balance between goods and leisure is not perfect, but the continuing increase in the percentage of women working and of men holding more than one full-time job suggests that the desire for additional goods—"contrived" though it may be —remains strong.

Many of those who worry about affluence are concerned because they feel that the present emphasis on private production interferes with the attainment of socially desirable objectives. For example, they argue for a major increase in the nondefense activities of government in order to achieve a more desirable balance between the public and private sector of the economy—and especially for a massive expansion in the area of education and research to eliminate poverty and toil and to allow us as a nation to play our proper role in the expansion of knowledge. But changes of this sort will be promoted by—in fact probably cannot in practice be achieved without—economic development. Admittedly the changes in question are *possible* without development; we shall see that relatively far more resources have been devoted to education in Russia than in the United States. And it may be that development will achieve little; perhaps our "contrived" desire for a dishwasher which taxes now prevent us from meeting will in time be replaced by an equally urgent and equally "contrived" desire for a helicopter. But even if relative public and private shares remain the same, rapid economic development at the very least means that the absolute quantity of production to meet public needs will rapidly increase. Hence I believe that the best argument for a massive expansion of education and research is the contribution it will make to economic development and the best way of achieving a massive expansion is to make sure that economic development is rapid!

Nothing in what has just been said should be construed as arguing for the importance of the production of cars with chrome-plated fins or of juke boxes decorated with neon lights. We may conceivably use our increasing capacity to produce in a deplorable fashion. But it is equally true that a vast increase in our capacity to produce—which is what is meant by economic development—is essential, even for the United States considered separately from the rest of the world, if we are to achieve the sort of America most of us would like—without poverty, without slums, without burdensome toil, and with *both* the goods *and* the leisure to achieve what I, at least, would consider affluence.

Economic development in world perspective

We cannot, moreover, consider the United States apart from the rest of the world: we cannot, whether we would like to or not, proceed in splendid isolation. We are engaged in a struggle with Communism. It seems likely that the purely military phase will come to an end in the not too distant future simply because an all-out nuclear war is likely to become too devastating to contemplate. To the extent that this is correct, the struggle—if it is to continue at all—must become primarily economic. While it is true that, during the military phase, the speed of modern war is such that existing weapons rather than productive capacity may be decisive, productive capacity returns to its former importance as soon as the struggle becomes primarily economic. As the Soviet Union is developing—and, it will be suggested, is likely to continue to develop—unusually rapidly, the need for rapid economic development if America is to keep pace seems obvious.

Finally, even if our struggle with Communism were to come completely to an end—and even more so as long as it continues—it seems to me that we must inevitably concern ourselves with world-wide economic development. I find it hard to believe that we can expect to progress in perhaps 40 years to a $9,500 average income per worker for a thirty-hour week unless the rest of the world is also making steady, even if less rapid, progress. Arnold Toynbee, the historian, has predicted that, in the perspective of history, the twentieth century will be notable, not for its wars or its atomic bombs, but for "having been the first age since the dawn of civilization . . . in which people dared to think it practicable to make the benefits of civilization available to the whole human race." To do so seems to me less an opportunity than a necessity if we are to look forward to the steady progress for ourselves and for our children which we tend to take for granted, but which has as yet been realized in only a small part of the world. As soon as one starts to consider what is involved in world-wide economic development, the optimism generated by past achievements—and the concern about affluence—disappears rapidly and completely.

The role of value judgments in economics

As the previous sections have shown, this book deals with many matters where value judgments play an essential role—to a degree unusual in a volume designed for possible use in an introductory course. For this there are a number of reasons. In considerable part it results from the nature of the subject matter. Because economics has not provided either a kit of analytical tools or a body of empirical data for dealing with problems of economic development, the presentation must inevitably involve a greater exercise of judgment than when generally accepted tools and data are available—just as the analysis of business fluctuations depended heavily on judgment before Keynesian tools and national income data became available. Undoubtedly there are economists who feel that introductory courses in economics should confine themselves to those areas where there is a considerable agreed body of understanding to be conveyed to the student. Whether this is desirable is, of course, itself a value judgment. My own is that, in selecting the subject matter for the introductory course, economics might usefully put more stress on *those areas where significant improvements in economic performance are possible.* There is, unfortunately, little correlation between what we happen to know at this time and what we need to know to improve economic performance in the future.

It may well be that this emphasis will tend to distress those who feel that economics should be "scientific" in the sense of confining itself to presenting results which have been empirically verified or conclusions which follow inevitably from stated assumptions—in short, that economics should be "positive." Obviously we need better tools and better data—*especially* in the study of economic development! It is, therefore, easy to sympathize with those who stress the importance of "positive" economics. The difficulty with the purely "positive" approach, however, is that, if followed logically, it severely limits the help that economics can give regarding the day-to-day decisions that every economy has in fact to make. Nothing could be said, for example, about the over-all desirability of free enterprise, because the extent to which production objectives should be established by consumer spending and income distributed in proportion to a factor's productive contribution obviously involves a value judgment. Admittedly in the final analysis what is sometimes called "normative" economics is nothing but "positive" economics plus value judgments. But in relating the two to concrete problems, "normative" economics provides insights that are not otherwise likely to be available.

One result is that, even where texts profess a "positive" approach, "normative" matters do receive consideration. In fact, what frequently happens is that, in attempting to appear "scientific," value judgments are concealed rather than avoided. But I am rather sceptical as to whether any particular purpose is served by making the student ferret out the author's value judgments. In any event this is an activity that will require little of the student's time in this volume. At the risk of considerable repetition I have throughout tried to indicate wherever judgments appear to be involved—especially where my judgment appears to differ from the consensus of economists. All that "scientific" method requires, as I see it, is a careful distinction between objective knowledge and value judgments. Whether I have succeeded in keeping the two sufficiently separate, and in labelling the value judgments sufficiently frequently, to qualify this book as "scientific" is up to the reader to decide.

PART ONE

MEASUREMENT AND DIFFERENCES

CHAPTER ONE

MEASUREMENT OF LIVING LEVELS

The meaning of economic development

This volume deals with "economic development." With what, then, is it concerned? "Development," defined by the dictionary as "passage from a lower to a higher stage," is a term which implies improvement. We could, of course, have dodged the issue by entitling this section "economic change." Sooner or later, however, someone is going to want to know whether the change has been for better or worse, so that this would at best postpone the matter. The problem might as well be faced at the start.

Note that this section does not deal with development in general. Whether we have been moving toward a "better" state is quite beyond its scope. All we are concerned with is whether we are better off from an *economic* point of view. Unfortunately no easy or complete definition of "economic" is possible; the essence of the problem, however, is whether we are better off in *material terms*—in terms of the *goods and services* that are available to us. Even from an economic point of view this is not enough; we must also take into account the *effort and sacrifice* that go into obtaining such goods and services and the number of us that are involved in producing them. Clearly more goods obtained by more of us working longer hours or under more adverse conditions would not involve improvement. But when we *obtain more goods and services for less effort and sacrifice per person,* then we may say that there has been economic development.

When economic development occurs, does it mean that we are necessarily better off in any general sense? Certainly not. In fact, for those who are convinced that it is easier for a camel to get through the eye of a needle than for a rich man to get to heaven, it seems to follow as a matter of simple logic that the more economic development we have, the farther we are from heaven! There is no doubt that our desires can increase quite as fast as—or for that matter a lot faster than—we can develop economically. It is perfectly possible, therefore, that the more material things we have, the more we will want—and the more unhappy we will become. Moreover, we may use our increased productive capacity to produce all sorts of things which—for noneconomic reasons—most of us would agree were completely undesirable. Does economic development, therefore, mean only more chrome, more neon lights, more singing commercials, and bigger and better upswept fins with no assurance that anyone will actually be any happier? It *can* mean nothing more; *as economists,* we would say that such changes represented economic development. So long as we are able to produce more goods and services which satisfy our material desires with less effort and sacrifice, economic development has taken place, even if the result is to make us less happy than ever before. In short, economic development is like scientific knowledge: it may be used for good or evil.

But it can be used for good; economic development can mean more leisure, better health, more time to read—even more time to contemplate the good life. In other words, economic development is at best but a means to an end, not an end in itself. But because economic development is a highly important means toward improvement in general well-being, it is worth extended consideration even if we can offer no guarantee whatsoever that improvement in general well-being will in fact result if in practice the opportunities made possible by economic development are misused.

Effort and sacrifice

In measuring economic development we will be concerned mostly with measuring the quantity of goods and services that are available, disregarding, in the main, the effort and sacrifice side of the picture. This will be particularly true in Part IV, which deals with underdeveloped areas; but even in Part II, which deals with development under free enterprise, effort and sacrifice will receive little consideration. To this there is one important exception: wherever possible, especially in Chapter 3, which summarizes what has been achieved in developed free enterprise areas, we shall attempt to bring hours worked into the picture as the best available approximation of effort and sacrifice. We shall find that their inclusion is far more than a refinement; economic performance in terms of goods and services per man-hour often differs significantly from goods and services per person or per worker.

There are several reasons why effort and sacrifice will receive, in general, relatively little attention. One is that information regarding hours worked is not always available for the United States and only rarely available for other countries. But, in addition, the very fact that hours worked are only an approximation of effort and sacrifice itself raises complications which are hard to resolve. There can be no doubt that the intensity of effort per hour can vary over a wide range, and the sacrifice may also differ greatly with differences in the conditions under which the work takes place: intense labor at an uncongenial task under adverse conditions can involve vastly more effort and sacrifice than congenial work at a reasonable pace in pleasant surroundings. On the other hand, it is quite possible that the practical difference is exaggerated. One man's meat is the next man's poison: some find a routine job with complete freedom from responsibility after the whistle blows at five o'clock highly desirable, while others find routine work utterly boring. People, of course, tend to take the job which, other things equal, they find most congenial in the light of their tastes and interests. As a result, differences in effort and sacrifice among jobs are obviously far less than if the jobs had been assigned at random to people with the same tastes and interests.

Even so there is no denying that many jobs have been in the past, and today remain, disagreeable—though for this very reason they are often well paid relative to the skills and abilities that are required. The real issue, however, is whether there has been any general change in the effort and sacrifice involved in work beyond that measured by changes in hours worked. Perhaps there was a period during industrialization when effort and sacrifice per hour worked increased; certainly the picture of the worker as no more than a cog in an assembly line set to operate at the fastest possible pace has troubled many observers. But the contrast with the past may well have been exaggerated, as the drudgery, hardship, and loneliness of agricultural work probably never made as good copy as the iniquities of the factory system. In any event, at least in developed economies, labor has become so expensive that management tries hard to eliminate routine tightening of nuts—and to make such routine work as is necessary as congenial as possible. Further, an important gain of unionization is the control it gives over working conditions—directly to unionized workers and indirectly to those in other areas.

In short, in my judgment it seems unlikely that the effort and sacrifice involved in an hour of work has, in the United States at least, increased. Thus it seems possible to measure effort and sacrifice, approximately, by changes in hours worked. This does not mean that this whole matter is not worth more attention than can be given it in this volume. When comparisons between countries are made, for example, it is a matter which must inevitably be considered: to what extent do the far longer hours worked even in nationalized industry in Great Britain compared with the United States reflect a British preference for long hours at low intensity rather than short hours at high intensity? It would be desirable to know far more than we do about what is involved. In contrast to the capitalist who can supply his capital without himself being present, laborers have to be present when the labor they sell is performed, so that the character of working conditions is of real significance in any full analysis of economic development. In quantitative and historical terms, however, concentration on the output of goods and services appears permissible. Man probably has never worked consistently more than 80 hours a week and even today on a full-time basis rarely works less than 40; changes in the quantity of goods and services have been of far greater magnitude.

Standard of living and level of living

It is the quantity of goods and services available to a person in any period which determines his "level of living." What we are concerned with is how a person actually lives, not how he might like to live. "Standard of living" formerly was often used by economists to refer to the way a person actually lived, but "standard" may be held to imply what a man should have, rather than what he actually has. Hence the neutral word "level" has come to be substituted in economics for "standard" when the reference is to actual living conditions; we will conform to the prevailing usage.

Measuring living levels

How can living levels be measured—in other words, how can we measure the quantity of goods and services available? What we are most interested in is the quantity that becomes available during a period of time such as a year rather than the quantity available at a point of time. Quantity at a point of time represents all production surviving from the past and is, therefore, a measure of *wealth*. While knowledge of the *stock* of wealth is important for certain purposes, it is, in general, less useful than estimates of the *flow* of production during a period of time, which we shall see is equal to the *income* of the period. For it is the flow of production which determines what can be continuously utilized from period to period without depleting the stock of goods inherited from the past. There is by no means complete agreement as to how the flow of production may best be measured, but by far the most widely used estimates in the United States at the present time are those published by the Department of Commerce. Let us, therefore, first see how the estimates of the Department are constructed, and then consider some of the implications of the method that have troubled other estimators.

We may start with the fact that in any period—conventionally a year—vast quantities of goods and services are produced. But many of them are used up during the period in creating other goods and services. If wheat is milled into flour and the flour made into bread, we obviously do not want to total the value of the wheat, the flour, and the bread. To do so would involve double counting and overstate the production achieved. There are two conceptual ways in which such duplication may be eliminated. We may include in the total only the *value of output at the point of final purchase*—as when bread is sold to the housewife —and in this way eliminate intermediate production. Or we may measure the *value added at each stage of production*. For, in the case of bread, the sum of the original value of the wheat (all of which is added by the farmer) and the value added by the miller to the wheat, by the baker to the flour, by the distributor to the bread as it comes from the bakery, and by the retailer to the bread bought at wholesale will be equal to the value of the bread sold to the housewife.[1] When double counting is eliminated by one or the other of these techniques, we obtain the *gross national product*, which is nothing more than the *total production of all goods and services, adjusted to eliminate duplication*. This is the broadest available measure of production; it is quite widely used, usually being referred to as the GNP.

Net national product and national income

In any period the capital equipment of a country deteriorates. Mostly this is the result of the actual use of such equipment to make the production of the period possible. But equipment also deteriorates even when it is standing idle or, as a result of the availability of new and im-

---

[1] To make the two approaches completely identical it is necessary that increases or decreases in inventories of unfinished goods be treated similarly. This can be done, for example, by treating inventories as a special point of final purchase or a special stage at which value is added. Detailed discussion of the handling of inventories does not appear warranted in this volume.

proved technology, becomes less valuable even though unchanged physically. If businessmen are to maintain their capital intact—so that they have as much capital at the end of the period as they had at the start—they must systematically set aside *depreciation allowances* equal to the decline in value of their capital occurring in each period. Actually the allowances used by the Department of Commerce are mainly those which the Treasury permits corporations to charge off before becoming liable for corporate income tax, as the Treasury is our main source of information regarding depreciation allowances. One difficulty to which this procedure gives rise is that the allowances permitted by the Treasury are based on the *original cost* of the equipment and are, therefore, inadequate when prices are rising. More generally, such allowances are inevitably subject to a considerable margin of error, as they attempt to estimate the economic rather than the physical life of the capital equipment involved.[2] In any event, however calculated, depreciation allowances, together with certain other minor deductions, are collectively called *capital consumption allowances* and have to be deducted from gross national product to determine the quantity of goods and services that are available as a result of the production of any year without reducing the stock of capital in existence at the start of the period; this is called the *net national product.*

One further deduction is necessary. In Department of Commerce usage, the contribution of government to production in any period is taken as equal to government purchases of goods and services (including the services of those employed by government), which we may for short call the cost of government. But part of the cost of government is met by taxes on the businesses of the country. These *indirect business taxes* have to be deducted from the net national product if we are to get the goods and services which directly accrue to the general public (including in such goods and services that part of the cost of government which is paid for by the general public rather than by business). The result is called the *national income.* Table 1-1 illustrates the magnitudes involved.

Thus in 1957 *gross national product,* or the total value of all the goods and services produced by the American economy with duplication eliminated, was $440 billions. Of this, business as a whole set aside $37½ billions in *capital consumption allowances* to offset the depreciation of its capital equipment, so that *net national product,* or the production available without depleting capital, amounted to $402½ billions. Of this $38½ billions was contributed by business, in the form of *indirect business taxes,* toward meeting the cost of government, so that the *national income,* or the amount accruing to the general public, was

[2] The adequacy of depreciation allowances is considered further in Chapter 8 in connection with the concept of net saving.

$364 billions. Of this total, in turn, $284½ billions was spent on personal consumption, $31 billions was saved and invested (gross investment less capital consumption allowances), and the remaining $48½ billions went to pay for that part of the cost of government which was not covered by indirect business taxes.

TABLE 1-1. NATIONAL INCOME AND PRODUCT IN 1957

(Billions of Dollars)

Gross National Product	440.3	Gross National Product	440.3
Capital consumption allowances	37.7	Personal consumption expenditures	284.4
Net National Product	402.6	Gross investment	68.8
Indirect business taxes	37.6	Government purchase of goods	
Minor items	1.0	and services	87.1
National Income	364.0		
Compensation of employees	254.6		
Rental income of persons	11.8		
Net interest	12.6		
Income of unincorporated enterprises	43.0		
Income of corporations	41.9		

SOURCE: *Survey of Current Business,* July, 1958, Tables 1, 2, and 4.

Why are three concepts necessary? Because they illustrate different aspects of the quantity of goods and services being produced. In wartime, for example, it may be possible to postpone the replacement of capital; in that case it is the gross national product which we will want to consider, as it indicates the goods and services that are available in the short run. But for the long run, when we want to know how much will be permanently available, it is the net national product which provides the answer and also gives the value of output at actual *market prices* (which inevitably include the indirect taxes that business pays). Finally, if we want to know how much is actually paid out or credited to the factors of production (land, labor, and capital)—and by the same token, the value of output in terms of the *factor costs* (including profits) embodied in such output—then we must utilize the national income.

Any number of detailed breakdowns of these basic concepts are possible, some of which are presented in the remainder of Table 1-1. National income, for example, can be divided into compensation of employees, income of corporations and unincorporated enterprises, net interest, and rental income of persons. Gross national product may be broken down into personal consumption expenditures, gross investment, and government purchases of goods and services. In each case, just what is included should be determined before the category is used. "Rental income of persons," for example, has little to do with rent in the economic sense, being, predominantly, interest paid on the capital embodied in the country's stock of houses.

The equality of income and the value of production

A characteristic of this system of accounts is that the value of the goods and services produced in any period is equal to the incomes earned in their production. This follows from the way the terms are defined—in other words, is true by definition rather than requiring proof. For cost payments by business are income to those receiving them. This is obvious in the case of wages, interest, or the rent of land—payments to the factors of production. But other business costs, such as payments for raw materials, ultimately resolve themselves into such factor payments plus profits. When we consolidate all cost payments for the economy as a whole, therefore, we have all income payments except profits. It follows that when we add profits to other income payments to get total income, we have something which must be equal to the value of production; for profits are defined as the difference between the value of the goods and services produced and their cost of production! One way of understanding what is at issue is to realize that if costs turn out to be larger than the value which business receives for production, profits will be negative. This is exactly what happens at the bottom of a severe depression; at such times business as a whole suffers losses (negative profits) because more is paid out as costs than is received from the sale of the goods and services. In short, profits—positive or negative as the case may be—when added to costs give the value of production; but equally, when added to all income payments except profits (the same thing as costs), they give total income. Hence, total income is inevitably equal to the value of all goods and services produced.

Some conceptual difficulties

If what has just been presented appears straightforward—if not simple—it is because many problems have been concealed. Take, for example, an expansion of government activity. Some activities—roads, parks, presumably education—are of direct benefit to consumers. But what of an expansion of military expenditure? If, for example, such expenditure rose from 10 to 20 per cent of income—leaving 80 per cent rather than 90 per cent for consumption—would "production" be unchanged? As calculated by the Department of Commerce it would be;

for the Department measures the contribution of government to "production" by the cost of government without regard to the services which government renders. In essence the problem is whether military expenditure should be treated as if it were of direct benefit to the consumer —in which case production would obviously be unchanged—or as merely facilitating the production of things useful to the consumer. In the latter case, production would decline, just as it would if depletion of resources required a doubling of the effort needed to grow wheat without any increase in the bread which was available.

There is no "right" solution to a problem of this sort—any more than gross national product is a "righter" measure of the goods and services produced than net national product. The choice depends on the purpose to which the estimate is to be put. If we are concerned with changes in the productivity of the economy, the Department of Commerce approach is likely to be most useful; but if we are concerned with the current flow of goods and services to consumers, an alternative would be preferable. In short, when using any estimate it is essential to bear in mind the way in which the particular series is constructed. Thus if since 1940 Swedish income measured by the Department of Commerce approach had increased as fast as in the United States, it would justify the conclusion that the performances of the two economies had been similar in regard to production but it would not mean that goods available to consumers had increased by similar amounts.

The impact of industrialization on the estimates

The sort of problem raised by the proper treatment of government is, unfortunately, not unique. In a small town a man may walk to work; in a large city he may commute from a considerable distance. If he moves from town to city, the service of transporting him to work each day will be considered an addition to production. If his wife takes a job and hires a maid to take care of the house, production will increase by the value of both his wife's work and that of the maid. The industrialization and specialization that have been going on in the United States for more than a century mean that we increasingly buy things which were previously made at home. And there has been a steady increase in the percentage of the population in the labor force. Both of these involve increases in reported income and production which undoubtedly overstate the gain in welfare, because the production which formerly took place in the home was not counted. Alternatively the recent "do-it-yourself" movement works in the opposite direction.

Frequently the theoretically desirable procedure cannot be followed because information is lacking. It is, for example, obvious that the government owns much useful capital such as our network of roads, but government capital is not credited by the Department of Commerce with making any contribution to current production. The reason is that the contribution of private capital can be measured by the interest and profits which the owners of such capital receive. But this cannot be done in the case of the government because there is no necessary correspondence between the size of the government debt and the quantity of government capital. For government debt may arise from wars or deficits on current account without an increase in capital, and capital may be financed on a pay-as-you-go basis without an increase in debt. As a result no estimate of the contribution of government capital to current production is included in the national income.[3]

Usefulness of the system of income accounts

Do all these problems mean that our estimates of income and output are of little value? Far from it; the estimates have added greatly to our understanding of the production of our economy and the way in which it is distributed. But they are *estimates* based on a series of decisions which must ultimately be made with reference to the purpose for which the statistics are to be used. In the short run, so long as the estimates are consistently made, most of the problems we have been discussing are not very important, though the impact of war is an obvious exception. But the complications which we have considered should leave the student aware that comparisons between countries—especially if the estimates have been made by different estimators—and comparisons over long periods may involve major errors as a result of purely technical considerations. Hence all comparisons need to be made with full recognition of the difficulties and uncertainties that are involved.

[3] Government interest payments, social security payments, military pensions, direct relief, and a wide variety of minor items are classified as "transfer payments," which involve payments made to people for reasons other than in return for their current productive services. While "transfer payments" are included in "personal income," they are not a part of national income and are not discussed because no use is made in this volume of the concept of "personal income."

CHAPTER TWO

DIFFERENCES IN
LIVING LEVELS

Differences in national income

The United Nations has published a comparison of average national income per person in 55 countries for the period 1952-1954. The sums involved were converted into dollars at prevailing rates of exchange—a method which we shall see leaves much to be desired. Let us first look at the results and then consider their significance. Table 2-1 gives income per person in dollars, with the countries ranked in descending order of income per person.

The broad conclusion that emerges from the table is the well-known fact that at the present time there are substantial differences in living levels between countries. The countries with the highest third of incomes per person are predominantly either European or British Dominions; the United States, Iceland, Venezuela, Israel, and Argentina are the exceptions. On the other hand, no European country is among those with the lowest third of incomes per person in column three. The broad regional differences are summarized in Table 2-2, which presents income per person by continental divisions. But the differences within continents are also worthy of note: the European range is from $1,010 in Switzerland to $200 in Portugal, the South American from $540 in Venezuela to $120 in Peru, the African from $300 in the Union of South Africa to $50 in Uganda, and the Asian from $470 in Israel and $310 in Malaya to $50 in Burma.

TABLE 2-1. INTERNATIONAL DIFFERENCES IN AVERAGE NATIONAL INCOME
PER PERSON FOR THE PERIOD 1952-1954
(In Dollars)

Country	Income per person	Country	Income per person	Country	Income per person
United States	1,870	Puerto Rico	430	Dominican Republic	160
Canada	1,310	Ireland	410	Guatemala	160
Switzerland	1,010	Austria	370	Ecuador	150
New Zealand	1,000	Chile	360	Honduras	150
Australia	950	Cuba	310	Philippines	150
Sweden	950	Italy	310	Paraguay	140
Luxembourg	890	Malaya	310	Egypt	120
Belgium	800	Union of		Peru	120
Iceland	780	South Africa	300	Ceylon	110
United Kingdom	780	Lebanon	260	Rhodesia and	
Denmark	750	Colombia	250	Nyasaland	100
France	740	Panama	250	Thailand	80
Norway	740	Brazil	230	Belgian Congo	70
Finland	670	Greece	220	Korea	70
Venezuela	540	Mexico	220	Pakistan	70
Germany	510	Turkey	210	India	60
Netherlands	500	Portugal	200	Kenya	60
Israel	470	Japan	190	Burma	50
Argentina	460	Jamaica	180	Uganda	50

SOURCE: Statistical Office of the United Nations, *Per Capita National Product of Fifty-five Countries: 1952-1954* (Statistical Papers Series E, No. 4, 1957), Table 1.

Significance of the estimates

How meaningful are these comparisons? In essence the broad rank-ing is probably significant, but the absolute differences are not. In other words, the table purports to show that an American is economically 37 times better off than a Burmese. To the extent that the comparison has any validity when the range is so great, the real difference is in all probability very much smaller. For this there are a number of reasons. The most obvious is the use of exchange rates in converting foreign currencies into dollars; for exchange rates, which reflect only the prices of goods which move, or are capable of moving, in international trade, give a rather poor indication of the relative purchasing power of cur-rencies.

To illustrate what is involved in using exchange rates it will be necessary to digress for a moment to explore the general problem of comparing the production of, say, France and the United States. To make such a comparison, the goods and services produced in each country must be valued in a common set of prices. But should we use

TABLE 2-2. INCOME PER PERSON BY CONTINENTAL DIVISIONS

North America	1,820
Oceania	960
Europe	580
South America	265
Africa	135
Asia	90
World Average	445

the prices prevailing in the United States or in France? Substantial differences are involved, as things which are plentiful are generally low in price. Thus if we use American prices to value the two sets of outputs, France does relatively well, because the relatively high American price for wine is used to value the large French production of wine. But if we use French prices, then France does relatively poorly, because the relatively high French price for cars is used to value our large car production. This is nothing but a particular example of what is called the "index number problem" that is inevitably involved in making comparisons either between countries or within a country over time. No single correct answer is possible, but a range within which the correct answer falls can be established by using both sets of prices. This was done in a recent study of four European countries and the United States.[1] Table 2-3 gives estimates of 1950 gross national product per person in each of the European countries as a percentage of American gross national product per person on three bases: when the comparison is made in American prices, in the prices of the country concerned, and by using exchange rates.

In every case without exception the comparison based on exchange rates gives a lower result than that obtained by using *either* set of prices. This means that the results contained in Tables 2-1 and 2-2 have a systematic bias in the direction of exaggerating the differences between the United States and other countries. The reason for this is, as already suggested, that only the prices of those goods which move, or are capable of moving, in international trade influence exchange rates; in addition, exchange rates may be set, temporarily at least, at "artificial" levels by government action. The strong competitive position of the United States in regard to goods that are traded internationally and the efforts of other governments to encourage their exports and discourage their imports in the face of American competitive strength have led to the establish-

[1] Milton Gilbert and Irving B. Kravis, *An International Comparison of National Products and the Purchasing Power of Currencies* (Paris: Organization for European Economic Co-operation, 1954).

ment of dollar exchange rates which do not fairly reflect the *internal* purchasing power of most currencies.

TABLE 2-3. GROSS NATIONAL PRODUCT PER PERSON IN FOUR EUROPEAN COUNTRIES AS A PERCENTAGE OF GROSS NATIONAL PRODUCT IN THE UNITED STATES ON VARIOUS BASES

United Kingdom	
Comparison in dollars	63
Comparison in pounds	49
Comparison by exchange rates	37
France	
Comparison in dollars	53
Comparison in francs	39
Comparison by exchange rates	35
West Germany	
Comparison in dollars	43
Comparison in marks	30
Comparison by exchange rates	26
Italy	
Comparison in dollars	30
Comparison in lira	18
Comparison by exchange rates	16

Estimates of the magnitudes involved are presented in Table 2-4. In it the actual income reported by the United Nations for the United States in 1952-1954—$1,870—has been multiplied by the percentages for both sets of prices as reported in Table 2-3 and the results compared with the actual United Nations figure for the country concerned. First note that the United Nations figure is below the lowest otherwise derived in every case with the single exception of France. But, in addition, the wide range and general lack of consistency of the estimates— for countries with relatively adequate statistics—illustrate the sizable margins of error that are inevitably involved in comparisons of this sort.

Comparisons between developed and underdeveloped countries

The bias introduced by the use of exchange rates applies to all international comparisons, as do the various problems that were discussed in Chapter 1 in connection with the significance of national income estimates. Where countries are broadly similar in structure and degree of development, however, meaningful solutions are generally agreed to be technically possible. But when the attempt is made to compare the level of living of underdeveloped and developed countries, the magnitude of the problems that arise becomes so great that there are those who doubt if results of significance can be obtained. In underdeveloped countries the market sector is small and most production takes place in self-sufficient family units—just as it did on the American frontier a century or so ago. In such units, food is not only grown but also made ready for consumption. Under the circumstances, by what American price should the food grown on a Korean farm be valued: the price on the farm, at a processing plant, at wholesale, or at retail?

TABLE 2-4. ESTIMATES OF RELATIVE INCOME PER PERSON
(In Dollars)

United Kingdom	
Comparison in dollars	1,178
Comparison in pounds	916
Actual UN estimate	780
France	
Comparison in dollars	991
Comparison in francs	729
Actual UN estimate	740
West Germany	
Comparison in dollars	804
Comparison in marks	561
Actual UN estimate	510
Italy	
Comparison in dollars	561
Comparison in lira	337
Actual UN estimate	310

One is tempted to say at retail, since the Korean product is consumed and an American product's value nearest its point of consumption is its retail price. One difficulty with this solution is that information regarding retail prices is hard to obtain, in large part because products often differ at the retail level. Thus most rice in Korea is eaten "unpolished"—unshelled—which means that it contains all its vitamins, which are concentrated in the shell. We, however, like our rice "polished." For long, this meant that we lost most of the vitamins, but recently the polished rice has been "fortified" by the addition of the vitamins distilled out of the discarded shells. Should we multiply Korean rice production by the retail price of polished and fortified rice in the United States? Hardly; presumably something valuable has been added by all the processing. But how much should we adjust the reported retail price?

Again, the retail prices of American products typically include advertising, transportation, wholesaling, and retailing. If a village cobbler in Korea makes and sells a pair of shoes identical in quality to a pair made in an American factory, should it be valued at the American retail price even if it is never advertised, transported, wholesaled, or—in the American sense—retailed? To the extent that these distribution costs are incurred merely to make factory production possible (presumably being more than offset by the economies of such production) and add nothing to the satisfaction the consumer derives from the shoes, this seems the proper procedure. But if we do use retail prices, we end up crediting Korea with doing many things which are in fact not done there at all! This point can be carried further. People apparently get born and buried on Korean farms without benefit of professional midwives or undertakers. Should the estimate of Korean production include an allowance for such services? Again, Korean families display a well-developed sense of family responsibility and can be counted on to take care of a man's widow and children. Should we, therefore, make an allowance for the "life insurance" they provide? How about barbering services? Or recreational facilities?

What do all these questions and qualifications add up to? China's income level is probably little above the lowest reported in the United Nations tabulation. But a careful comparison of American and Chinese income per person using more appropriate prices than the factory or wholesale price usually used led to the conclusion that American income per person was perhaps 12 times that of China—which would give a difference equal to perhaps a third of that suggested by the U.N. tabulation.[2] To the extent that it has any meaning when the countries compared are so different, the "real" range, although substantial, is clearly very much less than that reported by the tabulation.

Comparisons in physical terms

In view of the complexities of comparisons of this sort, attempts have been made to throw light on the matter by comparisons of physical quantities. One approach has been to compare calories consumed per person. This is done in Table 2-5, which repeats some of the income estimates of Table 2-1, again ranking the countries in descending order of income per person. As is to be expected, the correlation between income and calories is not perfect. Agricultural countries, such as Argentina and Ireland, are not always able to trade their food for other products on reasonable terms and as a result may consume far more calories than

[2] Ta Chung Liu, *China's National Income, 1931-1936* (Washington: Brookings Institution, 1946).

their income position would appear to justify. But the general correlation between income and calories consumed nonetheless remains, and the over-all range—from 1,683 to 3,498—is vastly less than for income. In fact, if allowance is made for the smaller average size of people in most Asian countries, the differences per pound of person would be very small indeed.

TABLE 2-5. COMPARISONS OF INCOME AND CALORIES CONSUMED PER PERSON

Country	Income	Calories consumed	Country	Income	Calories consumed
United States	1,870	3,088	Austria	370	2,726
Canada	1,310	3,114	Chile	360	2,344
Switzerland	1,010	3,109	Cuba	310	2,682
New Zealand	1,000	3,337	Italy	310	2,531
Australia	950	3,005	Union of South Africa	300	2,706
Sweden	950	2,996	Brazil	230	2,353
Luxembourg	890	2,944	Greece	220	2,498
Belgium	800	2,944	Turkey	210	2,647
United Kingdom	780	3,058	Portugal	200	2,385
Denmark	750	3,295	Japan	190	2,160
France	740	2,846	Philippines	150	1,957
Norway	740	3,118	Egypt	120	2,319
Finland	670	3,108	Peru	120	2,077
Germany	510	2,839	Rhodesia and		
Netherlands	500	2,828	Nyasaland	100	2,447
Israel	470	2,721	Pakistan	70	2,018
Argentina	460	3,106	India	60	1,683
Ireland	410	3,498			

SOURCE: Food and Agriculture Organization, *Yearbook of Food and Agricultural Statistics* (Rome: 1955), Table 81, p. 205.

On the other hand, it is easy to conclude too much from this sort of comparison. Many of the Asian countries are at, or close to, a level below which survival is impossible, while an American who consistently consumes significantly more than the typical calory intake in the United States will be both overweight and have a relatively short life expectancy! In fact, in many cases we already pay extra to eliminate calories from the things we eat. Further, the bare calory figures are rather misleading. The difference between the average Indian's 1,700 calories and the average American's 3,100 may not seem large. But the average Indian's calories are obtained overwhelmingly from perhaps a pound a day of a staple cereal, while the average American consumes perhaps four pounds of food (or drink) a day, drawn from the various items that are summarized in Table 2-6. Clearly comparisons of calories consumed, taken alone, are not too helpful.

TABLE 2-6. MAJOR COMPONENTS OF THE AMERICAN DIET IN 1955
(Approximate Pounds Per Person Per Year)

Dairy products	471	Potatoes	110
Fruits and vegetables	346	Sugar	95
Meats (incl. fats, oils, fish)	217	Poultry (incl. eggs)	69
Grains	167	Miscellaneous	24

But if we turn from food to other physical measures, the results vary with the measure chosen. If we take a typical product of industrialization such as the car or telephone, the range can be immense: America is estimated to have 1,250 times as many cars and almost 1,000 times as many telephones per person as China. Is there any way that telephones, cars, and calories can be combined into a meaningful total? Let us recall that what real national income attempts to measure is the total production of all goods and services, and that differences in the total production of goods and services are responsible for differences in living levels. Only to the extent, therefore, that physical measures of living levels can be selected and combined in such a way as to give a result which is representative of the total production of goods and services can they help in facilitating comparisons of living levels.

Can this be done? The most elaborate effort made thus far is a study by M. K. Bennett, who computed, with ingenuity and painstaking care, 19 physical indicators of living levels for the period 1934-1938.[3] When each indicator is given the same weight, it appears that the range from the richest country (United States) to the poorest (French West Africa) is somewhat more than 6 to 1. But when an effort was made to allow for the relative importance of the areas covered by the indicators, the range increased to more than 8 to 1.

The probable range of living levels

Both Bennett's physical measures and the previously mentioned comparison of real income per person in the United States and China apply to the thirties and suggest a range of 8 to 12 to 1. It is probable that the range has increased since then as the heavy unemployment of the Great Depression in the United States has been eliminated. Over-all, therefore, it seems likely that, to the extent that comparisons are meaningful where the differences are so great, the range between the most and the least prosperous countries at the present time falls somewhere between 10 and 15 to 1—rather than the 37 to 1 range suggested by the United Nations tabulation of income per person.

[3] *American Economic Review*, September, 1951.

PART TWO

DEVELOPED AREAS

CHAPTER THREE

WHAT HAS BEEN ACCOMPLISHED

Introduction

The discussion of economic development is divided into three parts. The first deals with areas where substantial development has taken place—predominantly under free enterprise. In this section main emphasis will be placed on Great Britain and the United States. Next we will consider development under Communism, concentrating on the Soviet Union. Then we will conclude with a discussion of some of the problems of underdeveloped areas.

The following section, which covers developed areas, starts with a summary of what has been achieved over the 75 years for which reasonably detailed statistical information is available and then considers some of the factors that have been responsible for the differences in the speed with which development has taken place in these areas.

The achievement of seventy-five years

Tables 3-1 and 3-2 summarize 75 years of American economic development. They are complicated tables because they summarize a lot of material, but they will repay careful study. Throughout, all income estimates are expressed in terms of what the dollar would buy in 1950—not in terms of what it would buy when steaks were a quarter and the fixings were thrown in free. In other words, the income estimates measure, as far as it can be done, the actual quantity of goods and services produced in each period; for such goods and services are in each case valued in terms of the prices which prevailed in 1950.[1] Let us start with the over-all picture and then examine the individual items more carefully.

In 1875 the United States was a country with 46 million people— roughly the present size of Great Britain—of whom 15 millions were in the labor force. For their work in 1875 Americans received the equivalent of $16 billions; income per person averaged $350 and income per worker roughly three times as much. To earn this amount they worked 65 hours a week—roughly six 11-hour days—and received for each hour they worked 33 cents. By 1950 population had increased more than threefold, the labor forces fourfold, and income fifteenfold. As a result, average income per worker was more than three and a half times and average income per person four and a half times as large as it had been in 1875. To earn this income the average worker put in 40 hours a week—say five 8-hour days—and received for his labor just under $2 an hour, which was almost *six times* as much as his forefather had received in 1875. It would be hard to exaggerate the importance of changes which are capable of making an hour of man's labor six times as valuable in a space of time which is only a little more than average life expectancy in the United States.

The margin of error of the estimates

How accurate are these estimates? In Part I we considered some of the problems that are involved in the measurement of the national income. But the historical comparisons just presented raise special problems of their own. The farther backward we go in time the less adequate is the basic statistical information which underlies all our estimates. The existence of a decennial census insures that the margin of error in the case of population is relatively small, but it is larger in the case of the labor force and even larger for the number of hours worked. The income estimates not only suffer from the difficulties of measuring income years ago but also are subject to errors that arise in adjusting from past prices to those prevailing in 1950. With the exception of population and the labor force, all other estimates are probably subject to a *minimum* error of 10 per cent; it is quite possible that subsequent work will find

---

[1] Just as using dollar prices in Table 2-3 tended to "favor" other countries, so using 1950 prices tends to "favor" other periods. Hence the estimates tend, if anything, to understate the actual increase in production.

TABLE 3-1. PHYSICAL MEASURES OF AMERICAN ECONOMIC DEVELOPMENT

Date	Population [a]			Labor Force [b]			Hours Worked [c]		
	Millions	Index	Percentage change per decade	Millions	Index	Percentage change per decade	Number	Index	Percentage change per decade
1875	46.2	100	—	15.2	100	—	64.7	100	—
1880	51.1	111	—	17.5	115	—	64.0	99	—
1890	63.9	138	25	22.9	151	31	61.9	96	− 3
1900	76.4	165	20	29.3	193	28	60.2	93	− 3
1910	92.7	201	21	38.1	251	30	55.1	85	− 8
1920	107.6	233	16	42.3	278	11	49.7	77	−10
1930	123.4	267	15	48.9	322	16	45.9	71	− 8
1940	133.0	288	8	54.7	360	12	44.0	68	− 4
1945	140.8	305	—	61.4	404	—	44.5	69	—
1950	152.4	330	15	61.8	407	13	40.0	62	−10

[a] SOURCE: Simon Kuznets, *Capital Formation and Financing in the United States: Trends and Prospects* (to be published by the National Bureau of Economic Research; reproduced by permission of the Bureau and Professor Kuznets), Table 37, p. E-18. Five-year moving average centered on year involved.

[b] SOURCE: Simon Kuznets, *ibid.*, Table 39, p. E-25. Five-year moving average centered on year involved.

[c] SOURCE: J. Frederic Dewhurst and Associates, *America's Needs and Resources—A New Survey* (Twentieth Century Fund, 1955), Appendix 20-4. The estimate for 1875 is an average of those for 1870 and 1880.

the error to be substantially larger. But the estimates are the best that are now available. While later revisions may well alter specific magnitudes and precise timing, it is quite unlikely that they will change the broad pattern of development with which we are primarily concerned.

Population, labor force, and hours of work

As is relatively well known, the rate of increase of our population declined steadily from the Civil War to World War II. After the turn of the century the decline would have been even more noticeable had it not been for heavy immigration; it was, in fact, the cessation of immigration that explains in large measure the small increase during World War I. But it was the Great Depression of the thirties that brought the population increase to its lowest ebb. Since then there has been a remarkable reversal to a rate of increase that is significantly higher than before World War II. Actually between 1900 and 1950 our population almost exactly doubled. If the present rate of increase continues—as it gives every indication of doing—our population will have doubled again—to a total of 300 millions—by the end of the century.

Since 1875 in almost every period the labor force appears to have expanded more rapidly than population. In part this is misleading—as is the comparable increase in national income. For wives of farmers are not included in the labor force. But as farming has decreased in importance, wives in families which moved to urban areas often took paid employment and so were reported as a part of the labor force—though they may well have worked less hard than they would have if they had remained on the farm! Quite apart from this statistical addition to the labor force, however, there has been a steady increase in the extent to which women—both before and after marriage—undertake paid employment. The causes of the shift are many, but among them are the broad "emancipation" of women from restrictions which frowned on paid employment, and the greater leisure made possible by better appliances within the home and more processing of products before they are purchased. It seems likely that this trend will continue, though at a decreasing rate.

Of the physical measures, hours worked is the one about which we have least direct evidence, but in the nature of the case it is doubtful if the estimates can be very far off. Broadly two periods were marked by major decreases in hours worked: that from 1900 to 1920, when the 60-hour week was replaced by the 48-hour week; and that of the Great Depression, which set the pattern for a 40-hour week, though its full realization did not come until the prosperity that followed World War II. That there will be further decreases in hours is certain, but the speed with which they will come is harder to determine. Both the rise in the number of married women who work and especially the sharp recent rise in the number of men holding two more or less full-time jobs indicates that, in many cases and for a while at least, the desire for additional income is strong, so that the decline in actual hours worked may be slower than had been anticipated. This is, of course, not inconsistent with a reduction in nominal hours, which, by increasing payments for overtime, increases earnings without necessarily affecting the number of hours actually worked.

The income measures of development

Although in the light of the limitations of the basic estimates it is hard to know how much weight to place on differences from decade to decade, the increase in income appears to have been far less steady than, say, the increase in population. The slowness of the increase during the thirties obviously reflects the Great Depression, and the rapid increase of the forties—the most rapid of the entire period—reflects the fact that 1940 was a year marked by considerable unemployment. These estimates do not allow for unemployment; as a result the increase in income slows down as unemployment develops and speeds up as it declines. If we look at the period 1930-1950 as a whole, income doubled. This is rather less of an increase than took place between 1890 and 1910, but rather more of an increase than occurred between 1910 and 1930. The factors responsible for these variations are by no means fully understood, but it seems fair to conclude that the Great Depression and World War II have not on balance led to any significant retardation of the rate of increase in income—at least in comparison with rates of increase that have been achieved in the past.

When we go beyond the total increase in income, there is at least tentative evidence that the performance of the economy is improving. Recall that this "improvement"—in line with Department of Commerce usage—*includes* production of military products; the increase in civilian production has not been nearly as marked. But, as Chapter 1 makes clear, it is total production of all kinds of goods which best measures the actual achievements of an economy; it is this, therefore, on which we are going to concentrate. Income per person is a rough measure of our average achievement—rough because it makes no allowance (among other things) for changes in the effort put into production. The most striking thing about its behavior is its relatively rapid increase in recent years: not only was the increase in the forties the most rapid ever recorded, but even during the Great Depression the increase was as or more rapid than in three of the previous decades. In part this was the

TABLE 3-2. INCOME MEASURES OF AMERICAN ECONOMIC DEVELOPMENT
(Dollar Amounts in Constant 1950 Prices)

| | National Income [a] | | | National Income per Person [b] | | |
Date	Billions of dollars	Index	Percentage change per decade	Dollars	Index	Percentage change per decade
1875	16.1	100	—	350	100	—
1880	24.2	150	—	472	135	—
1890	33.9	211	40	531	152	13
1900	50.5	314	49	659	188	24
1910	72.4	450	43	779	223	18
1920	91.9	571	27	854	244	10
1930	121.0	752	32	981	280	15
1940	150.0	932	24	1,128	322	15
1945	240.4	1,493	—	1,707	488	—
1950	240.0	1,491	60	1,575	450	40

| | National Income per Worker [b] | | | Hourly Income per Worker [c] | | |
Date	Dollars	Index	Percentage change per decade	Dollars	Index	Percentage change per decade
1875	1,062	100	—	.33	100	—
1880	1,372	129	—	.43	130	—
1890	1,484	140	8	.48	145	12
1900	1,721	162	16	.57	173	19
1910	1,878	179	9	.69	209	21
1920	2,175	205	16	.88	267	28
1930	2,474	233	14	1.08	327	23
1940	2,742	258	11	1.25	379	16
1945	3,915	369	—	1.76	533	—
1950	3,883	366	42	1.94	588	55

[a] SOURCE: Simon Kuznets, *Capital Formation and Financing in the United States: Trends and Prospects* (to be published by the National Bureau of Economic Research; reproduced by permission of the Bureau and Professor Kuznets), Table 26, p. C-45. Though 1925 estimates are for net national product rather than national income and are a five-year moving average centered on year involved. No adjustment to national income has been made as Kuznets' NNP Variant III exceeded the Department of Commerce's estimates of national income by only 3.2 per cent during 1929-1938. Thereafter estimates are from the Department of Commerce for specific years. Adjustment to 1950 prices throughout is by the price index implicit in the GNP of the Department of Commerce as reported in Table 41 of the 1954 National Income Supplement.

[b] SOURCE: Simon Kuznets, *ibid.*, Table 40, p. E-30 for estimates through 1925, adjusted to 1950 prices by the above procedure. Thereafter results are the estimates of income derived as explained above divided by Kuznets' estimates of population and labor force.   [c] National income per worker divided by weekly hours times 50.

result of an increase in the numbers working at a time when the increase in population was slowing down. But it is also somewhat misleading; in previous periods—especially the decade of World War I—much of the increase in real income took the form of a sharp decline in the number of hours worked.

In fact, there is probably no better single measure of the performance of the economy than real income per man-hour—the measure presented in the last column of Table 3-2. The estimates assume, for want of information, 50 weeks of work a year over the entire period. Hence the increase is understated to the extent that vacations have become longer in recent years. One result that emerges is that the apparent retardation of the increase in income between 1910 and 1930 was not the result of a decline in the performance of the economy, but rather of a sharp decrease in effort as measured by decreased hours of work. Actually by this measure it appears that the performance of the economy steadily improved from 1880 to 1920, and the decline in the rate of improvement during the twenties would probably have been negligible if the terminal year had been 1929 before the effects of the Great Depression were felt in 1930. The impact of the unemployment of the Depression shows clearly; the estimates measure earning per hour of the prevailing average full-time work week—in other words, per "available" hour—rather than per hour actually worked. But note that the 16 per cent increase achieved in the Depression is not greatly below that attained in previous decades.

Perhaps most striking of all is the fact that, for the 20-year period from 1930 to 1950, the rate of increase achieved appears faster than for any other 20-year period. Thus between 1900 and 1920 hourly income per worker rose from 57 to 88 cents, or by 54 per cent, while from 1910 to 1930 it rose from 69 to 108 cents, or by 56 per cent. But from 1930 to 1950 the rise was from $1.08 to $1.94, or by 80 per cent. It is still rather too soon to know just how much weight to attach to these comparisons. Some part of the more rapid recent increase, for example, reflects the fact that the unemployment of the Great Depression had already started in 1930. But at the very least it seems fair to conclude that there is no evidence whatsoever of any slowing down, or maturing, of our economy as judged by the rate at which productivity is increasing. While this is encouraging, it also means that as a "young" nation we did not progress particularly rapidly; in fact, the recorded change, at least between 1880 and 1900, was the smallest of the entire period. Hence to the extent that it is fair to judge by historical parallels alone, the argument that the recent rapid progress of the Soviet Union can be explained entirely because it is a "young" economy is obviously without merit.

British achievements

How has the development of the United States compared with that of Great Britain? An outstanding difference is the slower growth of British population, which increased by 50 per cent while American population tripled. It is obvious that an American businessman who overexpanded could expect to be bailed out by population increase in a way which his British opposite number could not possibly count on. Between 1910 and 1930 the total increase in British population was only a little over a million. Despite the increase since then, it is now antici- pated that not more than an additional 3 millions will be added to the population before the total starts to decline. In short, in looking ahead for the next 50 years, the British businessman can pretty well disregard population increase, while the American can expect the increase—if it continues—by itself to double the market for his goods.

Reflecting the slower rise of population, the increase in total British income was slower than in the United States, but the rise in in- come per person was also in general less rapid, especially after 1900. Two other differences stand out: the war decades hurt Britain far more than the United States, and the decade of the Great Depression was one in which Britain appears to have made *more* progress in terms of income per person than in any decade since the turn of the century. Though detailed information is not available, the decade of World War I in Britain, as in our own case, was marked by a considerable reduction in hours worked, so that the indicated decline in income per person was at least accompanied by a reduction in effort. This did not, however, occur to anything like the same extent during World War II; the burden of war on Britain has been real. Moreover, the apparent lightness of the impact of the Depression during the thirties, when British income per person increased rapidly, represented less of an improvement in the performance of the British economy than a cheapening of British imports relative to her exports. During the Depression, prices of raw materials declined more drastically than prices of manufactured goods. But this difference in price behavior was reversed as prosperity returned, so that much of the improvement in the thirties was of a purely temporary character.

Because the estimate for 1950 is computed on a somewhat different basis from the others, not too much reliance should be placed on exact comparisons between 1950 and either 1940 or 1945. Broadly it appears correct that after the thirties there was little additional increase in in- come per person until very recently. The over-all result is that by 1950 British income per person was rather less than two and a half times

TABLE 3-3. MEASURES OF BRITISH ECONOMIC DEVELOPMENT

(Pound Amounts in Constant 1950 Prices)

Date	Population [a]			National Income [b]			National Income per Person [b]		
	Millions	Index	Percentage change per decade	Billions	Index	Percentage change per decade	Pounds	Index	Percentage change per decade
1875	32.7	100	—	3.0	100	—	90.3	100	—
1880	34.4	105	—	3.3	110	—	95.0	105	—
1890	37.4	114	9	4.5	150	36	119.1	132	25
1900	41.0	125	10	5.7	190	27	139.3	154	17
1910	44.6	136	9	6.6	220	16	148.5	164	7
1920	45.4	139	2	6.7	223	2	147.6	163	−1
1930	45.8	140	1	7.7	257	15	167.5	185	13
1940	47.9	146	5	10.0	333	30	208.5	231	24
1945	49.1	150	—	10.7	357	—	218.3	242	—
1950	50.4	154	5	10.8	(360)	(8)	214.8	(238)	(3)

SOURCE: James B. Jeffreys and Dorothy Walters, *National Income and Expenditure of the United Kingdom, 1870-1952* in *Income and Wealth, Series V*, edited by Simon Kuznets (London: Bowes & Bowes, 1955), Table III, p. 14. The estimates are ten-year moving averages centered on the year in question. The estimate for 1950 was obtained by extrapolation.

[b] SOURCE: *Loc. cit.*, for all years except 1950. The estimates are ten-year moving averages centered on 1950. The estimates in the year in question adjusted to 1950 prices by a price index weighted 94 per cent by the index for consumer goods and services and 6 per cent by the index for capital goods presented in Table XVI, p. 39. Total income is derived by multiplying per capita income by population. The 1950 estimate for total income is from Table 1, p. 8, and the per capita estimate is derived from it.

higher than it had been at the start, while in America it was four and a half times higher.

This conclusion is intensified when allowance is made for the behavior of hours worked. It is likely that hours in Britain behaved in roughly the same manner as in the United States until the turn of the century. Thereafter, although World War I brought a sharp reduction of hours, the Great Depression did not. In the mid-thirties hours worked in British manufacturing industry were close to 48 at a time when comparable hours in the United States were under 37, and in 1950 hours in British industry were still around 46. Allowing for the longer hours typically worked outside of manufacturing, the following table presents some rough estimates of total hours worked and hourly income per person. Note that hourly income per *person* is not the same thing as hourly income per *worker* presented in the last column of Table 3-2, so that the absolute levels should not be compared.

TABLE 3-4. TENTATIVE ESTIMATES OF HOURS WORKED AND HOURLY INCOME IN GREAT BRITAIN

(Pound Amounts in Constant 1950 Prices)

	Hours Worked		Hourly Income per Person	
Date	*Number*	*Index*	*Shillings*	*Index*
1875	65	100	.55	100
1900	60	92	.93	167
1940	52	80	1.60	288
1950	50	77	1.72	309

To the extent that the estimates of Table 3-4 are correct, they suggest that hourly income per person in Britain a little more than tripled during a period in which hourly income per worker increased almost sixfold in the United States.[2] While further study may change the exact magnitude of this comparison, it is clear that there have been real and highly significant differences in the performance of economies even as closely allied by inheritance and language as those of Great Britain and the United States.

Economic development in other areas

Attention has been concentrated on Great Britain and the United States because the evidence available for these countries is considerably

[2] As hourly income per person rose more rapidly in the United States than hourly income per worker, the comparison in the text appears, if anything, to understate the performance of the American economy.

better than it is for other areas. But such concentration gives the impression of a quite superior performance by the United States. Recent studies have cast considerable doubt on the extent to which this is correct. While—to repeat—the evidence which underlies these studies leaves much to be desired and while later revisions drastic enough to halve the present estimated rate of increase in individual cases are entirely possible, nonetheless it is important for perspective to examine some of the presently available material. The following table presents estimates of the percentage change per decade in population, real national product, and real national product per person. The period covered is from approximately the turn of the century to the latest date for which information was available. The countries are ranked in the order of the increase in national product per person.

TABLE 3-5.   RELATIVE ECONOMIC DEVELOPMENT
(Percentage Change Per Decade)

Country	Population	Real National Product	Real National Product per Person
Sweden	7	38	29
Union of South Africa	21	50	24
Norway	8	34	23
Japan	13	38	22
U.S.S.R.	12	33	19
Canada	21	41	17
Denmark	12	31	17
U.S.A.	15	34	16
Eire	− 2	15	16
Switzerland	8	24	15
Italy	7	22	14
New Zealand	19	33	12
United Kingdom	6	17	11
France	1	11	10
Australia	17	28	10
Netherlands	14	25	9
Hungary	6	16	9
Germany	10	20	8
Spain	9	15	6

SOURCE: Simon Kuznets, *Economic Development and Cultural Change,* October, 1956, Table 1, p. 10.

It is clear that on this evidence the United States has not developed most rapidly nor Great Britain least rapidly among the nations of the world. This conclusion, however, makes no allowance for the reduction in hours worked. If the reduction were taken into account, it appears that results would be significantly altered, as declines in hours worked

show little correlation with the rate of increase in income.[3] Thus Great
Britain, New Zealand, and Australia, which fall in the bottom half of
the table, appear to have achieved relatively small decreases in hours
worked and therefore to have turned in an even poorer economic performance than the table indicates. Italy, France, the Netherlands, and
Germany appear to have attained relatively large decreases in hours
and hence to have achieved a better economic performance than indicated. Again, Sweden and Norway, close to the top of the table, appear
to have achieved relatively large decreases in hours—which suggests
that their economic performance has been outstanding. One thing that
does appear from the table is that there is no necessary relationship
between rapid population growth and rapid increases in income per
person: Sweden's population growth was less rapid than Spain's despite
the fact that Sweden is at the top and Spain at the bottom of the list.

Factors responsible for economic development

If this table serves no other purpose, it should demonstrate the
complexity of the problem of economic development. With this complexity very much in mind, we now turn to an exploration of some of the
factors responsible for the differences we have observed. As before, because so much more information is available, we shall in this section
concentrate on the United States and Great Britain—the former roughly
at the bottom of the top third of developed countries in terms of the rate
of increase in national product per person and the latter at the top of
the bottom third. Later sections will discuss development under Communism and in underdeveloped areas.

In presenting the factors responsible for development, no formal
theory of development is offered in the sense in which, for example,
the Keynesian analysis offers a theory of income determination. One
obvious reason for not offering a formal theory is that none has been
developed which commands any important measure of agreement among
economists. But the disadvantages of formal theory are sometimes over-
looked. Whenever a theory attempts to supply a complete explanation
of complicated and by no means fully understood phenomena, it can
do so only by establishing certain complex and inclusive relationships—
the complexity of which is often not fully understood by the theorist
himself. Any student familiar with the difficulties that were encountered
in clarifying the meaning of the Keynesian determinants of the level of
income will understand the point being made. This is not to deny the
usefulness of theoretical work. There can be no doubt that a theory of

[3] Information regarding hours worked is contained in Colin Clark, *The Conditions of
Economic Progress* (London: MacMillan, 1957), Chap. III.

the factors responsible for the level of economic development would be very useful. But a combination of the absence of any general agreement among economists as to what the factors are, together with the real difficulties of formal theorizing in so complicated an area, explains why no formal presentation of a theory of development is attempted in this volume.

Instead, we shall discuss some of the factors that appear important in explaining differences in the level of economic development. We shall start with a discussion of research in all its aspects, next consider the process of innovation by which the results of research are utilized, then turn to the role of saving in providing the capital that development requires, go on to explore the importance of resources in connection with development, and conclude with a chapter entitled "Other Factors." The order and extent of the treatment of the various factors reflect in a very rough fashion my estimate of their relative importance. But because this entire presentation is not offered as a formally complete theory of development, we may stress that throughout the discussion is incomplete and that it is particularly incomplete in the final chapter, which tries to go beyond the conventional bounds of economics. The whole field of economic development is one to which modern economists have only recently given major attention. It hardly needs to be pointed out that as yet they do not by any means have all the answers.

What has been omitted

Because no claim to formal completeness is made, much that has a bearing on the level of development but does not appear crucial has not been discussed. Thus when Adam Smith considered the "wealth of nations"—which was his way of describing their level of development— he laid great emphasis on specialization and exchange. The change from the typical farm household of a century or so ago, when most economic production took place within the household unit, to the mechanized single-crop farm family which feeds itself on frozen food bought at the supermarket obviously has a lot to do with our present higher level of living. And one has only to look at the coffee and bananas that are likely to be on the typical American breakfast table to realize that present-day specialization and exchange take place on an international rather than a purely national scale. But this is so generally understood to be a characteristic of development that it has received little or no consideration in what follows. In the remainder of this section, when attention is concentrated on the differences between countries with as similar backgrounds as Great Britain and the United States, discussion of much that from a broader point of view is undoubtedly relevant has been omitted in order to concentrate on what appear to be more "strategic factors" for the countries involved. In dealing with the Soviet Union and underdeveloped areas, on the other hand, the discussion is inevitably broader, though even so, it is still by no means complete. The Soviet Union, for example, is just as dedicated to the use of specialization and exchange—in the functional if not the market sense of "exchange"—as any capitalistic economy; it is also fully convinced regarding the superiority of money over barter—and perhaps even more convinced regarding the importance of capital accumulation than the most "capitalistic" economies! Hence considerations of this sort have been omitted to permit concentration on those factors which appear more crucial in explaining the differences with which we are primarily concerned.

CHAPTER FOUR

THE ROLE OF
FUNDAMENTAL RESEARCH

Some definitions

First, by changes in technology we shall mean changes either in end products or in the techniques by which they are produced. Second, by research we shall mean activities which make changes in technology possible. Broadly research is of two sorts: that which adds to fundamental scientific knowledge and that which applies such knowledge to particular problems, resulting in at least an improvement or, if it is important enough, in an "invention." Finally, we shall mean by innovation the actual commercial introduction of an invention or other improvement that research has made possible. Clearly these are all aspects of matters so closely related that they cannot always be separated. Rarely does a new product or a new technique become available which is fully developed and ready for exploitation. In most cases it is from a sequence of interacting improvements and innovations that the final result emerges. Nonetheless it will be useful to distinguish scientist, inventor, and innovator as representing three main aspects of research and innovation.

How does an innovator in this sense differ from an "entrepreneur"— the person responsible for making business decisions? Does not innovation used in this way cover all entrepreneurial activity? The answer is that a distinction can be drawn between the inevitable choices that an entrepreneur has to make among *existing* techniques of production in order to minimize his costs and maximize his profits and *improvements* in such techniques. Admittedly the two are closely related, but the distinction is in line with most theorizing in economics, which in general assumes that there is a body of existing technology from which the entrepreneur selects the products and techniques he believes best for his needs *without in the process improving them.*[1] Hence when economics studies price and output determination in the short run, it does so on the assumption that the entrepreneurs involved are not innovating.

The role of research and innovation in promoting development is not usually discussed systematically in introductory courses. It is not a matter on which economics has anything to offer remotely comparable to the body of doctrine that has been developed over the years as to how scarce means of production are allocated among the alternative uses to which they may be put. But there is, in all probability, nothing more important in raising material well-being over even short periods of time than effective research and innovation. Hence a discussion of research and innovation cannot be avoided. The student should, however, be clearly warned—and therefore aware—that the absence of any agreed upon body of doctrine makes the discussion of these chapters subject to an unusually wide margin of error.

The importance of research and innovation

Is it possible to determine the importance of research and innovation in the fourfold increase in real income per person that took place between 1875 and 1950? During that period the increase in capital per person can be estimated; it appears to have been roughly threefold. How much would the mere fact that each worker had three times as much capital to work with have increased production if nothing else had changed? Even without precise measurement, it seems obvious that if present production were confined to the products and technologies known in 1875, it would be very much lower. All that we would be working with would be more elaborate and carefully made capital equipment of the sort that existed in 1875, and all we would be producing would be products known in that year.

Any effort at more precise measurement involves an estimate of the relative importance of the contribution of capital and labor to total production. One way in which this can be done is to take the share of the national income received by capital and by labor as measuring their

---

[1] The assumption of unchanged technology has to be made if unique cost curves are to be obtained. For if an entrepreneur were to improve on available techniques as he utilized them, his costs would not be predictable and it would be impossible to discuss reversible movements along a "given" cost curve.

relative importance. This does not by itself solve the problem. While the shares of total income going to capital and labor have not changed greatly, the fact that capital has increased three times as fast as labor means that the reward per unit of capital has declined significantly. We get, therefore, rather different results if we measure the importance of the increase in capital on the basis of the high return per unit it was receiving at the start of the period or on the basis of the low return per unit it was receiving toward the end of the period. This is another example of the "index number problem" discussed in Chapter 2. Neither procedure is intrinsically "right," but the truth undoubtedly lies between them.

Estimates on both bases have been made by Moses Abramovitz.[2] When the importance of capital is measured by its relatively low return toward the end of the period, he concludes that the threefold increase in capital over the period might by itself have brought about a mere 14 per cent expansion in production; even when the importance of capital is measured by its relatively high return at the start of the period, it appears that the increase by itself would have been responsible for no more than a 44 per cent expansion. Whatever the importance attached to these particular estimates, it seems fair to conclude, in view of the fact that production per person actually increased by 300 per cent, that the increase in capital alone has not been of major relative importance in explaining the increase of production in the United States. Moreover, it seems likely that the relative importance will decline even further as development continues.

Are research and innovation responsible for the remainder of the increase? The answer appears to be for most of it, but not for all. We know that the increasing portion of the population included in the labor force has been more than offset by decreasing hours of work, so that man-hours per person have decreased over the period. But the quality of the man-hours worked—as a result of better education, better health, and the decline in hours itself—is undoubtedly higher, despite possibly more frequent trips to the water cooler. In addition, there have been changes in both the quantity and the quality of the raw materials that we use. Moreover, the broad institutional arrangements which are the subject of Chapter 10 are also important and may also have changed for the better over the period. Because we cannot measure these changes, we cannot separate out their influences from that of research and innovation. But granting that other factors have played a role, it seems impossible to deny, in the light of the vast changes in products and technology that have taken place since 1875, that research and innovation

2 Moses Abramovitz, "Resource and Output Trends in the United States Since 1870" (*Occasional Paper 52*, National Bureau of Economic Research, 1956), p. 11.

have been overwhelmingly responsible for the changes in real income that have occurred.

The background of research

Historically additions to fundamental knowledge have been predominantly a by-product of the educational system. In recent years the relative importance of educational institutions probably has declined—as government and industry have expanded their research activities, as necessary equipment has become more expensive, and as the increasing numbers attending college have diverted academic energies. In some areas of knowledge this trend may have been reversed since World War II by the rapid expansion of government research grants to educational institutions. Although sometimes liberal in scope, such grants generally have had the acknowledged purpose, not of increasing fundamental knowledge as such, but rather of achieving reasonably foreseeable military benefits. As a result, they have certainly distorted the balance between academic disciplines in favor of the physical sciences, and may conceivably have had the over-all effect of reducing fundamental research by diverting to practical applications talent that otherwise might have been adding to basic knowledge.

Government's contribution to both fundamental and applied research has a long history, quite apart from the contribution government has made to educational institutions. The main reason for this is that state experiment stations and the federal Department of Agriculture have between them been responsible for most research in agriculture. Such research as has been done by private enterprise has been done, not by the individual farmer who is by and large too small and too poor, but by firms supplying agriculture, which in most cases are large in size and few in number. The over-all result is that productivity in agriculture has been increasing steadily—and in recent years quite rapidly—but not, in the main, as a result of research done by private industry.

In fact, turning to industry's contribution to research, it can be argued that, the closer an industry is to being perfectly competitive, the worse is likely to be its research performance. To this there clearly are exceptions. Moreover, satisfactory research performance is hard to define because what can be invented is not known till the invention is made. But at least tentatively the contention appears to have merit. Such technologically "backward" industries as bituminous coal, textile spinning and weaving, housing construction, and the garment trades are all highly competitive (in the sense of having many small producers), while industries which would generally be conceded to be "progressive"—oil, automobiles, chemicals, electric utilities, the American Telephone and

Telegraph Company—are either oligopolies or regulated monopolies.[3] Note that at this point we are discussing research considered separately; we shall see that the situation regarding innovation is likely to be somewhat different.

The present research situation

The relationship between the organization of free enterprise and research performance is a matter to which we shall want to return. But let us first examine more fully the prevailing pattern of research. Table 4-1 summarizes some estimates of total expenditure on research. Starting with the source of funds, it appears that government in 1953 financed half and industry just under half the total. By 1956, on the basis of partly estimated results, it appears that the government's financial share had risen to almost 60 per cent and that of industry had fallen to 38 per cent, with educational institutions contributing out of their own resources a mere 3 per cent. In that year almost half of all research performed by industry was financed by government, with the percentage reaching 61 per cent in the case of electrical equipment and 87 per cent in the case of aircraft. In terms of what is desired from research, the source of financing is perhaps the relevant breakdown. But almost three quarters of all research was performed in 1956 by industry, with government undertaking four sevenths and educational institutions three sevenths of the remainder.

Three aspects of research by industry are especially significant: such research is concentrated heavily in large firms; it is concentrated in particular industries; and the amount of fundamental research undertaken is miniscule.[4] As Table 4-2 demonstrates, the percentage of companies undertaking research increases steadily with the size of the firm. Further, companies with over 5,000 employees, which provided 40 per cent of employment, were responsible for 72 per cent of research expenditures, while firms with less than 500 employees accounted for only 10 per cent of expenditures, although they provided 35 per cent of employment.

Research classified by industry is similarly concentrated. In 1956 of 14 groups of industries distinguished, 3—aircraft, electrical equipment, and machinery—account for 60 per cent of reported expenditures; at the other extreme, 7 groups—just half the total number—were responsible for

[3] A "monopoly" is an industry in which there is only *one* producer, while an "oligopoly" is an industry with only a *few* producers.

[4] Evidence for these conclusions is contained in National Science Foundation, *Science and Engineering in American Industry* (Washington: Government Printing Office, 1956).

less than 11 per cent of total research spending. Concentration is encouraged by government research contracts, 80 per cent of which were received by the aircraft and electrical equipment industries alone.

TABLE 4-1.   RESEARCH IN THE UNITED STATES
(Millions of Dollars)

	1941	1946	1951	1953	1956
Government					
Research financed					
Amount	370	910	1,980	2,820	5,300
Per cent	41	51	59	52	59
Research performed					
Amount	200	470	700	970	1,400
Per cent	22	26	21	18	16
Industry					
Research financed					
Amount	510	840	1,300	2,370	3,400
Per cent	57	47	39	44	38
Research performed					
Amount	660	1,190	2,300	3,870	6,500
Per cent	73	67	68	72	72
Colleges and Universities					
Research financed					
Amount	20	30	80	180	300
Per cent	2	2	2	4	3
Research performed					
Amount	40	120	360	530	1,100
Per cent	5	7	11	10	12
TOTAL RESEARCH SPENDING	900	1,780	3,360	5,370	9,000

SOURCE: Bureau of Labor Statistics, *Scientific Research and Development in American Industry* (Washington: Government Printing Office, 1953), Table C-1, p. 58; National Science Foundation, *Basic Research: A National Resource* (Washington: Government Printing Office, 1957), p. 28; and National Science Foundation, *Reviews of Data on Research and Development* (Washington: Government Printing Office, May, 1958, Number 10). "Other Institutions," accounting for less than one per cent of performance or financing, have been grouped with "Colleges and Universities." The results for 1956 are preliminary and partly estimated.

Finally, in 1953 of the total of $3.9 billions of research performed by industry, only $170 millions, or 4 per cent, went for basic or fundamental research.[5] Even when account is taken of the $220 million of

[5] Defined as projects "not identified with specific product or process applications, but rather (having) the primary objective of adding to the over-all scientific knowledge of the firm." Estimates are from National Science Foundation, *Basic Research: A Natural Resource*, p. 29.

basic research performed by educational institutions and the $45 million performed by the federal government, the total for fundamental research is still only $435 millions, or 8 per cent of total research expenditures. In other words, expenditure as a whole was overwhelmingly for "product-improvement" or "product-development" types of research.

TABLE 4-2. CONCENTRATION OF RESEARCH IN LARGE FIRMS

Number of employees of firms	Percentage of firms undertaking research
Less than 100	8
100–499	22
500–999	42
1,000–4,999	60
5,000 and over	94

To summarize: at the present time research expenditures of all sorts, though they have been expanding rather rapidly, are still around 2.5 per cent of the national income and expenditures on fundamental research probably not more than one fifth of 1 per cent. Of total expenditures more than half are spent primarily to obtain improved military products, so that research expenditure to improve products of general economic usefulness probably does not much exceed 1 per cent of income.

Research and the logic of free enterprise

The Introduction has shown why it is that, if certain assumptions are accepted, free enterprise tends to bring about an "ideal" allocation of resources—"ideal" at least in relation to the assumptions involved. But there is no comparable rationale for the amount of research that takes place under free enterprise. Not only does the government currently finance close to 60 per cent of all research, but in addition the government determines the character of the patent system, which has much to do with the level of private spending on research. Further, we have suggested tentatively that the closer an industry comes to being highly competitive, the more inadequate is its research performance likely to be; this suggestion has been confirmed by the fact that the percentage of firms undertaking systematic research increases as they increase in size. It does not, of course, follow that the government has itself to undertake whatever research may be lacking, but it does mean that the broad pattern of research is something which needs to be consciously determined —as, say, the amount of education—rather than a matter which can be left to the automatic operation of a free enterprise system. The issue will repay detailed examination: the remainder of this chapter will concentrate on fundamental research, while the two following chapters will deal with practical research.

Free enterprise and fundamental research

If enterprises sought exclusively to maximize their profits, it is by no means certain that they would undertake any fundamental research whatsoever. Fundamental additions to knowledge cannot be patented; they can, therefore, accrue to the exclusive benefit of a firm only to the extent that they can be kept secret—which is by no means easy so long as research personnel are free to move among the firms involved. Only where the number of firms is small and the returns from basic research extremely high is there likely to be a direct profit incentive for a firm to undertake expenditures on basic research—and, to the extent that the information is not secret, its competitors will have received exactly the same benefit without having incurred any of the cost. It is possible, of course, that business may undertake basic research for reasons not related to direct profits: as a form of institutional advertising, for example, or as a social duty—similar to business contributions to education or to charity. But it is obvious that this sort of consideration is most likely to apply to large enterprises or to small enterprises controlled by rich men.

There is, in fact, no agreement among businessmen that basic research is a business responsibility. We have seen that business expenditures on basic research amount to only 4 per cent of total business research expenditures. True a company such as Du Pont has undertaken basic research for more than 30 years and today believes that it spends more than any other company on such research—currently $15 millions a year or perhaps 8 per cent of the business total. Moreover, Du Pont has benefited greatly, as nylon was a practical application of some of Du Pont's fundamental research.[6] Yet the president of Du Pont—himself a chemist of distinction—considers fundamental research to be primarily the responsibility of educational institutions.

Much of fundamental importance has, of course, come from commercial laboratories, with outstanding honors going to those maintained by General Electric and American Telephone and Telegraph. Both have produced Nobel prize winners and made major contributions to fundamental knowledge. That basic research can pay off in practical results

---

[6] The extent to which practical results need not accrue to the company responsible for the basic research is illustrated by dacron, which stemmed from the same basic research but was developed and patented by a small British chemical company from which Du Pont has a license.

perhaps has been most spectacularly demonstrated recently by the transistor, which bids fair to replace the vacuum tube. But the list of industrial laboratories which have made, or appear likely to make, similar contributions is not long. In the opinion of *Fortune Magazine* they exist in the chemical, oil, and drug industries, and in Eastman Kodak and International Business Machines—all areas which are oligopolistically organized—but nowhere else in American industry.[7] Conspicuously absent is any company in the automobile industry. The case of General Motors is particularly notorious. Though its sales are larger than those of any other company in the world and its profits have been over a billion dollars a year, GM has only product-improvement research to its credit. The attitude that has marked General Motors in the past is typified by its one-time President, Charles Wilson, who scornfully dismissed basic research as worrying about "what makes grass green and fried potatoes brown."

The need for fundamental research

How much fundamental research is socially desirable? This is a question which, of course, goes well beyond economics. For fundamental research seeks to add to knowledge, and it is the possession of knowledge that distinguishes man from other animals. Hence the question really becomes: how much knowledge do we want? Let us be clear that the knowledge provided by fundamental research may or may not have practical benefits. For the essence of such research is that it does not seek to answer practical questions; it merely seeks to answer questions.

To illustrate: Langmuir, the Nobel prize-winning scientist of the General Electric Laboratory, one day became curious as to why water vapor in air did not turn into snow when the temperature fell below freezing. Experimenting in nothing more than a home deep freezer, he found that the water vapor did not condense by itself until the temperature dropped to thirty-odd degrees below zero: apparently prior condensation is prevented by the surface tension of the minute droplets. But when conditions are right, a chain reaction can be started either by cooling any part of the cloud sufficiently, as with dry ice, or by introducing silver iodine crystals, which resemble snow crystals and induce condensation rather as a celluloid egg induces a chicken to lay. What did all this experimenting achieve? Well, first—and in a basic sense most important—it satisfied Langmuir's curiosity. Second, General Electric got nothing; in fact when an effort to seed a cloud with dry ice coincided

---

[7] The inclusion of Eastman Kodak can be questioned. The development of the color process, for example, owes much to the work of two musicians whose research laboratory was a bathroom.

with a blizzard, the Company's lawyers issued an urgent cease and desist order for fear that everyone in whose yard snow had fallen would sue the Company for damages! Third, a fair amount of money is today being spent by farmers and growers who think that seeding clouds with dry ice or silver iodine affects rainfall, even though there is as yet no general agreement that in fact it does.

But suppose the Langmuirs are still curious. Should they be allowed to spend more than one fifth of 1 per cent of the national income satisfying their curiosity—money which the rest of us might otherwise spend for things we want? The increasing recognition of the importance of basic research has led to what may be a three- or fourfold increase in the level of spending in the last decade—amounting to perhaps a doubling in real terms.[8] Is even more necessary? Obviously the answer involves a value judgment and should be labeled as such. But in my opinion, despite the progress made, no present use of funds is likely to be more "productive" in the sense of increasing future economic well-being than a further substantial expansion of expenditure on basic research. This opinion is based on two subsidiary judgments. First, I believe that the pursuit of knowledge for its own sake will continue to yield, as a by-product, much which can be applied to the solution of practical problems. Examples of practical achievements resulting from basic research, in addition to those already mentioned, are so numerous and well known that further elaboration of this point hardly seems necessary. Second, it seems to me that continued solution of practical problems at a rapid rate is essential—for the same reasons that continued rapid economic development is itself essential.

A program for basic research

If an expansion of basic research is necessary, how can it best be achieved? The National Science Foundation, in outlining a program designed to encourage basic research, has proposed the following steps:

1. That private industry increase its support of basic research, both by more work in its own laboratories and by larger contributions to educational and other research institutions;

2. That state governments, with appropriate federal assistance, increase their support of basic research at state universities;

3. That the tax laws be changed to encourage additional philanthropic giving for basic research; and

4. That government agencies reduce the amount of development work under contract with educational institutions and increase significantly their support of basic research at all educational institutions which lack

[8] National Science Foundation, *Basic Research: A National Resource*, p. 2.

adequate private support—the federal support to be provided with minimum restrictions on the freedom of the scientist and the institution.[9]

Undoubtedly the basic requirement for the acceptance of any such program is a wide-spread recognition of the importance of knowledge for its own sake. So long as explorations of why "grass is green and fried potatoes brown" are considered to be an immensely inferior activity to the production of cars with bigger and better chrome-plated fins, we can expect to have an inadequate level of basic research. More specifically, achievement of the program requires, on the one hand, adequate financing and, on the other, appropriate organizations to perform the additional research. In the last analysis there are only two possible sources of financing: government and industry. It is hard to say whether it will be easier to persuade a congressman, up for election every two years, that he should raise his constituents' taxes to allow some long-haired scientist to fuss around with the weather than it will be to persuade the directors of General Motors that it is important to their stockholders that the way clouds develop should be understood. But if a significant increase in fundamental research is to be achieved, one or the other must be done. For neither educational institutions, hard-pressed by rapidly expanding enrollments, nor private foundations have the sums that are required.

In the case of industry, the choice is between doing more fundamental work itself or making more funds available to educational institutions. Almost certainly, both alternatives are needed, and we need not concern ourselves with the exact balance between them. In the case of government, and especially the federal government, the problem is that, for research as for expenditure in general, spending for destruction is acceptable but spending for constructive purposes controversial. This is perhaps better than nothing; had it not been possible to make an atomic bomb, it is hard to see how we would have achieved atomic energy. And there is no doubt that in many areas the present vast federal spending on military research is achieving results which are useful outside the military field. But with 85 per cent of the total being spent by either the Department of Defense or the Atomic Energy Commission, the present heavy emphasis on the practical improvement of military hardware is inevitable, with the repercussions on fundamental research at best incidental and at worst adverse as able scientists are diverted to the solution of practical problems. The current effort, for example, devoted to the development of solar energy is relatively insignificant, yet ultimately solar energy may well turn out to be as important as, if not more important than, atomic energy. True a start on

[9] Adapted from *Basic Research: A Natural Resource*, pp. 6 and 7.

encouraging basic research has been made: appropriations for the National Science Foundation have risen from $225,000 in 1951 to $40 millions in 1957. But the size of the job which remains to be done is immense. To indicate its size, I suggest that, if the Foundation were to be made the dispensing agency for the encouragement of basic research, its appropriation might well be raised within five years to a billion dollars a year—which would still leave expenditures on basic research at less than one half of 1 per cent of national income.

The suggestion that expenditures of this size are desirable does not imply that the research need be performed by either the federal government or the Foundation. Because the results of basic research are particularly difficult to predict, the greatest possible variety—confusion, if you will—of actual performance seems desirable. In fact, a case can be made that we are behind in rockets, not because of too much rivalry between the armed services, but because of too little competition between rocket systems and too early efforts to determine the system with the greatest potential in the interest of eliminating duplication.[10] Much of the funds at issue could be expected to go to educational institutions, including separate research institutes (such as the Institute for Advanced Study at Princeton). Grants, particularly matching grants, might also be made to outstanding industrial laboratories, with work in the government's own laboratories expanding only to the extent that they were best qualified to perform the research in question. Further, to the extent that industry, either directly or by grants to educational and research institutions, picked up the burden, the activity of the federal government might be equivalently reduced.

But, to repeat, the job to be done is immense and will be costly. Part of the high cost results from the fact that our educational system, which must inevitably undertake much of the work, is already being asked to cope with unprecedented numbers of students—with little expansion of personnel and even less of plant. In addition, the cost will be high because, to a significant extent, a vacuum is being filled: neither industry nor government, thus far, has accepted responsibility for the encouragement of nonmilitary fundamental research. That expenditures on such research will "pay off" seems certain; the main danger is that we will invest inadequately.

[10] Burton Klein, *Fortune,* May, 1958.

CHAPTER FIVE

THE ROLE OF
PRACTICAL RESEARCH

Practical research in the United States

Compared with basic research the importance of practical research is easy to understand. Everyone is aware that our life is being continually changed by the development of new and better products, made in new and better ways. Almost all large firms, as we have seen, have product-development programs, and total research expenditures have been increasing rapidly. But there appear to be two main problems which remain. First, in areas where the total level of spending is large, the emphasis is all too often on highly "practical" research of the "product-improvement" sort, which leaves what we may call "basic applied research" seriously neglected. Second, there are many areas of the economy where the firms typically operate on such a small scale that they cannot afford to finance expensive research programs of any sort. Of the two the latter is probably more important quantitatively, but let us consider the former first because it applies to all areas of the economy.

The importance of basic applied research

While product-improvement research obviously is of use, by itself it is clearly not enough. To illustrate: Pratt and Whitney, Curtiss-Wright, and the Allison Division of General Motors dominated the transport aircraft engine field in 1940. Although all three spent large sums on research, none made any important contribution to the development of gas turbine engines; yet within two decades from 1940 such engines will probably have almost entirely replaced the reciprocating engine for air transport use. Actually the most important single contribution on the Allied side was made by a junior officer of the RAF, who started work before World War II in a ramshackle shed on a government grant of a few thousand pounds!

Again one would have thought that the Radio Corporation of America, the outstanding research organization in its field, would have been responsible for the development of FM (frequency modulation) radio. Instead its director of research went on record in the early thirties that FM radio was impossible. The invention and the commercial exploitation were both brought about by Armstrong, who developed the equipment and built a transmitting station to demonstrate FM's superiorities to a sceptical Federal Communications Commission. This, ironically enough, he was able to do as a university professor because he had previously sold an invention to RCA for close to a million dollars. Despite the fact that the invention turned out to be useless, its sale provided the funds which made the development of FM possible! Though it has been suggested that RCA did not want FM developed for fear that it would have repercussions on the monopoly profits (resulting from physical limitations on the available number of channels) being earned by its broadcasting subsidiary, let us give RCA the benefit of the doubt and credit the failure to an error of judgment on the part of the research director. But, whether through error or by intent, the fact remains that FM radio is an important improvement which did not result from industrial research despite its obvious commercial value.

What is needed, then, is more emphasis on basic applied research—research not designed merely to improve existing types of aircraft engines but to explore quite different ways of using fuel to move aircraft. To the extent that businessmen accept the need for more fundamental research, they are also likely to accept the need for more basic applied research. But, to the extent that the need for fundamental research is met by financing by government and performance by educational institutions, a major problem will remain. Though the student should be warned that this is still another matter on which there is little agreement among economists, I believe that the problem has two aspects: first, rewards from basic applied research are likely to be so small as to reduce significantly the extent to which such research is carried on; and, second, the competitive organization of industry does not necessarily promote such research in the most effective manner.

The rewards from basic applied research

It may well be that the more important an invention is, the less important it is to the individual firm involved. What is at issue here is more than the fact that research costs may not be covered by the direct benefits achieved. For "inventing" may frequently be carried on at a direct loss—as witness the fact that there are few if any firms which support themselves by selling inventions.[1] The incentive for research frequently comes, not because it is directly expected to "pay off," but because without it the firm fears that it will lose out in the over-all competitive struggle. But, if the invention is basic enough, it cannot be denied competitors and therefore is not likely to have any significant effect on the competitive struggle. To the extent that this analysis is correct, it suggests that there is very much less incentive to undertake basic applied research than the routine research which is so important in determining the short-run competitive position of the firm.

To illustrate: the importance of few inventions was as clearly foreseen as in the case of television. Yet RCA—very much to its credit, as millions had to be invested before any commercial benefit was achieved—alone among producers of radios attempted the development of TV.[2] Why in the mid-thirties did Philco, then producing more radios than RCA, decide not to spend money on TV development? The most plausible explanation appears to be that Philco was sure that, if RCA was successful, patent licenses would have to be made available—and made available more cheaply than a patent position could be achieved by independent research. In this judgment Philco was almost certainly correct. For the extent to which the antitrust laws have been construed to bring about what comes reasonably close to compulsory patent licensing has been steadily increasing in recent years. Perhaps the most striking case involves the Aluminum Company of America, which had had a monopoly of primary aluminum production before World War II and held a valid patent on the best available production process but, nonetheless, was induced to license its patents to Kaiser and Reynolds—presumably through fear of continuous antitrust prosecution in the event that licenses were withheld.

RCA itself, moreover, was convicted and fined in 1958 under the anti-

[1] Many firms sell research services, but such services are bought for the same reasons that firms carry on their own research.

[2] The efforts of the Farnsworth interests to establish a marketable patent position is one of the few cases I know where an attempt was made to make money from substantial investment in the development of an important invention.

trust laws on several counts, including: (1) the stifling of competition by an agreement which gave RCA the sole right to license the patents in its field belonging to General Electric, Westinghouse, and American Telephone and Telegraph; (2) the stifling of research and development by its refusal to license its patents except in packages which included thousands of patents a licensee might or might not want; and (3) the reduction of international competition in both sets and patents by various agreements with foreign producers. One can agree completely that the elimination of the practices objected to by the Department of Justice will have the immediate effect of increasing competition and, at the same time, be concerned over the extent to which the Department's action vindicates the decision that Philco made in the thirties not to engage in television research. For it is obvious that if the decision to license one's patents in packages stifles competition, the decision not to license them at all would be even more unacceptable. In short, why should Admiral today invest money in research on color television or American Motors invest money in studying the application of gas turbines to automobiles? When color catches on commercially or the gas turbine proves superior, the patents will obviously be available to all comers. But, if everyone waits for the development work to be done by someone else, is it likely to be done as rapidly as is socially desirable?

Competition and basic applied research

Nothing is harder to decide in advance than the best way of achieving a desired result. Thus preliminary work suggested five methods of obtaining the material for an atomic bomb. Because we were at war, all five were tried. "As it turned out, one of the methods least favored in the early betting because it appeared so fantastically complicated—an electromagnetic separator—was actually the one that produced the material for the first bomb." [3] How can we be sure that all five alternatives get explored in peacetime? At first glance it might seem that the competitive organization of industry would automatically ensure the exploration of all likely alternatives. But there is little reason to believe that, if there are five possibilities and five firms in the industry, each possibility will be systematically explored by one of the firms. Instead each may concentrate on the most likely solution. Economists know relatively little regarding the research strategy of competitive firms. There may well be cases where the small firms gamble on the unorthodox alternative; an example would be the development of fluorescent lighting by Sylvania when the company was restrained by General Electric's patent monopoly

[3] Klein, *Fortune* (May, 1958), p. 113.

from efforts to improve incandescent lighting. But it is generally agreed that fear of loss of competitive position is likely to be a stronger spur than hope of gain; and fear of loss dictates doing whatever the other firms are doing so as not to be "caught short."

How can these problems be dealt with? Obviously the worst possible way of handling the matter would be to centralize the basic applied research of an industry and then, in the interests of efficiency or economy, to concentrate entirely on what presently appears to be the most likely alternative. But what if central direction assigned one of five alternatives to each of five firms? It seems likely that assigning a different alternative to each semi-independent "trust" is the way in which the central research director of a Russian industry would proceed. We know in any event that the Russians are ready to permit considerable "duplication" and "confusion" so long as results are achieved. Might not something similar insure more rapid results in the United States?

Before considering further the general problem of how basic applied research can best be encouraged, let us turn first to a discussion of the second of the two main problems presented at the start of the chapter: the difficulties raised by areas of the economy where production is organized on such a small scale that relatively little research of any sort is carried on—whether basic or otherwise.

Small-scale industry and research performance

Cotton growing is the poorest paid large segment of agriculture; several of the states involved have average incomes which are among the lowest in the United States. Hence the need for increased productivity is obvious and urgent, and now gives signs of being met. It looks as if it might be possible, in many areas at least, to cut the labor required in growing cotton by ultimately as much as 90 per cent. Why was so revolutionary a development so long in arriving? The main reason is that the solution was beyond the scope of any firm connected with the growing of cotton. Approximately as much labor is required in weeding and thinning out the cotton plants early in the season as is required in picking the crop after it has ripened, so that if a large amount of labor is to be released, both picking and weeding must be simultaneously mechanized. Knowing this, cotton growers have not been particularly enthusiastic about mechanical cotton pickers. For they knew that, unless they retained labor on a year-round basis by devices such as sharecropping, they would be unable to get the weeding done.

As a result, though the need for a mechanical picker was obvious, its development was slow. In fact, the first successful model was produced by an individual inventor working with quite limited resources rather than by the farm implement industry. Real progress was not made until the oil and chemical industries, looking for outlets for their products, developed flame and chemical weed killers which gave promise of substantially eliminating hand weeding. It is the combination of mechanical picking and chemical weeding that bids fair to revolutionize cotton growing.

What remains to be done is to redesign the cotton plant to meet the needs of mechanical pickers. Actually much work along these lines is regularly being done, predominantly by government research stations. As a result of one such development, which made available a new type of cotton suitable for growing in California, that state since World War II has become, in addition to its other achievements, the fourth largest producer of cotton (after Texas, Mississippi, and Arkansas).

In short, a revolution of vast significance for the South has been slow in coming, largely because no one invention or improvement is involved. A full solution is going to require joint action by the agricultural implement industry, the chemical industry, and the government's research stations. Only the cotton grower himself is not involved! Is there any way that so promising a revolution might have been brought about more rapidly? Would not a more systematic search for a solution have helped?

The case of bituminous coal

Or take the case of bituminous coal—an example deliberately chosen because it is less one-sided. The opportunities for coal are immense. It is available in far larger quantities than any other fossil fuel, and, in contrast to Great Britain where people apparently still like open fires, the American demand is overwhelmingly for the BTU's the coal contains rather than the coal itself. The challenge is how the BTU's can be most efficiently made available. Coal mining is not only dangerous but until very recently has been appallingly wasteful of manpower. Historically, after the coal had been blasted loose, it was broken into lumps of manageable size by hand picks and loaded into mine cars with hand shovels. The work involved was—and is—extraordinarily hard physically, especially as the humidity frequently runs close to 100 per cent. By the time of World War II, most coal was undercut mechanically; but less than half was mechanically loaded and productivity (measured in tons per man-shift) was only twice what it had been in 1890. There was no other industry in America which, as late as 1940, manhandled so large a tonnage of so basic a commodity. Clearly the social performance of the industry left much to be desired.

On the other hand, there are many possibilities of a revolutionary sort. One is to turn the coal into gas underground. Technological developments in drilling make it possible to drill horizontally with extreme accuracy, so that it is possible to ignite the coal underground, control its combustion by controlling the inflow of air and water vapor, and get a usable gas as a product. Experiments under the auspices of the Bureau of Mines in this country have been disappointing, but Russia is said to produce as much as 20 per cent of its manufactured gas by underground conversion. Alternatively, machines are available which remove coal from the seam and carry it to the surface in a continuous operation, without cutting or blasting, so that musclepower is completely eliminated. Once the coal is on the surface, revolutionary kinds of transportation are possible. Powdered and mixed with water, coal is now being moved by pipe line. Or coal may be converted into gas or electricity at or near the mine, eliminating transportation. In the past, when coal was used for house heating, in locomotives, and in other small-scale furnaces, lumpy coal was desirable and brought a premium price, which in turn made full mechanization difficult, as mechanization tends to reduce lump size. But powdered coal loses none of its BTU's and has long been burned successfully by power plants appropriately equipped with mechanical stokers, which are sure to increase in importance as house heating and locomotive use declines and which will bring with them significant increases in the cleanliness of cities. In the other direction, powdered coal may be recombined into briquets of ideal size for use without mechanical stokers.

It is, however, hard to see how possibilities of this sort can be developed by small-scale firms engaged in such rigorous competition that their survival is often a matter of doubt. Nor have those who supplied machinery to the industry been much better off, as they too have been small-scale. But under the impact of the expansion of oil and natural gas in the postwar period—which cut coal use 30 per cent in the two years following 1947 and even more by 1954—significant changes have taken place. In 1948, productivity (tons per man-shift) was 21 per cent higher than it had been in 1940; seven years later it had increased an additional 65 per cent. Over the entire period from 1940 to 1955, productivity doubled—an increase as large as had taken place in the previous fifty years. Between 1950 and 1955 productivity increased *five times* as rapidly as before 1940. This is an impressive achievement. But it was not achieved until competition from oil and natural gas became devastating. Is there any way in which the recent gains could have been achieved sooner? And how can the immense possibilities which remain be rapidly realized?

Practical research and the patent system

The question which these examples of cotton and bituminous coal have raised is the extent to which private industry, particularly when it is organized on a small-scale and highly competitive basis, can be depended on to provide the socially desirable amount of practical research. The main incentive—itself the result of specific government action—for undertaking private research is the patent system, which gives to an inventor the exclusive use of his invention for seventeen years. While a system which permits an inventor to monopolize the benefits of his invention for a reasonable period of time seems clearly desirable, the actual reward that is involved is hard to anticipate. Just as a solution is reached, another inventor may patent the idea. Or the well-paid legal staff of a large corporation may break the patent by claiming that the idea was previously known. The first thing RCA did, for example, when it felt obligated to buy the invention, which proved to be worthless but enabled Armstrong to finance FM, was to see if the idea had not been anticipated. They found that an Englishman had indeed patented something similar, but had subsequently joined the Colonial Service and was then stationed on the Upper Nile. When an emissary at long last reached him, RCA received a cable which read: "Patent bought by a man named Armstrong." Such foresight on the part of a college professor so impressed RCA that they paid out the million dollars without further delay. But without it Armstrong's invention might have brought him nothing. When the rewards are so unpredictable, it would indeed be a miracle if the amount of research by private industry that results from the availability of patents were to be the amount which is socially desirable.

On the other hand, it is obvious that the "socially desirable rate" cannot easily be given precise meaning; it depends on how much we are prepared to give up today to have more tomorrow—not only for ourselves but for our children. A selfish man who has no children may see no reason for undertaking any present expenditure unless the results will be available in his lifetime. But men acting together as a society feel quite differently about the matter, and even men as individuals are prepared in war to die to provide benefits to those who survive them. Clearly a full definition of the "socially desirable rate" is a complicated matter.

Evidence from agriculture

Even if we can say little with precision regarding the socially desirable amount of research, some of the magnitudes involved may be illustrated. Let us take agriculture as an example.

From 1910 to 1950 farm labor decreased by 28 per cent, but this was more than offset by the increased use of other factors of production, including land but more especially various forms of capital such as fertilizer and machinery, so that "inputs" as a whole increased. If the importance of "inputs" is measured by their relative prices in 1946-1948, the increase was 14 per cent; if the 1910-1914 prices are used as weights, the increase was 33 per cent. But over the same period output increased 75 per cent, so that productivity (output per unit of input) increased between 32 and 54 per cent depending on the weights used. As a result in the year 1950 "inputs" were from $9,600 to $16,200 millions—again depending on the weights used—less than they would have been had there been no increase in productivity after 1910. But in 1950 state experiment stations and the federal Department of Agriculture spent only a little over $100 millions on research, with extension work costing a further $75 millions, or an over-all total, including private agricultural research, that may well have been under $200 millions.[4] Had this rate of spending on research and innovation been maintained for 40 years, the total would have reached $8,000 millions—which is *less than the smaller measure of "inputs" saved in 1950 and less than half the larger measure.* Hence Professor Schultz's conclusion appears hard to deny: "It is our belief that an economic analysis will show that, while the expenditures [on agricultural research] are large relative to past outlays and compared to what other countries spend for these purposes, the resources committed annually would have to be increased very substantially before the rate of return from this stream of inputs would not exceed that obtained in production activities generally." [5]

Alternatively let us look to the future. An estimate has been made of the country's probable food requirements in 1975. Two alternatives were investigated: one assumed that productivity would increase from 1950 to 1975 at 1 per cent annually, the second that it would increase at 2.4 per cent annually. With the same amount of land (10 per cent more than at present) meeting 1975 food requirements under the first alternative was estimated to require 21 per cent more labor, 24 per cent higher current costs other than labor (gasoline for tractors, fertilizers,

[4] Theodore W. Schultz, *The Economic Organization of Agriculture* (New York: McGraw-Hill, 1953), pp. 108-109, 119, 120.

[5] Schultz, *op. cit.*, p. 113.

and the like), and 39 per cent higher capital costs (tractors and other mechanized equipment).[6] Because we do not know what it would cost to achieve a 2.4 per cent rather than a 1 per cent rate of increase in productivity, it is not certain that achieving the higher rate is the most economical way of meeting our needs. But the labor alone that would be saved would amount to more than a million workers, and the total costs of producing 1975 requirements would be perhaps 20 per cent lower. Further this would be a permanent and continuing saving in production costs, while the research that made the saving possible would have to be paid for only once. Thus even if the cost between 1950 and 1975 of the additional research was exactly equal to the saving in production costs that such research achieved up to 1975—so that we were no better off till 1975—we would still be very much better off at that time, as costs would continue to be 20 per cent lower even if research expenditures were then terminated. Hence the probability that the cheapest way of meeting our 1975 food requirements is by stepping up research in the interim seems high indeed.

Research in other areas

Is this conclusion likely to apply to other areas besides agriculture? Any answer is an opinion and should be labeled as such. But I believe that a relatively rapid doubling of the present level of expenditure on nonmilitary practical research in all probability would provide a higher rate of return, in terms of future increases in national income, than any alternative use to which the funds at issue could be put (barring only the increase in fundamental research already proposed). It may well be that an even greater increase might ultimately be desirable when time permits facilities to be increased and additional staff to be trained. The chapter which follows will be devoted to a discussion of how such an increase can best be achieved.

[6] Vernon W. Ruttan, "The Contribution of Technological Progress to Farm Output: 1950-1975," *Review of Economics and Statistics,* February, 1956.

CHAPTER SIX

THE ROLE OF
PRACTICAL RESEARCH (*Continued*)

Problems to be solved

The case for the social desirability of an expansion of practical research is clearer than the manner in which such an expansion can best be achieved. To the extent that the foregoing analysis is correct, there are two main problems to be solved. First, a general encouragement of research in the small-scale, highly competitive areas of the economy is needed. Second, the achievement of more basic applied research in even the areas of the economy marked by large-scale production and relatively adequate over-all research expenditures is required. For the first problem, two sorts of solutions appear possible: increases in the scale of production in the hope of improving research performance within the free enterprise framework; and government encouragement of research. Both alternatives are controversial—the former being anathema to liberals who distrust large-scale business and the latter anathema to conservatives who distrust large-scale government. The discussion which follows, therefore, is unlikely to command wide-spread agreement. Regardless of whether the desirability of increases in the scale of production are accepted, a discussion of the relationship between research performance and large-scale production should clarify some aspects of our present-day American economy. Let us start, therefore, with a consideration of the contribution to improved research performance that might be made by changes in the scale of production and then consider possible encouragement of research by government action.

Research, large-scale production, and oligopoly

"Large-scale production" means merely that a firm produces on a relatively large scale—say, is among the firms with over 5,000 employees which provide 40 per cent of total employment. Conversely "small-scale" means just the opposite—say, that the firm is among those with less than 500 employees which provide 35 per cent of total employment. Again "oligopoly" merely means that there are few sellers in the industry or market with which we are concerned. The two terms, therefore, do not necessarily mean the same thing. If the industry or market is large enough, it may have many large-scale firms; if it is small enough, it may have only a few small-scale firms. In general, however, there is likely to be considerable correlation—if only because scale is usually defined with reference to the situation which currently prevails in the economy.

Undoubtedly there are cases in which more research is undertaken by an industry with many small-scale producers than by one with a few large-scale producers. But these are likely to be very much the exception rather than the rule. We have seen that the larger the firm, the more likely it is to have a research program. And there are clearly types of research—such as those which require large expenditures and much equipment—which cannot be undertaken by small-scale firms. Moreover, it is hard to think of research that can be done by small-scale firms which cannot also be done by firms operating on a larger scale. Hence, although not all economists agree that increasing the scale of production will typically bring about an expansion of research, it appears to me likely that, other things equal, large-scale production will be correlated with large-scale research expenditures and therefore with the probability of a more rapid increase in productivity.

Note that the word used is "probability." One reason that there is so little agreement on this matter is that the oligopoly likely to be associated with large-scale production can have many results. If it results in a market-sharing device or, more specifically, an agreement to restrict research expenditures and to hold up the introduction of new products, then obviously the probability will not be realized and the oligopoly in all regards will be inferior. But agreements tending to restrict research appear to be rare among American oligopolies (though more frequent in Europe), so that this sort of danger seems unlikely to be of practical importance in the United States.

Excessive profits and rapid development

Perhaps the most general objection to oligopoly is that it is likely to lead to excessive profits. It can readily be shown, however, that if more extensive research under oligopoly leads to development which is only a little more rapid than would otherwise occur, the resulting more rapid development will quickly offset whatever adverse affects the possibly higher profits may have on the distribution of income.[1] Total corporate profits amount to approximately 12 per cent of the national income. Suppose that oligopoly profits, on the average, amount to 18 per cent while competitive profits average 6 per cent. (The assumed difference is probably extreme; it is quite unlikely that oligopolies are three times as profitable as competitive industry.) With profits taxed at the present approximate rate of 50 per cent, however, half of the 12 per cent of additional profits assumed to be received by oligopolies, or 6 per cent, would be paid to the government in additional taxes on the income of the oligopoly. If government expenditures were unchanged, other taxes could be proportionately reduced, so that the welfare of those not owning oligopolies would to this extent be unchanged. Hence replacement of competition by oligopoly would leave nonowners with 6 per cent less income initially—the portion of the original 12 per cent increase retained by oligopolies after additional taxation. Of this 6 per cent, half would typically be saved by the corporation and half distributed to its owners as additional dividends. To what extent do these uses have adverse effects from the social point of view?

On the ground that the added income is not deserved, let us completely disregard any pleasure that owners of oligopolies may derive from the increase in their dividends. We cannot treat additional saving in the same way; as Chapter 8 makes clear, saving is socially important. But, to avoid determining how important, let us see how much more rapidly productivity would have to increase to offset initial declines in nonowner income of both 3 and 6 per cent. (The 3 per cent figure in effect assumes all corporate saving is socially useful; the 6 per cent figure in effect assumes that corporate saving is of no use whatsoever.) Since 1870 the increase in productivity per capita has averaged 1.9

---

[1] There are, of course, other objections to oligopoly. Some economists argue that it tends to increase costs and to cause underutilization of capital, though I do not find such arguments convincing except for the short run when the oligopoly is being established. Excessive profits also have a tendency to misallocate resources, but Arnold C. Harberger has shown that the welfare loss involved is miniscule (American Economic Association, *Proceedings,* May, 1954). The argument of the text is presented in greater detail in the *Political Science Quarterly,* September, 1957.

per cent.[2] The following table summarizes the number of years that would be needed for various differences in the speed with which income increases to make up for the initial declines in the income of those not owning oligopolies.

TABLE 6-1.   YEARS REQUIRED TO OFFSET INITIAL INCOME DECLINES

Productivity difference	Number of Years Required	
	To offset 3 per cent	To offset 6 per cent
.2(1.8/2.0)	16	32
.6(1.6/2.2)	6	11
1.0(1.4/2.4)	4	7

What this table means is that, when productivity in the economy as a whole is increasing at 1.9 per cent a year, if oligopoly situations achieved a 2 per cent rate and competitive situations a 1.8 per cent rate of productivity increase, even the small 0.2 per cent difference would compensate nonowners for the higher income of owners in 16 years; were the difference as large as 1 per cent—2.4 for oligopolies and 1.4 per cent for competitive industry—the time required would be a mere 4 years. Clearly if large-scale oligopoly does develop appreciably more rapidly than small-scale competitive industry, the faster rate of development will rapidly compensate for the adverse income distribution, providing higher real incomes even for those who were originally adversely affected. To offset both the higher income of owners and the additional saving will take not more than 32 years. But this is not all. Although the relationship between an increase in saving and an increase in income is by no means precise, it is clear that additional saving may itself be expected to bring about a somewhat more rapid increase in income quite apart from the more rapid increase in productivity that may be likely under oligopoly. Even if this possibility is completely disregarded, the fact remains that, to the extent that there are significant differences in the rate of increase in productivity between competition and oligopoly, the adverse effect of the latter on income distribution will be rather rapidly offset.

Should large-scale production be encouraged?

If the higher profits that may possibly result from oligopoly are not particularly serious, then does it follow that large-scale production

[2] Moses Abramovitz, "Resource and Output Trends in the United States Since 1870" (*Occasional Paper* 52, National Bureau of Economic Research, 1956), p. 7.

should be encouraged as a matter of social policy even if it results in oligopoly? The danger that explains why most economists would in all probability deplore such a development is that the reduction in competition which today permits wider profit margins may tomorrow spread to other areas and activities, so that in time the few surviving producers may drift into market-sharing, live-and-let-live arrangements under which first innovation, and ultimately research itself, may be greatly reduced. That this is a possible danger cannot be denied; how probable it is is harder to estimate. In a particular highly competitive industry, the dangers inherent in oligopoly can be partially avoided by relying on oligopolistic suppliers to provide research and development. Unfortunately this is not necessarily a full or lasting solution, as the competitive industry may not have the financial resources to adopt new techniques— which in turn will inevitably discourage the development of improved technology by the industry's suppliers. And there is also no reason why the suppliers may not themselves in time drift into market-sharing arrangements.

Concentration, it is worth stressing, is not a new problem separately created by efforts to promote research and development. Rather it is a problem with which we have to deal in any event. Specifically it now appears highly unlikely that any new firms will ever again be able to enter the automobile industry and it is by no means certain that more than three will survive. The problem of making these three continue to compete is, therefore, one which we must in any event solve if free enterprise is to remain viable. It is not clear how much more difficult achieving a general solution would become if the number of oligopolistic industries were somewhat increased.

On the other hand, the benefits of large-scale production must not be overstated. At best it makes probable—but by no means guarantees —large research expenditures and more rapid development. We have seen that the highly competitive bituminous coal industry—at least under intense enough pressure from alternative fuels—has been able to develop rapidly, though the recent improvement has been accompanied by a somewhat greater concentration of production. And anthracite coal appears to be, if anything, even less progressive than bituminous despite the fact that it is organized oligopolistically. Here the problem appears to be that bituminous coal is a substantially cheaper source of BTU's than anthracite, which has enjoyed a special market, especially in house heating, because it produced less smoke. Hence an aggressive effort on the part of an anthracite producer to expand sales by lowering costs and prices would have involved trying to expand into markets where bituminous had a natural advantage. Instead, the response of the anthracite producers appears to have been to share the available special market—a response which has left the industry not only unprogressive but with its future prospects clouded. There can be no doubt of the fact that oligopolistic organization does not by itself guarantee that an industry will be technically progressive.

Over-all the desirability of encouraging large-scale production—and risking oligopoly—in my judgment is a matter of alternatives. In view of the smallness of the effective increase in profits under oligopoly and the probability that on balance development is likely to be significantly more rapid, encouragement of large-scale production does not seem without merit—provided that no effective alternative is available. Specifically, suppose that, instead of the present thousands of small-scale producers, the bituminous coal industry had been organized since World War I into an oligopoly with 10 to 20 large firms—in roughly the pattern that developed in the oil industry following the Supreme Court's dissolution of the original Standard Oil monopoly in 1912. Had oligopoly prevailed, I am inclined to believe that the technology of mining coal would by now have been revolutionized and the social performance of the industry have been substantially superior to what in fact it has been. It should be emphasized, however, that this judgment is only likely to be valid if the level of competition that prevails is not less than has been maintained in the United States in recent years; it is definitely not likely to be valid in an economy of cartels and monopolistic agreements. But in the American situation it seems hard to deny that the emergence of large-scale production—despite the accompanying expansion of oligopoly—has contributed significantly to the speed with which our productivity has increased.[3] Before attempting to reach a final decision on the over-all social desirability of encouraging large-scale production, however, let us consider whether as an alternative more rapid economic development can be better achieved by government encouragement of research.

Government and practical research

In view of the progress that America has made under free enterprise, any suggestion that the government should expand its activities and accept new responsibilities in connection with the encouragement of practical research is inevitably controversial. Let us, therefore, recapitulate the analysis which brought us to contemplate so dire a possibility. There is general agreement that, left to their own devices, people do not spend enough on education and that the performance of the economy

---

[3] Obviously, the question of the desirability of large firms raises issues which go beyond economics—as illustrated, for example, by the contention that such firms have excessive political power. While I happen to believe that the reverse is more likely to be true, discussion of the issues involved is beyond the scope of this volume.

benefits from the provision by government of additional educational opportunities. What is here being suggested is that, somewhat similarly, industry as presently organized does not undertake sufficient practical research and that the performance of the economy would benefit significantly from additional research. In contrast to education, however, it is not necessary for the government itself to provide the additional research—any more than the government produces planes or tanks or guns when they are needed. It is merely necessary for the government to accept responsibility for seeing that an appropriate level of research is achieved.

How could government best discharge such a responsibility? Some over-all direction would clearly be necessary. For an important purpose of the program would be to correct the present lack of balance in research expenditures. There is, of course, no reason why such expenditures should have any particular uniformity among industries; but it seems equally unlikely that the present pattern of expenditures is that which is socially desirable. Hence enough central control would appear desirable to permit reasonable concentration on areas with greatest needs and most promising prospects—perhaps chosen on the basis of joint recommendations by the National Science Foundation and the Council of Economic Advisers. But once reasonable balance among industries had been achieved, substantial autonomy would appear desirable. Even more than in the case of fundamental research, an approach emphasizing variety seems essential, to utilize to the fullest possible extent available facilities of industry, government, and educational institutions—much as they are today used to develop a guided missile.

The possibility of productivity institutes

A device which certainly would deserve serious consideration in the implementation of any program of government encouragement of research would be the establishment of government-sponsored productivity institutes in areas of the economy where increases in productivity seem especially urgent. Suppose, for example, a Cotton Productivity Institute had been set up in 1920 and had been promised 1 per cent of the value of the cotton crop for as long as it was able to make a significant contribution to the improvement of productivity in growing cotton. Would the revolution that now appears probable have come more rapidly? The answer obviously depends on the quality of the leadership of the Institute. The sum involved could easily be spent by incompetent people without achieving anything of consequence. But with reasonably competent leadership which attempted to enlist the aid of private industry by subsidy or otherwise wherever possible and undertook work itself only when there was no one else capable of doing it better, it seems probable that the revolution might well have been significantly expedited. Because of the small scale of the typical cotton grower and the interrelated character of the solution, a Cotton Productivity Institute might well have made an unusually important contribution, especially if it worked closely with the chemical and farm implement industries. In fact, given the practical impossibility of achieving anything remotely resembling large-scale production in the growing of cotton within the foreseeable future, it is hard to see how cotton-growing technology can be improved except by a device such as a productivity institute. The only alternative is to accept the rate of development that results from the fact that the chemical and farm implement industries, which supply cotton growers, happen to be oligopolies operating on a large scale.

Productivity institutes and basic applied research

Would a Coal Productivity Institute have made as important a contribution? In this case it is possible to place greater reliance on large-scale production, as mergers of present firms until production on the required scale was achieved is certainly technically possible. But a Coal Institute, nonetheless, might have made a contribution—especially in connection with the encouragement of basic applied research. It seems quite unlikely that, for example, the possibilities of underground gasification are today receiving the attention that they deserve. Again, technological help regarding radical improvements in the transportation of coal (such as movement of coal through pipe lines) is currently being provided by the electric power industry—ironically enough, mainly as a result of the vast demand for electric power created by the atomic energy program. But it is by no means certain that all promising alternatives in regard to transportation are being explored to the extent desirable.

These particular instances are merely examples of a problem that we have suggested may be quite general throughout American industry: that there appears to be inadequate profit incentive in many areas of the economy to provide the socially desirable level of basic applied research. Would the wide establishment of productivity institutes provide an effective solution to this problem? The possibility is one on which, in the absence of actual experience, we can do no more than speculate. If the productivity institute made its results available to all at reasonable fees, it is quite likely that its only effect would be to relieve everyone in the industry of any sense of obligation to undertake basic applied research—just as most radio producers felt, as we have seen, no obligation to develop television. Undoubtedly this result would be even more likely if the institute were financed directly by the firms of the industry; in fact, if the amounts to be paid were controlled by the firms involved, the institute might well become a device to reduce research expenditures. And if the institute were to be granted any sort of monopoly over improvements by, for example, a requirement that all patents be sold to it at reasonable prices, the results would be infinitely worse than anything which presently prevails. In short, to the extent that the institutes were organized to undertake joint research *under the control of* the industry involved and *without government supervision,* there is no doubt that the idea raises serious dangers.

But suppose, alternatively, that the institute's funds come primarily from the government—either from taxes on the industry or from general revenues; suppose that the institute, while licensing all comers, charged the highest fees that the traffic would bear on the patents it came to hold; and suppose that, far from being granted any sort of monopoly, the institute operated in full competition with the research departments of all the firms in the industry. Particularly if individual firms were given, in the enforcement of the antitrust laws, somewhat greater freedom to exploit the inventions that they were able to develop in competition with the institute, it appears to me that institutes so organized might make a significant contribution. At the very least, the government would be in a position to ensure that resources were devoted to basic applied research in the amounts and in the areas where they seemed likely to do the most good—though mere devotion of resources to research of course carries no guarantee that results will be achieved. But the institute might also serve to *encourage private research* both directly by charging licensing fees which were *higher* than a private patent monopolist would now be likely to charge in view of our antitrust laws and indirectly by creating a climate in which higher fees on improvements developed in competition with the institute were tolerated.

Research, competition, and profits

Throughout the emphasis has been on creating effective competition in research. In all probability, the more practical the results sought, the more likely that they can best be attained within the framework of private competitive enterprise. This means that the institutes would generally devote relatively little effort to what we may call "practical applied research"—the design of specific product models or the improvement of particular tools or machines. Rather the institutes could best concentrate on encouraging basic applied research. But even in this connection reliance on competition and a variety of approaches appears highly desirable. Take, for example, the systematic exploration of alternatives, including those which do not now seem likely to be fruitful. It is by no means necessary for an institute to undertake all such work itself. It might well induce a firm to explore an unprepossessing alternative by a combination of subsidy covering an appropriate portion of research costs and the promise of a share of the profits if the research turned out to be successful.

Obviously in making arrangements of this sort abuses are possible; bribery and graft, rather than merit, may determine the allocation of research contracts. The possibility cannot be denied, but whether its likely quantitative importance warrants concern is less clear. In fact, there is much to be said for a general effort to increase the profitability of research. It is true that fundamental research is often undertaken by dedicated men little concerned with material rewards. But practical results can undoubtedly be more rapidly and economically achieved if satisfactory solutions carry with them the prospect of appropriate profits. Attempts, however well-intentioned, to reduce the rewards derived from successful practical research seem a rather clear-cut example of killing the goose that lays the golden egg. For, though the exact total is not known, the sum currently being paid for the use of patents is certainly so small that a doubling of the amount would seem a cheap price to pay if any important improvement in research performance were to result. Further, if in a particular case rewards which appeared unduly large were being received from a particular patent, an effort to limit such rewards by developing competing techniques or products seems a far more socially desirable approach than any direct effort to reduce the receipts obtained from successful research.

Large-scale production versus government encouragement

Once again the tentative and controversial character of the discussion just concluded needs to be stressed; these are matters on which there exists no general agreement among economists. To sum up: whether practical research should be encouraged along the unorthodox lines that have been suggested depends ultimately on a comparison of one's estimate of the benefits likely to flow from increased research and more rapid development with the dangers inherent in either an expansion of large-scale production (and the accompanying risk of oligopoly) or an increase in government "interference" through the creation of productivity institutes. My own appraisal is that the benefits of more rapid development are likely to be sufficiently great to justify both some increase in concentration in industries now marked by small-scale operations *and* the fairly general establishment of productivity institutes—with the exact balance between the two varying from industry to industry depending on the particular prevailing circumstances. Among those who agree that some action is desirable, those anxious to avoid concentration within an industry or among its suppliers are likely to favor productivity institutes, while those who oppose all such "interferences" with the private economy as the institutes would represent are likely to favor the encouragement of research through concentration of production.

Other alternatives

It is worth stressing, in conclusion, that the present discussion has by no means exhausted all the alternative ways in which research can be encouraged. Emphasis has been placed on devices that seem likely to yield immediate results. But it may well be that techniques designed to secure an increased expenditure on research have been unduly stressed. Certainly the creation of an environment favorable to research is of immense importance; in numerous cases in the past important discoveries have been achieved by talented people with a minimum of physical facilities. Perhaps no nation has been more successful in achieving much with little than the British—as evidenced by jet engines, radar, dacron, and penicillin, to name but a few obvious examples. And there can be no doubt that the creation of physical facilities does not guarantee even successful applied research. But it is also obvious that some facilities are needed, and there is no reason why the proposed productivity institutes, for example, should not back the talented lone wolf as well as the established laboratory. And there is also no reason why they should not back research into ways and means of improving research performance; for this clearly is a subject on which additional study is urgently needed.

CHAPTER SEVEN

THE ROLE OF INNOVATION

Conditions which favor innovation

Organizing an industry so that it performs research is no more important than organizing it so that it innovates—actually introduces commercially the invention or other improvement in technology that research has made possible. What conditions are likely to make for rapid innovation? Undoubtedly the most fundamental condition is an industry so organized that a firm which fails to innovate stands to get hurt—and get hurt seriously—because it fails to react to changed conditions. The other side of the coin is that a man who hurts his competitors—and does it for no immediately apparent reason except to make more money for himself—should at least be acceptable socially; it is even better if he is honored for his efforts. But while competitive pressures may be fundamental in bringing about rapid innovation, many other factors are involved; they range all the way from such predominantly economic matters as the organization of industry and the characteristics of competition to such broadly sociological considerations as general receptivity to change and the concept of fair play. Innovation by definition involves change and, therefore, inevitably conflicts with our increasing desire for security; while competition involves struggle, and our sense of fair play dictates that the struggle should be among equals, with no large corporation "bullying" a smaller rival.

In this chapter attention will be concentrated on the specifically economic factors which influence the rate of innovation, especially the relationship between the organization of an industry and the rate of innovation that it achieves. Though some of the broader influences will inevitably enter the picture, extended treatment of such matters will be postponed to Chapter 10. Let us start with two examples: one of an industry marked by rapid innovation and the other of an industry where innovation has been conspicuously slow, exploring the meaning of the term in connection with our first example. We will then try to apply the lessons learned to the major ways in which industries are organized both in the United States and abroad.

The meaning of innovation

Though an oligopoly, the American automobile industry has been marked by rapid innovation. It has also been subject, especially recently, to severe criticism. An examination of the criticism will aid in showing that in the last analysis "innovation" is as difficult a word to define as "development." In essence the criticism of the automobile industry is that: (1) it caters to consumer demand; and (2) it does not cater to consumer demand. Both at present are correct. For the industry, which is handicapped by the considerable length of time that must elapse between "locking up" the design of a model and its actual production, appears to have underestimated the extent of the demand for a "small" car. To the extent that the demand for such a car continues on a scale sufficient *to make its production economic,* there seems little doubt that it will be produced. In the nature of the case, however, the economies of mass production are inevitably accompanied by reductions in the choices that are available, as it is obviously not economic to produce in the United States a variety of small cars if the demand for each variety is limited. Hence foreign imports will undoubtedly continue and the American industry persist in not producing exactly what every consumer wants.

The opposite criticism—that the industry caters to consumer demand—is not usually made in just these words. The industry is, however, frequently criticized for failing to provide functional transportation. But cotton stockings and flat-heel shoes are more functional clothing than the high heels and sheer nylons the public prefers; I suspect that the number of car buyers who want functional transportation is about the same as the number of women who wear cotton hose. More sophisticated is the criticism that the industry creates the bad taste to which it caters. But over the last decade the industry has consistently offered an inexpensive black sedan with an economical six-cylinder engine—and the public has stayed away in droves. In fact, the company of the "big three" which during the early postwar years most consistently won the praise of consumer magazines sold fewest cars and was in danger of going bankrupt until it introduced a new line which was longer, lower, and had bigger fins than any of its competitors. And even in 1958, when sales fell and criticism rose, the two lines which stood out against the trend were the Oldsmobile and the most expensive version of the Chevrolet—both of which were loaded with more chrome than ever before.

The fact of the situation is that the automobile is today a fashion product which is bought with little more regard to economy or durability than a dress with the New Look. It is frequently argued that styles are deliberately created to render obsolete the consumer's existing inventory of goods and therefore increase the purchases that he has to make. But style changes are expensive for the automobile industry; the industry's profits in all probability would have been appreciably higher if model changes had been slower. In any event, just as a woman is likely to buy a dress sufficiently different so that her friends will know it is new, so car buyers have consistently preferred models which are noticeably different from those already on the road. Admittedly this may be conspicuous consumption—consumption for the benefit of the neighbors rather than for the intrinsic merit of the product—but, then, being social animals, do we ever act without considering the impact on others of what we do? In short, one may dislike much of what passes for taste in America and still believe in the desirability of allowing American industry to cater to our collective idiosyncrasies!

Even if catering to consumer demand is accepted as proper, the question remains as to the extent to which meeting its vagaries constitutes innovation. To what extent was the sack dress or the New Look an innovation? Confining innovation to "functional improvements" does not help. What is the "function" of a dress—to provide warmth and meet the requirements of modesty or to attract men? In essence this is the same problem that was discussed at the start of Chapter 1 in connection with the meaning of "economic development." There seems little need to repeat that discussion. Instead let us tie the two matters together by defining "innovation" as the *making of changes which contribute to economic development*. This means that a style change, to the extent at least that it adds to the economic value of a product, is a type of innovation. But we made very clear in Chapter 1 that economic development did not necessarily imply "improvement" in any more general sense of the term. In the same way not all innovation is necessarily for the "better" in any over-all sense.

The performance of the automobile industry

In the light of this discussion, what is the record of the American automobile industry in regard to innovation? Clearly it has been sufficiently rapid to bring about drastic changes in consumer preferences among producers, as Chart 7-1 makes quite clear. Further, there can be no doubt that the industry is organized so that firms can get hurt—and get hurt seriously—as the behavior of earnings in the following table demonstrates. Two firms went from comfortable profits to losses which

TABLE 7-1. AUTOMOBILE PROFITS PER SHARE

Date	American Motors	Chrysler	Ford	General Motors	Studebaker-Packard
1948	4.63	10.25	1.82	1.62	5.07
1949	6.04	15.19	3.35	2.44	2.59
1950	6.64	14.69	4.93	3.12	1.73
1951	3.73	8.27	2.39	1.88	1.88
1952	2.90	9.04	2.21	2.08	1.94
1953	3.25	8.59	3.14	2.24	1.88
1954	d1.95	2.13	4.31	3.03	d4.06
1955	d1.23	11.49	8.19	4.30	d4.80
1956	d5.36	2.29	4.38	3.02	d6.73
1957	d1.88	13.75	5.19	2.99	d1.73

d denotes deficit.

made their future uncertain, and Chrysler's average earnings declined significantly during the period. But in 1955 General Motors' earnings were 165 per cent and Ford's 350 per cent higher than they had been in 1948. All firms except the two leaders were hurt in various degrees. But many improvements which the average consumer—rightly or wrongly—wanted were achieved. Cars were made longer, lower, and roomier; engines were completely redesigned and made more powerful; performance and roadability were much improved; automatic transmissions became practically universal; and many new features, such as power brakes and power steering, were made available.[1] In addition, manufacturing techniques were steadily improved and manufacturing capacity greatly increased. In short, it seems clear that the industry, even though it was highly oligopolistic, was innovating rapidly.

[1] Evidence that the changes listed were what most people wanted is provided by the fact that the share of "middle-price" cars expanded steadily at the expense of "low-price" cars as long as the former were significantly longer, roomier, and more powerful, or offered a greater choice of gadgets. But, when the differences became insignificant toward the end of the fifties, the share of the "middle-price" group fell sharply.

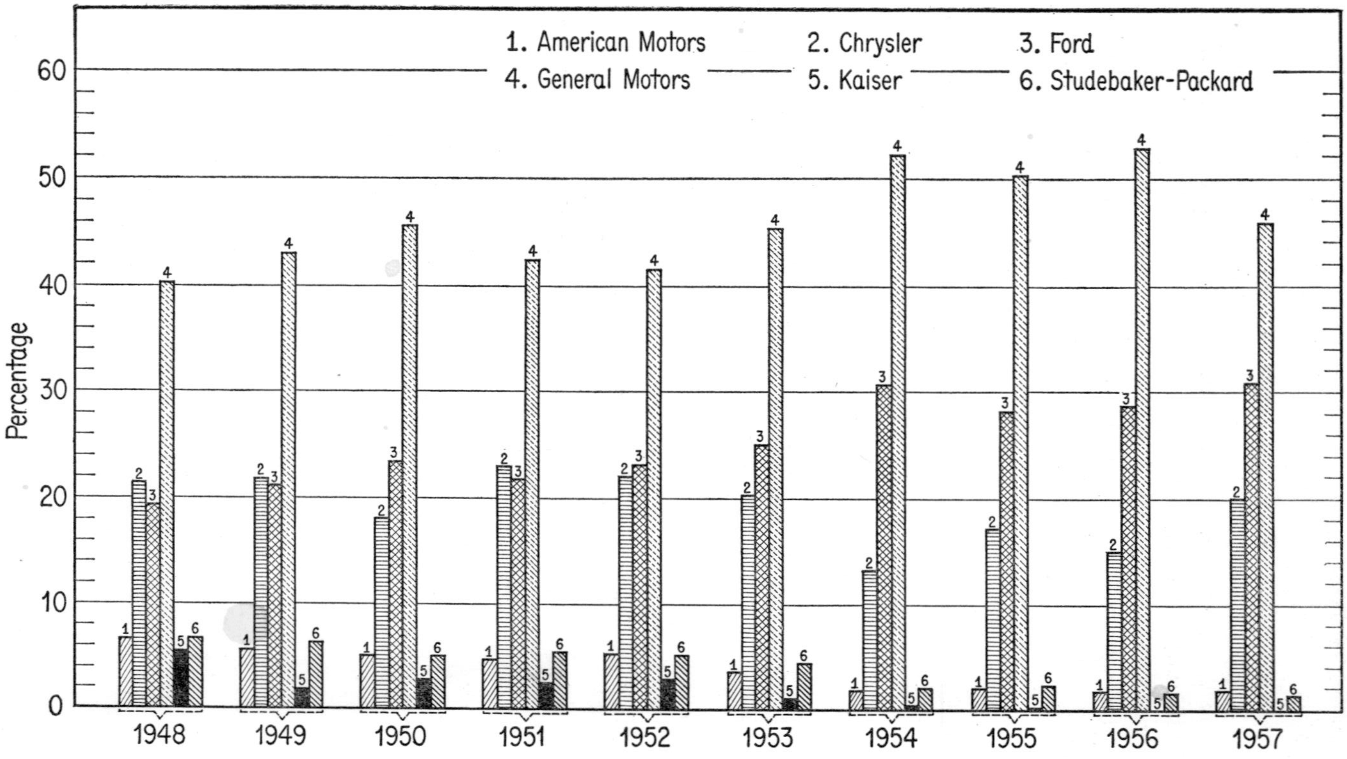
1. American Motors
2. Chrysler
3. Ford
4. General Motors
5. Kaiser
6. Studebaker-Packard
Percentage
0
10
20
30
40
50
60
1948
1949
1950
1951
1952
1953
1954
1955
1956
1957

CHART 7-1. PERCENTAGE OF TOTAL CAR PRODUCTION SECURED BY AMERICAN PRODUCERS BETWEEN 1948 AND 1957

Another way of getting at the factors promoting innovation is to examine the extent to which there is open or tacit market sharing in an industry. Each firm in the automobile industry appears dedicated to the proposition that it is permanently entitled to the highest percentage of the total market that it has ever achieved in the past and is prepared to do almost anything—short of cutting prices—to gain the share of the market to which it feels it is entitled. So long as an adequate number of firms fail to achieve their objective permanently—so that oligopoly is not reduced to duopoly or monopoly—an industry so organized appears likely to achieve rapid innovation. Economists have, in fact, long suspected that the best of all monopoly profits is a quiet life. On this basis the automobile industry was clearly not monopolistic.

An example of slow innovation

On the other hand, the worst possible way to organize an industry from the point of view of innovation is to permit rigid market sharing and price fixing. Neither is typically permitted under the Sherman Act, though price fixing is allowed under fair trade laws and required under mandatory fair trade. Hence the best available example is probably the British coal industry after the Coal Mines Act of 1930, which authorized the setting of fixed quotas and minimum prices for each company. (Lest we feel smug, recall that the American coal industry sought exactly the same solution through the Bituminous Coal Act of 1937; the only difference is that our Act, under the impact of the war-induced expansion of demand, was allowed to expire in 1943.) Of the two, price fixing at the manufacturing level is likely to be relatively unimportant if changes in the product are possible, as such changes may in themselves permit significant competition. Market sharing, however, has a devastating effect on innovation because it greatly reduces the rewards that innovation can be expected to achieve. Indeed rewards for product improvements—except to the extent that the improvement of one firm's product expands the demand for the industry as a whole—are completely eliminated.

Moreover, improvements in techniques of production are undoubtedly most easily made in connection with expansions of capacity; many small changes which may not be worth making in an existing plant can make an appreciable difference when a new plant is established or a new mine opened. Thus where an industry as a whole is expanding, innovation is likely to be relatively rapid. But where firms can expand at the expense of their less efficient rivals, innovation may also be rapid even if total output is not growing or is only growing slowly. It is not, of course, essential for a firm to succeed in expanding at the expense of its rivals. If, as is frequently the case, the rivals feel that they have no alternative but to undertake retaliatory investment, then the final result is likely to be that inefficient plant is retired far more rapidly than it otherwise would have been even if relative market shares are in fact unchanged.

Expansion of production is not always necessary. Profits will be increased if costs are reduced even with output unchanged. But, in contrast to the case in which the firm expects, or at least hopes, to use both new machinery and old, with unchanged output old machinery will inevitably have to be scrapped. Moreover, as capital costs are in most cases a relatively small part of total costs, significant cost savings with unchanged output usually mean that labor will be released without even the hope that it can be reabsorbed by an expansion of sales. Further, labor in the typical situation probably has more control over changes in existing job categories in an existing plant than when new techniques are established in a new plant. Thus, while the role of labor in connection with innovation will be more fully examined in Chapter 10, workers, in general, can be expected to oppose strongly those changes which lead to the inevitable displacement of labor—perhaps to the point at which management is significantly deterred from attempting to innovate.

In short, when a firm is prohibited from expanding at the expense of its competitors—which means hurting other firms by taking away their market and perhaps ultimately driving them out of business—much of the incentive to innovate will have been lost. Why under such circumstances should a firm try to develop a better mousetrap or risk a strike by its labor force in order to reduce costs if nothing it can do will enable it to increase its sales faster than those of the industry as a whole? In the case of British coal the result of market sharing was that little coal was undercut up to World War II (when expanding output and shrinking labor supply forced some improvement), productivity was significantly lower than in both the United States and Germany (partly but not wholly because of the inferior seams which had to be worked in Britain), and there came to be general agreement by both the Labour and Conservative Parties that the coal industry should be nationalized as rapidly as possible.

Innovation under competition

With these examples of rapid and slow innovation in mind, let us explore the relationship between different types of industrial organization and the rate of innovation. We may start with highly competitive, small-scale industry approximating "perfect competition" such as exists in agriculture. Whatever its merits from the point of view of resource allocation, it is not a form of organization which necessarily promotes rapid innovation. It is often hard to get the "entrepreneur" involved to utilize the results of research—which means that a farmer, dead tired from a day's work, finds it hard to read up on the latest developments in contour plowing. As a result reliance on market pressures alone has not been deemed sufficient in agriculture; instead, to ensure a satisfactory rate of innovation, around $75 millions annually is spent on an elaborate system of bulletins, county agents, and demonstration farms—developed by the extension service of the Department of Agriculture in conjunction with state experiment stations.[2]

In addition to having difficulty in learning of innovations, firms operating on a small-scale may also be unable to finance desirable changes, especially if increases in the scale of production are involved. Thus far this has not been a serious problem in agriculture. The efficient scale of production has remained small, though there is some evidence that increasing mechanization may in the future enlarge the efficient farm to the point at which the sums needed for financing will become difficult for an individual to raise. But outside agriculture, when substantial expansions in the scale of production have become desirable, financial difficulties have frequently retarded innovation if the industry is composed of a large number of small firms. Even when organized as corporations— which avoid the special difficulties associated with the unlimited liability of partnerships and proprietorships—it is not easy for small firms to attract capital. For, no matter how optimistic he may have been regarding the automobile industry, it was not easy at the start for an investor to choose General Motors or Ford among the thousands of firms that at one time or another made cars in the United States. Admittedly the rewards of those who picked the successful companies were high and the desire to take a long chance may have offset, to some extent at least, the conservative attraction of more oligopolistic areas where the certainty of participation was likely to more than offset a lower anticipated rate of growth. While this is not a matter on which a great deal is known, the extent to which small firms have had in the past to grow predominantly out of their own resources makes it probable that on balance financial difficulties have significantly slowed down innovation in areas where small-scale firms predominated.

The situation in this regard has undoubtedly become appreciably more difficult in recent years under the impact of higher corporate taxation and the efforts of the Securities and Exchange Commission to eliminate the flotation of securities by means of fraudulent or misleading information. Lower tax rates for "small" corporations help, but major differences in rates encourage the proliferation of subsidiaries designed entirely to make use of the tax advantage. Hence only limited relief from

[2] Theodore W. Schultz, *The Economic Organization of Agriculture* (New York: McGraw-Hill, 1953), p. 119.

differences in tax rates appears administratively feasible so long as substantial revenue is to be obtained from corporate taxation. In the case of
the SEC the problem is that the cost of arranging to underwrite a new
security issue—costs such as investigating the company, checking the
legality of the issue, and printing the prospectus required by the SEC,
which must be incurred before new securities can be sold—are often little
different for an issue of one or ten million dollars, so that the percentage
of the funds taken by underwriting costs increases rapidly as the size of
the issue decreases. On the other hand, in recent years there has been a
considerable movement toward "diversification" on the part of large businesses, probably not so much to increase total profits (there being no
reason to believe that the new areas will on the average be more profitable than the old) as to promote a more peaceful life by eliminating the
headaches that arise when profits fluctuate as a result of changes in business conditions in a particular area of the economy. This development
has been much aided by the same tax laws that retard the growth of
small firms. For an existing business may offset its mistakes in one field
against the income earned elsewhere—and this very fact makes it attractive to conservative investors. Thus while they may have had little *over-
all* effect in retarding innovation, the tax laws and the SEC—however
justified they may be on other grounds—certainly have made innovation
more difficult in industries organized on a small-scale, competitive basis.

In short, problems involving the quality of available entrepreneur-
ship and difficulties in financing expansion may well retard innovation to
a significant extent in a competitive industry marked by small-scale
firms. The difficulties can, however, easily be exaggerated; so long as
there are no restrictions on price competition or entry into the industry,
the retardation of innovation is likely to be relatively small.

Innovation under restricted competition

Perhaps the main difficulty with competition as a way of organizing
industry is that people tend to feel sorry for the firms involved just because they are small. Thus taxicabs in New York City are one of the
clearest available examples of a technical monopoly: not only are fares
rigidly controlled, but the number of hack licenses issued by the Police
Department has not changed for a number of years, so that entry is possible only by buying an existing license. Further, it is possible to estimate
with a high degree of accuracy the capitalized value of the monopoly
profits which result from the possession of a hack license; this may be
done by subtracting from the total price paid for a cab with a hack license the readily ascertainable value of the cab alone. The value of a license determined in this way is currently about $15,000, which in turn

means that for this reason alone hundreds of dollars more each year must be paid for the use of cabs than would be the case if entry were free. All the same, only the most devoted advocate of laissez faire is likely to argue that it should be free in the light of hours and earnings of cab drivers!

If nothing more than cab drivers were involved, the matter would not be worth our attention. But it is sympathy for the poor proprietor which is basically responsible for such diverse matters as fair trade and the farm program. Furthermore, similar movements in many other countries have gone much farther—in some cases to the point at which it is felt that, once a man opens up a small business, he should, in effect, be guaranteed the right to continue it indefinitely. It is easy to sympathize with the objectives of those who want to reduce competition. The thought of a man losing his life savings by being forced out of a long-established business—especially if his rival is a well-heeled corporation—represents a type of bullying that is repugnant to our sense of fair play. Nevertheless, it is important that we understand what happens when we interfere with competition. When price competition alone is restricted, as it is by fair trade laws (which permit a manufacturer to control the price at which his product is sold by retailers), excessive costs and social waste are likely, caused by both underutilization of capacity and the provision of services which the consumer does not want. When, in addition, entry is restricted, monopoly profits typically ensue, as in the taxicab case just outlined. Thus restrictions on competition clearly distort the pattern of resource use.

But what we are particularly concerned with at this point is that restrictions of this sort are likely to have effects which are even more serious socially because they make innovation more difficult to achieve. The most extreme situation—such as prevailed in British coal mining—is where prices are fixed, entry limited, and rigid quotas established for each producer. With the exception of certain aspects of the farm program, formal quotas have not played much of a role in the American economy; in fact, formal restrictions on entry have also not been particularly important, though they are involved in such things as oil proration and taxicab or liquor licenses. But restrictions on price competition have been widespread, either as a direct result of fair trade or indirectly because of pressure from manufacturers to maintain customary margins. Undoubtedly the problem is most generally acute in the area of distribution. This is true not only because firms are usually relatively small—so that there is great public sympathy with efforts to mitigate the full impact of competition—but also because product variation, which does much to offset rigid manufacturing prices and profit margins, is considerably less important at the retail level.

Broadly since the turn of the century cost savings in distribution have not kept pace with the reduction in manufacturing costs made possible by techniques of mass production. As a result the relative cost of distribution has been rising. For this reason economies in distribution are particularly desirable. Substantial changes are now in progress; it is not too much to say that they would have been greatly retarded had it not been for the broad collapse in restrictions on price competition that marked the end of postwar shortages—roughly from 1950 on. So long as "regular" outlets could sell all the goods that they received at list prices, supplies to "discount" houses were inevitably limited. But, though the timing varied from line to line, as supplies became more generally available, sales through "discount" channels soared. Three main factors were at work: increased consumer knowledge—as a result of the expansion of both consumer organizations and a whole host of "how-to-do-it" publications—which reduced reliance on the "reputation" of the retailer; general car ownership, which facilitated mobility over a wide area; and more leisure time, which permitted extensive comparative shopping. The result was that, when department stores and "regular" outlets tried to hold the line, their sales of hard goods declined drastically. In self-defense they were forced into price competition, which in turn caused an increasing number of manufacturers to abandon efforts to enforce either fair trade or conventional margins.

Closely related has been the development of supermarkets and self-service. The movement started during the depression in food distribution, where price competition has always been substantially unrestricted, and has slowly spread. Again leisure, mobility, and the refrigerator with deep freeze have been involved. The spread has not been without setbacks: it was the reaction of thousands of corner druggists to self-service in "pine-board" drug stores which was responsible for the original passage, during the depression of the thirties, of the fair trade laws. Despite such setbacks the broad movement toward both more supermarkets and more self-service has made steady progress in recent years.

To summarize: the broad process of adapting distribution to the changing character of American life has been most rapid in those areas where price competition has been most vigorous. Had there not been a general decline in restrictions on price competition in the years since 1950, it is probable that the process of innovation and adaptation would have been appreciably slower. In fact, in areas where mandatory fair trade prevails, there are no supermarkets, no self-service, and by definition no discount houses; as a result, unwanted services cannot be eliminated and underutilization of capacity remains chronic.

Oligopolies, cartels, and nationalized industry

Do oligopolies innovate rapidly? Our example of rapid innovation is drawn from such an area. Quality of management, ease of financing, and the character of our tax laws all combine to make innovation easy for oligopolies. Further, the firms that are hurt by the innovation of a rival are so large that they do not command public sympathy. Hence it seems clear that oligopolies *can* innovate easily and rapidly. *Will* they? The word itself, which as we have seen merely means "few sellers," tells us nothing. In terms of the automobile industry, the crux of the problem can be put very simply: will Henry Ford continue to wish to increase his share of the market and outsell Chevrolet or will he be content with his share and anxious to enjoy a quiet life?

It is my impression that *in general* American oligopolies not only attempt to increase their share of their present markets but also are willing to expand into any related field which appears likely to be profitable. The importance of the second of these two points should be recognized. A market-sharing agreement among existing producers will achieve little if the increased profit margins which result from the agreement immediately attract new firms into the industry. This impression of the behavior of American oligopolies should be labeled as tentative; full confirmation would require more detailed studies of industry behavior than we now have. Undoubtedly there are many individual cases in which market sharing occurs. At best the impression is based on present business conduct; there is no guarantee that it may not change in the future. Nor does it imply that there are not many oligopolistic areas where even more rapid innovation would be desirable. But, with all the qualifications in mind, innovation under oligopoly presently appears at the very least to be no less satisfactory than elsewhere and in all probability somewhat more rapid on an over-all basis.

The best guarantee that this situation will continue, and the unique aspect of American oligopolies, is that they operate under the Sherman Act. Little attention has been given to the Act because the changes in judicial interpretation or administrative policy that have occurred from time to time cast little light on basic issues. In fact, it is quite easy to argue that the Act has accomplished little or nothing; the number of companies that have been dissolved as monopolies is miniscule. The overriding fact, however, is that any arrangement for sharing markets is, under the Act, a criminal offense. The result is that, if share they must, American businessmen have either to risk being sent to prison or to rely on "Gentlemen's Agreements"; and available evidence appears to indicate that, in their business dealing at least, Americans businessmen are no gentlemen.

We can have a look at the other side of the coin by considering some of the factors that have retarded the development of British industry. Let us make clear at the start that the interpretation here presented is both controversial and incomplete. It is controversial in the sense that there are economists who feel that it is unduly critical of the performance of British industry; and it is incomplete in the sense that it presents some over-all generalizations which obviously do not apply in every individual case. But it seems to me that the organization of British industry is of major importance in explaining why over the last 75 years British real income per hour of work has increased only about half as fast as in the United States. For in Britain market-sharing arrangements are not only widespread but have only recently been subject to condemnation; in my judgment they have significantly contributed to retarding innovation in British industry. The main reason for this is that British market-sharing schemes have frequently produced results similar to those just described in the case of coal.

Take, for example, the treatment of the British Oxygen Company. After it had been investigated by the British Monopolies Commission, found to supply 98.5 per cent of the oxygen and dissolved acetylene sold in the United Kingdom, and judged to be operating against the public interest, it, nonetheless, was allowed to continue—with its prices and profits unregulated—after promising to engage in research, to offer its products on a nondiscriminatory basis, and to refrain from taking over the remaining 1.5 per cent of the industry! The comment of the London *Economist* summarizes the problem: "British anti-monopoly legislation makes no provision for the breaking up of any company into competing units. . . . But without some such power to restore competition, rather than chain monopolies by the leg, it might be as well to disband the reconstructed Monopolies Commission." [3] The contrast between the treatment of the British Oxygen Company and the Aluminum Company of America, which was not allowed at the end of the war to acquire any government-built aluminum capacity but rather was forced under threat of antitrust action to license its patents to two competitors, provides a measure of the difference in British and American attitudes toward monopoly.

Or consider the British match market, which historically has been split among six firms. Not only were rigid quotas fixed, but firms which exceeded their quotas agreed to pay an amount estimated to be equal to their profits on the additional output to those whose sales fell behind.

[3] January 5, 1957.

Such agreements are not illegal in Britain, although they cannot be enforced in the courts and, starting in 1957, have to be registered publicly and may thereafter be subject to condemnation. Although an investigation of the match industry was begun in 1949 and a report condemning the industry's agreements issued in 1953, as yet no important changes in the organization of the industry have been brought about.

Particularly where there is excess capacity, either cartelization or nationalization may well be a better way of organizing an industry than to preserve the appearance of competition and allow market sharing. Cartels take many forms, but what is probably the most important type involves a common sales agency and an agreed sharing of profits, with production allocated to the plant best qualified to handle it. If all plants had previously been working at, say, 50 per cent of capacity, the advantage of closing down half the plants and working half at 100 per cent is too obvious to need elaboration even when the costs of each plant are identical. It is just this, of course, which market sharing prevents. Further, in any practical situation the plants of different firms are likely to have different costs and to be working at different percentages of capacity. But even where all firms are working at full capacity and have uniform costs, it is still true, in general, that further expansion can be most economically achieved by modernizing and expanding particular existing plants or opening up entirely new plants. This is what a cartel or a nationalized industry can do. It is, in fact, exactly what was done by the German coal cartel during the interwar period, so that productivity in Germany increased significantly. And it has also been what the coal industry in Britain has tried to do since nationalization in 1946. In short, where the allocation of production is centrally controlled, it can be undertaken by the plant with the lowest cost, and new, heavily mechanized plants can be established with the assurance that their expensive machinery will never be idle because decreases in demand can be concentrated on older, less efficient plants.

This is one of the reasons why socialists believe nationalization superior to competition; they contend that allocation of output to the best qualified plant will both reduce current costs and, of most immediate concern, make for more rapid innovation and development. This may well be correct if the alternative involves any important amount of market sharing. But what of the typical American oligopoly? How is output allocated under such conditions to the most efficient plant? The answer is, of course, that it is not done centrally but by the firm with lower production costs driving its competitors out of business and in this way allocating to itself the sales that were previously theirs. This is, if you will, a ruthless process which, if you oppose it, should be referred to as "the law of the jungle." However described, the point is that it works well. For, when its very survival may depend on remaining fit, no firm can allow either its product line to fall much behind or its production costs to rise much above those of its competitors. On the other hand, the various "productivity teams" that have examined British industry since the war have consistently reported that, while the best British technology is unexcelled, the worst is very poor, the range great, and the average inferior. The reason is, predominantly, that market sharing in Britain has been so widespread that superior firms have neither driven the inferior firms out of the industry nor forced them to modernize. Undoubtedly the competitive process can involve some wastage of the capital of the displaced firms, but over-all it appears to result in greater pressure and therefore more rapid innovation than is likely under any alternative arrangement.

Innovation by public utilities

This conclusion can be confirmed by considering the rate of innovation typically achieved by public utilities—which have the same ability to allocate output to the most efficient plant as is possessed by a cartel or nationalized industry. In general, the record, while not particularly bad, is also not particularly good. Take, for example, the American Telephone and Telegraph Company. We have seen that its research record has been first-rate, but as an innovator it has not been outstanding.[4] On more than one occasion it has held up the introduction of technically possible improvements until products embodying them were developed by Western Electric, its manufacturing subsidiary. Obviously in the long run its sales and earnings depend on its basic efficiency—if only because it is competing for the consumer's limited spending. But, equally obviously, it stands to lose very little if it holds up an innovation for a year or two; no competitor will take away its market. As a result its life has been quiet; the dividends paid, for example, remained unchanged at $9 a share from 1922 to 1958. And, while profits in the automobile industry varied in the way summarized in Table 7-1, those of the Telephone Company increased slowly but steadily from $9.86 to $13.00 per share.

Broadly the same is true of other regulated utilities, with variations depending on the closeness of competitive alternatives. When the Tennessee Valley Authority started, rates in the Tennessee Valley were high and current usage low; within a decade private rates had been greatly reduced and over-all usage was the second highest in the United States. In the same way, when the Rural Electrification Administration appeared on the scene, time and again private utilities suddenly found that

---

[4] John Sheahan, *Quarterly Journal of Economics,* May, 1956.

they could serve, and serve at a profit, consumers whom they had previously been unwilling to supply. And the real revolution that has taken place in rail transport—which in exactly one decade (1944-1954) raised the gross-ton-miles of freight trains powered by diesel locomotives from 4 to 84 per cent—has been vastly expedited because truck, pipe line, private car, and airplane have turned what was once a monopoly into a quite competitive business.

Competition and innovation

Just as was true in the case of practical research, there appears to be no substitute for real and effective competition if rapid innovation is to be achieved. But the form taken by such competition may be quite different from the "perfect competition" of many small-scale firms that can be shown to be "ideal"—within the assumptions of the analysis—in connection with resource allocation. In fact, we have suggested that innovation is likely to be most rapid under what may be called "competitive oligopoly"—where the scale of production is large but each firm, nonetheless, makes vigorous efforts to increase its share of the market. On the other hand, innovation in highly competitive areas with small-scale production may be fairly rapid provided that entry is free and prices uncontrolled; but even under such conditions difficulties in connection with learning about research results and obtaining necessary financing may retard innovation. As a result it is hard to determine whether a highly competitive industry is likely to innovate more rapidly than a regulated utility, cartel, or nationalized industry. In each of the three latter cases competitive pressures are obviously reduced, but information and financing are likely to be readily available, so that no general choice among the alternatives appears possible. But it does appear possible to suggest that the greater the extent of restrictions on price competition and, particularly, the greater the amount of market sharing in any industry, the slower is likely to be its rate of innovation— even though the industry may give the appearance of being "competitive" by being organized into a large number of small firms.

CHAPTER EIGHT

THE ROLE OF SAVING

Saving and capital formation

"Saving" is a word of many meanings; our first job, therefore, is to make clear what we mean by the term. In common speech, used in the plural, "savings" frequently refer to the total assets that a man has accumulated. This meaning will cause us least difficulty; it is almost never used in economics and hence can be dismissed without further discussion. Instead "saving" will be used to mean the part of the flow of income not spent on consumption or used to pay taxes in any period. In discussing fluctuations in economic activity, consideration is usually given to whether saving is or is not always equal to investment and the conclusion reached that, as normally used, the two *in any period* are always equal *for the economy as a whole*. This usage we shall follow, so that in any year the nation's saving can be taken as equal to its investment: both in turn will be equal to capital formation, which we shall use as an alternative term for investment.[1]

As explained in Chapter 1, all three of these concepts may be either "gross" or "net," the difference between them being accounted for by "depreciation allowances." These are the sums that business sets aside in any period to make good the wear and tear caused by the production of the period to the capital which was available at the start of the period

---

[1] Note that, however described, what is involved is the production of capital goods, which are those man-made things that help in the future production of goods and services.

—in order that the stock of capital shall be as large at the end of the period as it was at the start. Only when there is net saving will there have been an *addition* to the capital stock during any particular period. But a given amount of investment in a particular area of the economy may occur—even if there is no net addition to the total capital stock—if an equal amount of existing capital is not replaced in some other area. Hence both gross and net saving have a contribution to make to our understanding of the process of capital accumulation.

Sources and uses of saving

Table 8-1 provides a summary of sources and uses of saving in the United States in selected recent years. Let us start with some general words of warning. First, although the data are given in hundred millions (and even millions in the original source), they are in fact *estimates* subject to a sizable margin of error. Some indication of the margin involved is given by the behavior of the "statistical discrepancy." This discrepancy exists because investment and saving are estimated from different data. Theoretically, as we have just seen, the results ought to be exactly the same, but due to unexplained errors they actually diverge by the amount of the discrepancy. Second, the "sources" and "uses" categories are somewhat arbitrary, especially where an item can swing from positive to negative. Thus it would be just as sensible to put "government surplus" (the opposite of "government deficit") on the "sources" side (with of course the sign changed) as it is to place "government deficit" among the "uses." Finally, particular "sources" cannot be joined with particular "uses" with any certainty. All we can say is that the totals must be equal—just as in the case of a pond with several inlets and outlets, we cannot say which inlet feeds which outlet but do know that the total inflow must equal the total outflow if the level does not change.

With these warnings in mind let us examine the estimates for 1957. In that year "personal saving" was $20.7 billions. This was the amount saved by individuals, including those operating unincorporated businesses, in such widely varying forms as deposits in savings banks, contributions to pension funds, mortgage repayments, savings accumulated under life insurance contracts, direct purchase of stocks and bonds, or even, in the case of unincorporated businesses, outright purchases of buildings and machinery. In that same year corporations saved by retaining $7.9 billions of their after-tax profits, so that sources on this basis totaled $28.6 billions. The surpluses of all governmental units made available a further $1.7 billions, while the statistical discrepancy "provided" $.7 billions, so that if we add all "sources" in that particular year

we get a total of $31 billions. This total made possible net private domestic investment of $27.5 billions and net foreign investment of $3.5 billions.

TABLE 8-1.   SOURCES AND USES OF SAVING IN THE UNITED STATES
(In Billions)

	1929	1933	1939	1946	1950	1955	1957
Sources							
Personal saving[a]	4.2	— .6	2.9	13.5	12.6	17.5	20.7
Corporate Saving[b]	2.9	—4.6	.5	2.4	8.6	10.1	7.9
Net saving	7.1	—5.2	3.4	15.9	21.2	27.6	28.6
Uses							
Net private domestic investment[c]	7.6	—5.8	1.5	17.4	30.9	31.9	27.5
Net foreign investment[d]	.8	.2	.9	4.6	—2.2	— .4	3.5
Government deficit[e]	—1.0	1.4	2.1	—4.1	—8.2	—2.9	—1.7
Statistical discrepancy[f]	— .3	—1.0	—1.1	—2.0	.7	—1.0	— .7
Net uses	7.1	—5.2	3.4	15.9	21.2	27.6	28.6
National income	87.8	40.2	72.8	180.9	241.9	330.2	364.0
Net saving and uses as percentage of National Income	8.1	—	4.7	8.8	8.8	8.4	7.9
Depreciation[g]	8.6	7.2	7.8	10.7	19.1	32.0	37.7
Gross saving and uses	15.7	2.0	11.2	26.6	40.3	59.6	66.3
Gross National Product	104.4	56.0	91.1	210.7	284.6	397.5	440.3
Gross saving and uses as percentage of Gross National Product	15.0	3.6	12.3	12.6	14.2	15.0	15.1

[a] Line 2.   [b] Lines 3, 4, and 8.   [c] Line 13 less lines 5, 6, and 7.   [d] Line 14.   [e] Line 9.
[f] Line 15.   [g] Lines 5, 6, and 7.

SOURCE: *Survey of Current Business,* July, 1958, Table 5. References are to the numbered lines of Table 5.

Perhaps the most important thing about Table 8-1 is that it makes clear that the sources of saving are complex. Even personal saving is itself complicated, summarizing the actions of many individuals often undertaken for quite different motives; yet it is only one among several sources of saving. In 1950, for example, such saving provided funds equal to little more than 40 per cent of net private domestic investment; but in 1957 the amount provided had risen to 75 per cent. Corporate savings and government surpluses are the main other sources of saving. Some indication of their importance in the past, as well as a breakdown of personal saving, is provided by Table 8-2.

TABLE 8-2. DISTRIBUTION OF NEW SAVING AMONG SAVER GROUPS
(Percentage Shares)

Period	Farmers	Other individuals	Unincorp. business	Total personal	Corporations	Government[a]
1897–1906	1.3	61.2	5.8	68.3	25.1	6.6
1907–1916	—5.8	70.0	3.6	67.8	23.9	8.3
1920–1929	—2.1	62.8	3.4	64.1	20.4	15.5
1946–1949	7.2	51.8	1.4	60.4	25.3	14.3

[a] Includes nonprofit corporations.

SOURCE: Simon Kuznets, "International Differences in Capital Formation and Financing," contained in *Capital Formation and Economic Growth* (New York: National Bureau of Economic Research, 1955), Table III, p. 75.

It is obvious that, as a source of saving, retained earnings of corporations have a long history. But government, too, has often made a contribution, though the last two periods, both of which follow major wars, are somewhat abnormal, representing the maximum rather than the average contribution that government has made in the past.

The importance of saving

Why should we concern ourselves with saving? In no year for which information is presented in Table 8-1 did net saving amount to as much as 10 per cent of the national income; in no year did gross saving amount to more than 15 per cent of the gross national product. Why then is the matter of major importance? The answer is that the rate of saving is intimately related to the rate of economic development. Without net saving, improvements in technology can only be introduced as capital is replaced at the end of its useful life. In theory this would not rule out substantial development; if when a machine is replaced, the new machine, paid for by the depreciation allowances that have been set aside, is twice as productive as the one which has worn out, productivity will have doubled even without net saving. But this is true only for areas where replacement is undertaken regularly, and is not always true even for such areas.

To start with, assets of government and of consumers are rarely replaced systematically. While consumer durables are not usually considered a part of capital formation, our stock of housing clearly is; and almost no house owner sets aside, for example, 2.5 per cent of the purchase price of his house each year so that at the end of 40 years he can retire his old house and buy a new one. Thus in nonbusiness areas relatively automatic replacement in connection with depreciation allowances cannot be counted upon to bring about improvements in our capital stock. Second, depreciation allowances are based on the original cost of the capital equipment at issue. Hence, even in business areas where depreciation allowances are systematically set aside, the full benefits of improvements will only be obtained if prices have not risen over the life of the machine in question. For example, if a machine cost $1,000 when it was new 20 years ago and now costs $2,000 to replace, then in the absence of improvements mere maintenance of capital will require $1,000 of net saving. In periods of major price change such as took place after 1939, this means that businessmen have to save large amounts merely to maintain their capital intact. Of course, if the $2,000 machine were twice as productive as the original $1,000 machine, then the business would have been able to maintain its capacity without net saving, but the increase in productivity that would otherwise have taken place would have been eliminated. In short, whenever prices rise, the rise tends to offset the development that would otherwise result from the normal replacement of worn-out machines by new and improved models; where prices rise as fast as (or faster than) the average improvement in productivity, development will occur only if there is net saving even in the business area where depreciation allowances are systematically set aside.

These have been specific reasons why economic development requires net saving. In more general terms, additional capital and improvements in technology both tend to offset the utilization of wasting resources and render man's labor more productive. Between 1875 and 1950 capital per person roughly tripled. As a result not only has the reward per unit of capital declined greatly, but in recent years there also appears to have been a tendency toward a decline in the share of the national income going to capital as it became relatively more plentiful. Many economists, but especially Keynes, have projected this trend into the future and have suggested that a time may come when capital will be so plentiful as to have no scarcity value, which would lead, as Keynes put it, to the "euthanasia of the rentier." The prediction is, of course, the exact opposite of the picture which Marx foresaw of an ever-increasing share of income going to capitalists until revolution became inevitable. Any prediction that capital will lose its scarcity value assumes a slowing down, if not an elimination, of improvements in technology. For it is the opportunities for the employment of capital made possible by improved technology that have prevented the threefold increase in capital per person from resulting in an even greater decline in the return which capital has received. In fact, had not net saving been large since 1875, the share of the national income going to capital might quite possibly have risen—at least in the absence of public action to prevent such a rise. Thus, in periods when improvements in technology are rapid, appreciable net saving may be essential if an increase in the share of income going to capital is not to occur.

Saving and economic development

The importance of capital in connection with economic development can, however, be overestimated. Because economics has a fairly well-developed capital theory and almost no systematic theory regarding the factors responsible for development, capital frequently receives more attention than it deserves. While no precise measure of the contribution of capital to progress is possible, the estimates of Abramovitz presented in Chapter 4 suggest that the threefold increase in capital per person that took place between 1875 and 1950 might *by itself* have brought about an increase in production per person of 14 to 44 per cent depending on whether the importance of capital is measured by its low return at the end of the period or its high return at the start. Whichever figure is used, in view of the fact that production per person increased 300 per cent, it is clear that other factors have been far more important than capital.

It is also true that the higher the level of saving and depreciation, the smaller the importance of capital. This point can be illustrated by noting that in developed economies the value of reproducible capital tends to be roughly three times the national income, giving a capital-output ratio of 3 to 1. If saving were to reach 25 per cent of income —which we shall see it appears to have reached in the Soviet Union— then the economy involved could be expected to double its capital in 12 years, and capital would be relatively plentiful. On the other hand, if saving is no higher than 5 per cent of income—which we shall see is relatively high for an underdeveloped area—then the economy would require 60 years to double its capital, and capital would be relatively scarce. Again the United States, with net saving of less than 10 per cent, would probably be relatively short of capital if it were not for the fact that since 1946, depreciation has increased from 40 to over 55 per cent of gross capital formation. Hence where saving and depreciation are at relatively high levels, capital is likely to be relatively plentiful—and relatively unimportant in its influence on economic development. But, although its role may be exaggerated, net saving clearly is of importance in connection with development, especially in developing countries where depreciation allowances are small because there is as yet little to depreciate. Moreover, even in developed areas, it remains true that the more rapid the development that is desired, the more important does net saving become and the less can depreciation allowances alone be depended upon.

The behavior of saving

When budget studies are made of the way in which people spend their income, we find that, beyond a point below which people do not save (or actually dissave by drawing on their assets), on the average in any year the rich save a higher percentage of their income than the poor. In addition, from one year to the next, the over-all percentage saved tends to increase with increases in national income. When students were searching for an explanation of the severity and duration of the Great Depression, it seemed logical to suggest that nations, like people, might save more as they got richer. Then if investment opportunities were to decrease for reasons such as the end of the frontier or a slowing down in the rate at which technology improved, saving might tend to be more or less permanently in excess of investment opportunities and the economy subject to "secular (long-term) stagnation."

TABLE 8-3. THE IMPORTANCE OF SAVING

Decade	Domestic gross saving as percentage of GNP	Domestic net saving as percentage of NNP	Depreciation as percentage of gross saving
1869–1878	21.7	13.9	42.8
1879–1888	21.0	13.8	39.7
1889–1898	22.9	14.6	43.0
1899–1908	21.5	12.8	46.5
1909–1918	19.4	10.7	50.1
1919–1929	20.6	8.8	62.4
1929–1938	14.8	2.3	86.7
1939–1948	28.5	11.4	67.8
1869–1908	21.8	13.8	43.0
1909–1948	20.8	8.3	66.8

SOURCE: Kuznets, *op. cit.*, Table I-3, p. 62.

But when one looks at what has actually occurred, it appears from Table 8-3 that saving, if anything, has declined rather than increased. Results in recent years reflect the Great Depression—when income and saving were unusually low—and two World Wars—when saving was unusually high—so that comparisons between the start and end of the entire period are not easy to interpret. But even in the prosperous twenties net saving was lower and gross saving almost as low as in any previous decade, so that at the very least it is hard to argue that the expected increase has taken place. In fact, if one leaves out the decade of the thirties and allows for the fact that gross saving was high relative to net saving during World War II and again after 1950 because "accelerated depreciation" of war plants was permitted, perhaps the most significant thing that emerges is the stability of the long-term ratios.

How can this long-run stability be reconciled with the previously noted tendency of people to save more as their income rises? The answer appears to be that over time there is a "secular shift" upward in our willingness to consume. What this means is that a man with a $2,000 income in 1875 undoubtedly saved a significant amount—perhaps as much percentagewise as a man with an $8,000 income today—while a man with a $2,000 income today saves little or nothing. Clearly this is what must have happened or the percentage saved for the economy as a whole would have risen steadily.

Comparative rates of saving

What we are particularly concerned with in this chapter is the relationship between saving and the rate of economic development. We know that American economic development has been relatively rapid. Has our rate of saving been higher than that of other countries? At first sight this does not appear to be the case. A recent study found that our ratio of gross saving to gross national product was exceeded in recent years by 13 out of the 25 countries for which information was available, while our ratio of net saving to net national product was exceeded by 10 out of 16 countries.[2] But many of the countries with high ratios in recent years were repairing the dislocations and damage caused by World War II. If we look at a longer period, our rate of saving has been significantly higher than the two major European countries—Great Britain and France—for which long-term information is available. The estimates, which are summarized in Table 8-4, will repay careful study.

The difference between total investment (which of course equals total saving) and domestic investment represents foreign investment. If we compare the three countries period by period, we find that from roughly the Civil War to World War I, when real income in the United States increased appreciably more rapidly than in Great Britain or France, our rate of investment was significantly higher. This is particularly

[2] Kuznets, *op. cit.*, Table I-1, p. 60.

true of domestic net investment, which in our case slightly exceeded
net investment, as we were on balance borrowing during the period.
But Britain and France were substantial net lenders, the latter lending
on the average over 3 per cent and the former almost 4 per cent of
net national product. If repaid, foreign investment may be as productive,
or more productive, than domestic investment, permitting a country to
import more than it exports—as indeed Britain was able to do on a
large scale during the interwar period. But much foreign investment has
been lost: in the French case largely in Russia as a result of the Communist Revolution and in the British case because of the need to liqui-
date foreign assets to finance two major wars. Hence, although this is to
some extent conjectural, it seems quite probable that domestic rather
than total net investment comes closest to measuring the present usefulness of the investment activities of the period.

TABLE 8-4. COMPARISONS OF INVESTMENT RATES

Period	Total gross investment as percentage of GNP	Domestic gross investment as percentage of GNP	Total net investment as percentage of NNP	Domestic net investment as percentage of NNP
United States 1869–1908	21.7	21.8	13.6	13.8
Great Britain 1870–1909	13.8	10.0	12.1	8.2
France 1878–1911	—	—	8.3	5.1
United States 1925–1930	20.4	19.8	12.7	12.0
Great Britain 1925–1930[a]	14.1	13.0	6.6	5.4
France 1927–1930	11.7	9.8	9.0	7.0
United States 1947–1952	19.7	17.9	13.5	11.6
Great Britain 1948–1952[b]	16.8	15.7	8.0	6.8
France 1949–1952	18.5	18.6	9.1	9.2

[a] Domestic estimates for 1924-1930.

[b] Central Statistical Office, *National Income and Expenditure* (London: HM Stationery
Office, 1956), Tables 1, 6, and 54, pp. 1, 4, and 58.

SOURCE: Kuznets, *op. cit.*, Tables I-1, I-2, I-3A, B, and E, II-1, II-2, and II-4A, B,
and E, pp. 60, 61, 62, 64, 65, 67, 70, and 72. In some cases data in the tables have
been averaged.

Second, during the period Britain's depreciation allowances were
much lower than those in the United States—amounting to only 20 per
cent compared with 43 per cent of gross domestic investment. It is this
which explains why our total gross investment was almost 8 percentage
points and our net only 1.5 percentage points higher than in Britain.

How was such a difference possible? First, in Great Britain no depreciation whatsoever was permitted on buildings until 1918, and the rate allowed was only 1 per cent per year up to 1945. In addition, depreciation reflects more than physical wear and tear; it also depends on the anticipated decline in value quite apart from wear and tear. Consider an automobile used by business: it will have lost almost all its value in 7 or 8 years. But unlike the wonderful one-horse shay, it does not then fall apart; instead, by sufficient repair it could probably be made to last as long again. It is a *matter of business judgment* as to when it becomes more profitable to junk and replace rather than to repair. It is clear that in Great Britain business practice, which came to be embodied in the tax laws, was to depreciate capital much less rapidly than in the United States. The actual difference may be somewhat less than the statistics convey, as, if it were anticipated that equipment would be used for 20 years rather than junked in 10 or less, it might be built better. Nonetheless a country whose equipment has an average age of 5 years is practically certain to be able to produce more efficiently than a country whose equipment has an average age of 10 years—even if the older equipment was originally of somewhat better construction. Thus during the long period up to World War I the United States was ahead on every count: it was replacing its stock of capital more rapidly, its net investment was higher, and less of its investment was going abroad to run the risks of loss in revolution or war.

During the twenties the same broad pattern prevailed, but since World War II a sharp change appears to have taken place in both Great Britain and France, as the cumulative results of low depreciation and low capital formation became evident. In Britain depreciation allowances rose to 60 per cent of gross domestic capital formation as depreciation policy was liberalized to permit a 2 per cent annual rate on buildings, with a special initial allowance of 10 per cent on new buildings and 20 per cent on new equipment. But net investment, and especially net domestic investment, remained low, partly as a result of the impact of highly progressive taxation on saving by individuals. While the whole matter is still tentative, the evidence appears to justify the not unexpected conclusion that high rates of saving and investment appear to accompany rapid economic development. To the extent that this is correct, the fact that in recent years many countries have equaled or exceeded our rate should be of considerable interest.

Government and the rate of saving

If economic development is closely related to the rate of saving, how is such an important rate determined? Under free enterprise it is

mainly determined by the decisions of individuals as to how they allocate their income between consumption today and saving for the future—individual decisions, as Table 8-2 makes clear, having been directly responsible for 60 per cent or more of all saving in the United
States. Although the saving done by corporations is sometimes treated
as if it were done for the account of corporate owners, it has long been
recognized that such saving—accounting for 25 per cent of the total—
was in a different category, and the importance of the difference has
increased as corporate control has become increasingly vested in the
hands of self-perpetuating management groups.

In the past the contribution of government to saving has not been
large—never over 15 per cent in the period covered by Table 8-2. In fact,
conscious efforts by government to influence the rate of saving began
with the Great Depression. At that time, the fear was that people would
try to save more than businessmen would want to invest, so that income
received in one period would be less than spending in the following
period—leading to a cumulative decline in income and spending. The
proposal was that the government should absorb the excess saving by
borrowing it and spending it for worth-while purposes, thereby insuring
that it did not remain idle.

In recent years, when inflation has been the problem, the earlier
thinking was reversed and the government urged to run a surplus to
counteract inflationary pressures. But running a surplus may have more
of an influence on the rate of saving than is sometimes realized. Simply
reversing the depression procedure is clearly deflationary only if the
surplus flows into idle balances—just as running a deficit is fully ex-
pansionary only if it is financed with funds that would otherwise have
been idle. In periods of prosperity when inflation is a problem, however,
businessmen are anxious to borrow. If, therefore, the government uses
its surplus to retire government debt—as the federal government did,
for example, during the twenties—the holders of retired securities may
simply re-lend the funds they receive to private investors. Only if government holds the funds idle—or if those who received them in exchange
for their retired securities do so—will spending decline even in the
first instance by the full amount of the surplus. On the other hand, if no
funds flow into idle balances but instead are re-lent in full as rapidly as
they would have been spent in the absence of the taxation which
brought about the surplus, then no contribution has been made to reducing spending. But—and this is what is here important—*saving will have
been increased by the extent to which the funds involved would have
been spent on consumption if they had not been used to pay the taxes
responsible for the surplus.* Thus to the extent that funds derived from
debt retirement expand private investment beyond what it would have

been in the absence of taxation, government action to prevent inflation will, in fact, be significantly influencing the rate of saving and investment.

Thus far in the United States there is widespread recognition of the desirability of the government acting to prevent excessive saving from causing cumulative declines in economic activity and considerable recognition of the desirability of the government using its powers of taxation to counteract inflationary pressures. On the other hand, there has been little or no recognition of any comparable desirability for the government to concern itself with the rate of saving in general—largely because the rate that has actually been realized appears satisfactory. But in Great Britain, where many feel the rate in recent years has been too low, the matter has come in for more direct government attention, and the distinguished British economist, Sir Dennis Robertson, has written: ". . . the State has [now] claimed the right and assumed the duty of making and implementing on behalf of the community one of the most fundamental of economic choices, namely the distribution of productive resources between present and future uses. In other words, it has taken upon itself responsibility for determining the rate of growth of the community's real capital." [3]

But even though no such responsibility has been accepted by the American government, in practice both the anti-depression and anti-inflation policy of the government is in fact influencing the rate of saving at the present time, and the means are at hand for more extensive influence to be exerted if the government were to believe such action desirable. To illustrate: suppose that the federal government were to run a surplus of $7 billions. This would be equal to 25 per cent of private domestic capital formation in 1957 and would clearly have an important influence on the supply of saving. Yet such a surplus could be continued for 40 years without retiring the present federal debt, even if we assume that in the interim there was no occasion when a federal deficit would have been desirable. In short, while even in recent years the government has accounted for no more than 15 per cent of total saving in comparison with the 60 per cent contributed by individuals and the 25 per cent contributed by corporations, the means are at hand for the government to play a far larger role in influencing the rate of saving if such action were to appear desirable.

The contribution of saving

How can we summarize this discussion of the contribution of saving to economic development? Two points are perhaps most important. First,

[3] D. H. Robertson, *Utility and All That* (New York: Macmillan, 1952), p. 116.

the significance of saving varies greatly depending on the circumstances of the economy in question. In an underdeveloped area where the rate of saving is low and capital scarce, the provision of additional saving may well be essential if development is to proceed. But in a developed economy, where capital is relatively plentiful and depreciation allowances large, the need for additional saving may be relatively small. Second, especially in the case of developed economies, saving facilitates development rather than initiates it in the sense that large saving *by itself* may not lead to important increases in production but a considerable amount of saving is likely to be essential if improvements in technology are in fact to bring about significant expansions of output.

CHAPTER NINE

THE ROLE OF
NATURAL RESOURCES

Land, natural resources, and physical environment

In the Introduction it was explained that land, labor, and capital are the "factors" which made production possible. But what do economists mean by "land"? Obviously their meaning is broader than the usual way in which the term is used. Perhaps the best simple definition is "everything made available by nature that is useful for production." When defined in this way, the meaning probably comes closest to what is commonly meant by "natural resources," so that this is the term which we shall use in the discussion which follows. A discussion of natural resources by no means covers the full impact on man of the physical environment in which he finds himself; it is this broader impact with which the geographer is concerned. The economist, however, is more narrowly interested in the direct contribution of environment to economic activity in general and production in particular, and the direct contribution is made through natural resources as we have defined the term.

The question, then, with which this chapter is concerned is the extent to which differences in the availability of natural resources are responsible for differences in economic development among countries. We will examine the matter from two points of view. First, we will consider the essentially static question of the extent to which differ-

111

ences in resources are responsible for observed differences in living levels, which in the main reflect differing rates of development in the past. Second, we will consider the essentially dynamic question of the impact of resources on economic development treated as a *continuing process*. Starting from the first point of view, differences in the availability of natural resources would appear to influence realized living levels in three ways. If a country does not possess resources, it has to pay for them; let us examine, therefore, the payments that are made for the use of resources. Second, the resources have to be transported to the place of use; we will examine, therefore, whether transportation costs are important in connection with living levels. Finally, we will examine the extent to which inability to pay for "superior" resources is responsible for the use of "inferior" resources, and then consider the further question of whether it is the poor resources or the poor productivity explaining the inability to pay that should be blamed when "inferior" resources are used.

The meaning of economic rent

The payment for the use of land—or, in our usage, natural resources —is "economic rent." [1] Probably nothing has been more overemphasized in economics than economic rent. Ricardo, perhaps the greatest of the classical economists, came close to suggesting that the only ultimate result of economic development would be to benefit landlords by raising the rent that they received, while Henry George, thoroughly convinced by Ricardo as to the importance of rent, sought to solve the world's ills by a "single tax" on economic rent, which was to yield enough to finance all government activity. And generations of economic students have risked failure if they did not learn that "economic rent is not a cost of production." The importance of this statement can be exaggerated, but understanding its meaning will help us to understand the role of natural resources in economic activity.

Let us take farm land as an example—*not* because it is necessarily the most important natural resource of a developed economy such as the United States but because it is the example which has been conventionally used. Suppose we start by assuming that all such land is of uniform fertility. At any time there is a certain amount of land that can best be farmed by one man. If he tries to farm more land, he will not

---

[1] The student familiar with the concept of "quasi-rents" in connection with payments for the services of capital and labor should note that the concept is given no consideration in what follows since we are concerned, not with the concept of "economic rent" as such, but with the role of resources in economic development.

be able to cultivate all of it properly and his output will be less than if he cultivates a smaller amount of land more intensively. In the other direction, if he cultivates less than the proper amount of land, his output will again be smaller. Hence the particular amount of land involved is the amount which will produce the maximum, or optimum, output per farmer. Strictly the amount must be defined with reference not only to a given state of agricultural technology but also to a given quantity of capital embodied in tools, equipment, and, as we shall see, improvements of the soil itself; for changed techniques or amounts of capital can obviously alter the amount of land a man can farm.[2]

Now suppose, with given technology and a fixed quantity of capital, there is so much land available—of uniform fertility—that every farmer can have that certain amount which maximizes his output. Under such circumstances would land have any value? The answer is no value as a result of present use, though farsighted people might still be willing to pay something for it in the hope that population growth or some other change in circumstances might make it useful in the future. But if no one anticipated any changes in the future—believing instead that as much land as anyone wanted would continue to be freely available—then land would have no economic value and therefore earn no economic rent; it would in fact be a free good like the air we breathe.

What then makes land valuable? The obvious answer is that there is not enough to go around. Under such circumstances more and more labor will be applied to the land that is available; in other words, it will be cultivated more and more intensively. But there is an ultimate point beyond which additional labor does more harm than good. After each rice plant has been lovingly planted by hand in the tiny paddy that one man typically cultivates in Japan, there is nothing left to do but let the plant grow. Even if labor were free, there would be no point in utilizing any more of it. Just as before there was a certain amount of land that gave maximum output per farmer, so there is a certain amount of labor which will maximize the output that can be obtained from a given quantity of land (techniques and the quantity of capital still being constant).[3] Fortunately this point of maximum output has little application to developed areas, as they are relatively plentifully supplied with resources. But the fact that labor can become useless, even if free, helps to explain why in underdeveloped countries situations are frequently found where labor in agricultural areas is employed only part of the time

[2] For those familiar with the concept, the point involved is that at which the average physical product per unit of the variable factor—in this case of the labor of the farmer—is at a maximum.

[3] Again for those familiar with the concept, the point involved is that at which the total physical product is at a maximum.

or employed at tasks which really contribute little or nothing to production. The latter case is described as "disguised" unemployment; we shall see in Part IV that an important aspect of development in underdeveloped areas is finding ways of utilizing agricultural labor that would otherwise be unused or wasted on useless work.

Economic rent as a surplus

What, then, determines the level of economic rent? Let us recognize the obvious fact that land is not of uniform fertility; rich bottom land in Iowa is better for farming than the sandy wastes covered with scrub oak that make up much of Cape Cod. But let us disregard for the moment the fact that land is located differing distances from the market for its products. If we consider only differences in fertility, it is obvious that long before anyone would want to attempt to farm Cape Cod he would be willing to pay quite a lot for the use of land in Iowa. This, then, is the essence of the matter: *economic rent is a surplus paid for the fertility of particular parcels of land.* It is limited at any time by the availability of less fertile land which is "on the margin of cultivation"—just worth cultivating. Thus, if the demand for food increased enough, Cape Cod might be worth cultivating. Before doing so, however, a farmer would be willing to pay more for the use of Iowa land; but he would never be willing to pay as rent for Iowa land *more than the increase in the value of his output that he judged would result from farming Iowa land rather than land just worth cultivating on Cape Cod.* The individual farmer, if he wishes to continue farming, has, of course, no alternative but to pay the rent charged for Iowa land; it is part of his individual cost of production. From the social point of view, however, it is not a cost which has to be met; the land would still be available if nothing were paid for its services. This is the sense in which economic texts have stressed that "economic rent is not a cost of production" but rather a surplus the size of which is determined by the superiority of a particular parcel of land over land which, at the prevailing level of demand, is just worth farming.

What about the influence of differing distances from markets, which we temporarily set aside? In any full statement of specific differences in rent the effect of differences in location, as well as differences in fertility, clearly must be taken into account. But to the extent that the contention, which is shortly to be advanced, that transportation costs are relatively unimportant in explaining differences in living levels is correct, it follows that locational differences are likely to be of relatively minor importance in explaining the broad differences in living levels with which we are concerned. To the extent that it is possible to do so, however, we will take into account the influence of locational differences when we attempt to estimate the importance of actual rental payments in the section which follows.

In the light of this analysis, it is possible to understand Ricardo's pessimism. For he thought of development not so much as raising living levels as permitting more people to survive. With more and more people and a given amount of land, the conclusion that the future belongs to the landlords follows inevitably. What Ricardo underestimated was the extent to which improved technology and increased quantities of capital would permit more and more to be grown with little or no increase in the amount of land in use. It is this which has kept the landlords in their place, created a "farm problem" in the United States, and made possible the rapid expansion of our population. But in underdeveloped areas, where the increase in population has often outrun the improvement in farm technology, the share of the national income received by landlords often raises serious social problems.

In the explanation of economic rent just presented, the assumption that land was of uniform fertility was dropped. Were fertility uniform it would be considerably harder to explain the level of rent. In such circumstances land would have no value until all land was in use—speculations on the future again aside. But once all land was in use the level of rent would be fundamentally determined by bargaining between landowners and cultivators, with possible outcomes ranging from situations in which cultivators would receive little more than subsistence to those in which land ownership would be not particularly remunerative. Since in most countries there are wide variations in fertility, the point just made is not generally important; but it does help to explain why there are such wide variations in the share of agricultural output received by landlords in countries where population is dense, farm technology stagnant, and available land fully utilized.

The quantitative importance of economic rent

It is of greater general significance to stress again that the level of economic rent for any resource cannot be larger than the addition to the value of production that results from using that particular resource rather than one for which there is no present value, plus any additional payment that may be made because of the superior location of the resource in question in relation to the market for its product. What quantitatively does this amount to? How much economic rent do we today pay in the United States to those who happen to own privately the resources that were provided by nature and made valuable by general demand? The answer is that the over-all amount is unknown, because in practice the economic rent which is paid for what is made available by nature is in business accounts always combined with interest payments on the capital used to improve what nature has provided. Only in the case of agricultural land is information available; in 1950 such land appears to have been responsible for 17 per cent of the value produced on American farms.[4] But as agriculture in that year accounted for only about 8 per cent of total activity, the contribution of agricultural land to the national income would appear to have been less than 1.4 per cent. But this *overestimates* what is involved. For the value of "agricultural land" in this sense includes the value of the capital which has been embodied in breaking the prairie, clearing the land, ditching, draining, fertilizing, and the like. Probably less than half of agricultural rent—well under 1 per cent of the national income—represents payments for the "original and indestructible powers of the soil" that nature provided, which is what an economist means by "land."

Another way of getting at the same point is to stress that "rent," as the economist uses the term, bears no relationship to any other kind of "rent." Thus perhaps 30 per cent of the rent paid by the average person for a house is used to pay the taxes assessed on the property, and almost all the remainder goes to maintain and provide a return on the capital that was invested in building the house. Probably no more than 5 per cent of the "rent" paid by the average person is a payment for the use of the unimproved land on which the house stands. Nor are our national income estimates of any help. The "rental income of persons" which they report is roughly the rental value of the nation's stock of houses—the total largely imputed because of the extent to which houses are occupied by their owners. The estimate, therefore, is at once much too high for houses and too low because it omits payment for the use of all other resources.

Although the over-all amount is unknown, the amount of true economic rent paid is almost certainly small because our resources are not particularly scarce. In fact, despite the increase in population, land "in agricultural use" is today smaller than it was in 1910, though land "in farms" has increased by roughly 30 per cent as the feed lot replaced open grazing and farms came increasingly to include "nonfarm land grazed by livestock." Many areas of the United States which were farmed in the past have today no value whatsoever as farm land. New England is covered with abandoned farms; fields which were cleared of rock with back-breaking labor—as anyone knows who has seen what lies under what appears to be a small stone wall—now support only a crop of summer tourists. Even in the agricultural midwest large areas of marginal land in the "dust bowl" have been allowed to revert to pasture. And,

[4] Theodore W. Schultz, *The Economic Organization of Agriculture* (New York: McGraw-Hill, 1953), p. 138.

as a part of the farm program, considerable amounts of agricultural land have in recent years been removed from production and placed in a "Soil Bank." Clearly we are not short of farm land.

Nor has the value of urban land risen much in recent years. Perhaps the least defensible aspect of the private ownership of property is the possibility that large fortunes will be received, not in return for any service, but simply through ownership of land made valuable by the growth of cities. The Wendell sisters provide an excellent example: they were two maiden ladies who kept a lot assessed at a million dollars to exercise their poodle and died leaving $60 million—all because their father had the foresight to run a lumber yard in the Times Square district of New York and direct his executors to rent, but never sell, the underlying land! But, despite such spectacular individual cases, the rise in urban land values has also been limited by technical change. The mobility provided predominantly by the private automobile has vastly increased the amount of readily accessible land; and the resulting exodus to the suburbs—or even exurbs—has significantly restricted the rise in urban land values that would otherwise have taken place.

And the same would appear to apply to other natural resources. True, the Mesabi range in Minnesota—50 per cent or better pure iron— is now largely exhausted, but somewhat lower grade iron is available in large quantities in the United States and richer veins have been discovered in other areas. We have enough coal for hundreds of years at present rates of use, so that here again there has been little deterioration in availability—and, therefore, little rent paid for the more readily available coal that has been mined thus far. Clearly we will have to use inferior resources in the future and will become increasingly dependent on imports; and significant economic development on a world-wide scale, as is suggested in Chapter 14, would rapidly alter the present picture. But, thus far, resources have remained sufficiently available to hold down the general level of economic rent.

Undoubtedly the outstanding exception to what has just been said— and the first thing people think of when they think of a man made rich by exploiting resources—is the oil millionaire. There is no doubt whatsoever that a pool of oil is a nice thing to find under one's house. The fabulously rich Kuwait field was responsible for annual payments to the Sheik which, when divided among the original inhabitants of Kuwait, gave rise to average incomes higher than in Great Britain and not so far from those in the United States! But it is the total cost of economic rent rather than the spectacular individual case in which we are interested. Even when payments for farm land, for urban land, and for other natural resources are totaled, it is most unlikely that the sum is larger than a very few per cent of the national income. Hence the elimination of all payments of economic rent would make little difference. But, to repeat, economic rent is what we pay for the use of "superior" resources as compared with those which are just worth using and so receive nothing for their use. Hence, to the extent that payments of economic rent are small, it follows that ownership of "superior" resources by one country cannot be of any great significance in explaining its superior living levels—provided, of course, that the resources involved can be transported at reasonable rates to, and paid for by, other countries.

It is for this reason that economists have given little attention to Henry George rather than as a result of any logical flaw in his argument. By the very definition of resources—"made available by nature"— they would remain available, to society if not to the individual, even if no payment were made for their services. But even if all payments of economic rent could be captured by the "single tax" that George proposed, it would not begin to meet the present-day cost of government. And, in addition, because true economic rent is, as we have seen, so rarely distinguished from the interest on the capital that has been used to improve the resource, levying a tax that would extract the exact economic rent would be extraordinarily difficult administratively—just as Shylock found it hard to extract an exact pound of flesh. Yet if the tax were to impinge on the return on capital improvements, its inevitable effect would be to discourage the making of such improvements.

Living levels and transportation costs

If, then, the total paid for the use of natural resources is so small as to offer little help in explaining differences in living levels, is the fact that the resources may be concentrated in particular areas—thereby permitting such areas to minimize transportation costs—a factor of importance? This possibility we may dismiss rather rapidly. For water-borne transportation is remarkably inexpensive. There are many areas of the United States where American coal costs more than it does in London. And the cost of delivering Texas fuel oil to London is little more than the cost of delivering it to New York. As most of the major countries of the world can be reached by sea, it is hard to explain broad differences in living levels among countries in terms of transportation costs. Undoubtedly there are situations in which such costs are important, but they are probably far more important in explaining differences *within* countries than *among* countries. "Prices slightly higher west of the Rockies" is a well-known phrase; it is probably fair, however, to place emphasis on the "slightly." For not only are transportation costs rather small in relation to the value of most of the items which make up present living levels but also the bulky items, where transportation costs are important, are rather widely distributed over the face of the globe and therefore do not impinge, through heavy transportation costs, on the living level of any particular area. Because this may be an unexpected conclusion, it is important to stress that differences in transportation costs must obviously be taken into account in any complete explanation of differences in living levels. The point here being made is simply that *quantitative* differences in such costs are unlikely to be of importance in explaining the broad differences in living levels with which we are concerned.

Paying for natural resources

There remains the third possibility distinguished at the start of the chapter: that inability to pay for "superior" resources may force the use of "inferior" resources and in this way significantly lower living levels. This is undoubtedly the most complicated way in which natural resources influence living levels. While there are payment problems within countries, payment difficulties are greatest across international boundaries. Hence we are involved in the complications covered in the not insubstantial portions of elementary texts devoted to international trade. The discussion which follows, therefore, is inevitably quite superficial. In particular, all the short-run reasons why a country may find it difficult to finance imports—reasons which have been especially important in Europe since 1939—will have to be omitted in order to concentrate on basic considerations.

The basic question is why any country should work its own "inferior" resources if it can buy "superior" resources from abroad. While there have been from time to time interferences with imports—and since World War II an actual embargo on trade with the USSR in "strategic" supplies —most countries in the past have stood ready to export, and export freely, the raw materials that they possessed. To the extent that exports are freely permitted—and the remainder of the argument disregards the cases in which exports are restricted—every country has access to the most readily available natural resources in the world—at no more than the addition of transportation costs—*provided that* the country can pay for them. The essence of being able to pay for imports is to be able to make something that is wanted abroad—and to make it at prices as low as or lower than prevail in world markets. Once the ability to export on the scale necessary to pay for imports is achieved, a country is in a position to buy "superior" resources wherever they may be located.

Note the quotation marks used in connection with "superior" and "inferior." In each case the meaning has been physical or technical rather than economic; thus a "superior" resource is one which can be produced with less, while an "inferior" resource requires more, productive effort measured on some internationally comparable basis such as in terms of man-hours of work. But the technically superior resource is not always the cheapest for a given country. Suppose that the productivity of a country is uniformly low so that there is nothing that—if trade were suddenly to become possible—it would be in a position to export at prices prevailing in world markets. If it has urgent need for certain imports, it may still be able to buy them. But, as is made clear in discussions of international trade, efforts to pay for them will bring about either a depreciation of the country's exchange rate if it is not on the gold standard or an export of its gold holdings if the gold standard prevails. One or the other movement will continue until exports become sufficient to pay for the imports at issue. As its exchange depreciates or its prices decline as a result of gold exports, the country will find that its own technically inferior resources become cheaper in economic terms than the technically superior resources that are available abroad. The result is that a country which achieves high productivity and can, therefore, export easily is likely to add further to its level of living because the resources which are easiest to produce physically are also likely to be, for it, cheapest economically. But a country with low productivity and difficulty in exporting is likely to find that its own inferior resources are, for it, cheapest, and so have to be used despite the greater physical effort required for their utilization. This in turn brings about an even lower level of living than results from the low productivity we premised at the start. It is the first of a number of cases in which we shall find that the process of economic development is cumulative. "For whosoever hath, to him shall be given, and he shall have more abundance; but whomsoever hath not, from him shall be taken away even that he hath."

The classic example of this point is Switzerland: with few resources of its own except scenery and a location a long way from the ocean, it has achieved the highest level of living in Europe. The ability to produce high-grade watches more cheaply than they can be produced anywhere else does not by itself explain the Swiss achievement; the demand for watches is simply not that large. But it is representative of the abilities which have made it possible for Switzerland to export easily and in this way obtain needed resources wherever they were cheapest.

Inferior resources versus inferior productivity

What is involved in such circumstances: inferior resources or inferior productivity? Perhaps we can simplify the issues by thinking in terms of the reaction of two Vermont farmers to the opening up of vastly superior agricultural resources in the midwest. One sensible reaction would be for them to "Go West"; but this may be ruled out as no solution to international problems in an era of immigration restrictions. Suppose Vermonter Smith leaves his farm and develops the ability to produce something that the midwest farmer wants—and to produce it as cheaply as it can be produced anywhere else in the world. In this case Smith will be buying his food from the midwest farmer at prices higher than a midwest consumer pays by only the amount of the transportation costs involved—and his level of living will be high. But suppose Vermonter Jones continues to farm his rocky and hilly Vermont acres. Not only will he be using inferior resources to feed himself, but, because he will have little to sell, he will have to make for himself much of what his neighbor Smith buys from Sears Roebuck, and his level of living will be low. This, then, is the question: do we say that Jones' level of living is so low because he is farming a rocky Vermont hillside or because he did not behave like Smith?

Are differences of this sort important? Definitely. Take the British and American coal industries. In 1955 about 700,000 miners, or 3 per cent of the entire British labor force, provided each Britisher with 4.3 tons of coal; in the same year in the United States 210,000 workers, or one third of 1 per cent of the American labor force, provided each American with 2.8 tons of coal—more not being required because of the ready availability of substitutes. Rather more than eight times as many hours were required to mine a ton of coal in Britain as in the United States. Clearly the greater expenditure of labor in mining coal is a factor in explaining why the British level of living is lower than in the United States. But, as before, the question is: should the blame be placed on the inferiority of British coal resources or on the failure of the British to produce something which they could trade for the superior resources—which in this case might be oil—available elsewhere?

Basically the answer to this question depends on the alternatives that are taken as available. So long as we assume that Jones has no alternative except to remain on his farm, it is obvious that the rocky quality of his acres influences Jones' living level. But we get a different answer as soon as we open up the possibility of Jones following in Smith's footsteps. The whole emphasis of this volume is that alternatives are not to be taken as fixed; the *creation* of desirable alternatives is a proper— and very important—function of an economic system. Viewed in this light, whenever an economy is utilizing resources which are technically inferior in the sense of requiring more effort to work than resources available elsewhere (with appropriate allowance for transportation costs), it has open to it the possibility of retiring its inferior resources by developing new and better alternatives for the use of its labor force. This, of course, does happen: Cornwall's tin mines, once of major world importance, are now almost entirely closed down and Britain's tin comes from Malaya in exchange for exports. But, because Britain has been unable to develop exports sufficiently competitive in world markets to permit her to meet her energy requirements from cheaper sources than her own inferior coal seams, the same shift has not taken place in coal. And the fact that it has not is a part of the price that the British level of living continues to pay for the British economy's level of productivity.

Natural resources and the process of development

It is undoubtedly a great deal easier to suggest that Jones should follow in Smith's footsteps than for him actually to do so. For what we described Smith as achieving was not merely the production of something that was wanted but also its production at prices as low as those which prevailed anywhere else in the world. Thus far we have suggested, to summarize, that neither payments of economic rent for the use of natural resources nor differences in transportation costs appear to be of sufficient importance to help much in explaining actual differences in living levels. And we have also suggested that no economy needs to use technically inferior resources if only its degree of development and level of productivity is sufficiently high to provide it with goods to exchange for superior resources. But in the *process* of achieving a high degree of development and productivity, the availability of technically superior resources is undoubtedly helpful. For the availability of superior resources may have favorable repercussions on all the factors which we have discussed as likely to promote development. This is particularly likely to be true when development takes place without conscious planning. It was the availability of coal—and to a lesser extent iron ore—that led to the development of a steel industry in England. But it is perfectly possible, as the Japanese have demonstrated, to have a modern steel industry without raw materials. Again, the availability of a readily exportable natural resource may well make capital accumulation easier in the crucial initial stages of development by reducing the number of domestic man-hours required to achieve a given quantity of foreign exchange—and in this way minimizing the impact of development on the domestic level of living. It is especially helpful if the natural resource is such that considerable domestic employment must be—or can be—attached to it before export takes place. Even in the case of oil, for example, royalty payments are in most cases small in relation to the value of the oil at the time of export. The domestic labor that is, in the main, responsible for the added value might have been used to create something else that could have been exported; but it might well have been more difficult to do so. In other words, Smith, when he moved to town, might have developed insurance services for export to Iowa. But it might have been easier to get Iowans to buy if Vermont happened to have the raw materials needed to produce fertilizer—even if such materials were only a small part of the value of the fertilizer at the time it left Vermont.

Some conclusions

The role of natural resources in connection with economic development—and particularly the quantitative importance of resources—is not a matter which has received extended consideration by economists. As a result it is hard to know to what extent the emphasis of this chapter on the relative unimportance of resources reflects the consensus of the thinking of economists. It seems probable that few would deny the quantitative unimportance of economic rent or of transportation costs. Nor does it seem possible to deny, in the light of the accomplishments of a country such as Switzerland, the theoretical possibility that high productivity and a high level of living may be achieved without an abundance of natural resources. Undoubtedly differences of opinion are most likely to develop in regard to the role of readily available resources in facilitating the *process* of economic development. Nothing that has been said in this chapter in any way denies that abundant resources make economic development easier. What has been stressed is that, even without readily available resources, economic development is, nonetheless, perfectly possible—though it may well be more difficult.

CHAPTER TEN

OTHER FACTORS INFLUENCING ECONOMIC DEVELOPMENT

Introduction

Thus far we have attempted to explain economic development **in** terms of such predominantly economic factors as research, innovation, and capital formation. Actually there is almost no aspect of man's behavior or of his social organization that does not have a bearing on the rate at which development takes place. As a result this chapter cannot possibly hope to cover all the factors that are involved. It is included primarily to make clear that development is not the result of the operation of certain economic abstractions, but rather an integral part of the dynamic process of growth of a society. What we shall try to do is provide some examples of the way in which considerations broader than those normally included in the term "economic" can promote or retard development. *In no sense is what follows a systematic coverage of the broader influences on development.* Rather the examples have been chosen to show how small differences in emphasis can lead to wide differences in results. This will be achieved, in the main, by contrasting Great Britain and the United States. For the broad similarity of their cultural heritage makes the differences that have emerged of particular interest.

As we move from more strictly economic matters to those of broader significance, the question as to whether economic development—and

124

especially rapid economic development—is worth the costs that are involved will come increasingly to mind. The costs at issue are many and varied. Because development means change, there is involved an inevitable sacrifice of security. Old ways of doing things have to be discarded and new ones learned. In the short run at least, there is likely to be a reduction in leisure—if only in the form of sleepless nights as adjustments to changed circumstances are worked out. And the sort of competitive pressures that are so useful in promoting innovation are also very effective in promoting ulcers. Is the game worth the candle in a society which is becoming increasingly affluent? Obviously the fact that this book has been written indicates that in my judgment rapid development remains important and will continue to be worth the costs involved until a far higher level of living has been achieved for all mankind. Even among those who agree with this broad proposition, there is room for endless disagreement as to just how much development justifies just what cost in other benefits foregone. Clearly this is a matter in which value judgments are very much involved. In the discussion which follows no effort has been made to conceal the cost of economic development, so that those who feel that the game is not worth the candle can be guided by their own value judgments.

Materialism and economic development

Let us start with fundamentals. Economic development by definition involves an increase in the material well-being of a society. A belief, therefore, in the importance and desirability of material things undoubtedly helps to promote development. Conversely, if everyone were convinced that the length of time that they would reside in purgatory was a direct function of the quantity of material things they had acquired in their life, development would undoubtedly be slower. But this does not mean that, in seeking economic development, man seeks merely material things; in practice there are both material and non-material advantages. We would have far more material things today than we do in fact have if we were today prepared to work the 50 per cent longer hours that prevailed at the turn of the century. For, although there is likely to be hard work involved in achieving development, the fruits of development may be taken in the form of shorter hours and greater leisure quite as much as in the form of more material things. In fact, one of the things to be stressed about continuing development is that it will, in time, permit both leisure and material benefits rather than require a choice to be made between them. Material things, of course—as was stressed in Chapter 1—do not guarantee that a man will be "better off" in any ultimate sense; for they may be used for good or evil. But the potentialities for good that they represent are obviously immense.

Not only is society's attitude toward material things as such important; it is also important as it influences the innovators and entrepreneurs who are so largely responsible for development. If social prestige is reserved, let us say, for soldiers and statesmen while businessmen are considered to be engaged in menial work, then—*to the extent that they can*—those with ability are likely to enter the army or the government rather than business. The qualification is important: if the prestige occupations are restricted to those with qualifications other than ability while business is open to all, the inability of able people to enter the army or government may more than offset the lower prestige of business, leaving the average level of ability in business higher than it would have been in the absence of restrictions. Clearly the relationship among social attitudes, entrepreneurial motivation, and economic behavior is highly complex. But it seems reasonable to conclude that a society that wants to develop and honors those responsible is likely to develop far more rapidly than a society which has ·a greater regard for other values.

Labor unions and development

The conflict between values is well illustrated when we consider the impact of labor unions on development. In many cases unions impede economic development. When they insist that painting be done with a small brush when a paint spray could be used, limit the number of bricks that can be laid or the number of looms a man can tend, or insist on the employment of more workers than are needed—in short, promote "make-work" or "feather-bedding"—productivity is reduced and development retarded. But, equally, unions may expedite innovations if they convince workers that they will not be harmed by change but, instead, will receive their fair share of the resulting increase in production. How do these generalizations contribute to an explanation of differences between Great Britain and the United States? Basically the answer is simple: British unions have put more emphasis on security and less on development than unions in America. Historically, when Americans have lost their jobs, they have been able to "Go West"; in fact, they are still going to California! Mobility, in short, has been high—both between areas and occupations. But in Britain movement over even short distances—from Wales to the Midlands, for example—has been far more difficult, and a son has tended to follow the occupation of his father. Perhaps natural selection is involved: the forebearers, at least, of those who got to America had to be willing to travel; a few more miles one way or the other may, therefore, seem relatively unimportant to their progeny!

This is, in fact, one of the many situations in which more is given to him that hath. For the rapid growth of the American economy—both in population and production—has meant that relatively few industries or areas have declined on an absolute basis. Only rarely has labor been asked to accept changes which actually resulted in loss of jobs. This in turn has made labor more willing to accept changes, which in turn, by increasing productivity and expanding demand, has often eliminated job losses which might otherwise have occurred. Thus in an important sense insecurity can lead to security and excessive emphasis on security to insecurity.

This is not to suggest that the American labor movement has not sought seniority and job protection for its members. The point is that it has emphasized security far less and increased wages and reduced hours far more than labor in Britain. Contrast, for example, the attitudes of the two coal mining unions. John L. Lewis has at no time resisted mechanization of coal mining, contending instead that only through mechanization will miners ever receive the sort of wage to which they are entitled for the dangerous and disagreeable work that they do. Although between 1947 and 1955 coal production declined by 25 per cent and employment by 50 per cent, the union made no effort to slow down mechanization despite the fact that output per man-day increased in the 8 years as much as it had in the previous 27. True, to spread employment the union insisted on a work-sharing scheme which had the effect of increasing costs of production by keeping mines working at less than capacity when coal might more economically have been mined by shutting some mines down and working others more intensively. But these restrictions were clearly thought of as temporary and no effort was made to prevent, in addition to mechanization, consolidations, expansions, or permanent abandonments. In fact, Mr. Lewis has been quoted as saying some years ago that he would rather be the president of a union of 100,000 well-paid miners than lead 400,000 poorly-paid workers. When one realizes that, by implication at least, this means that Mr. Lewis has been prepared to see three quarters of the workers he once represented lose their jobs, this is a remarkable statement; yet in 1955 only 210,000 were at work, so that Mr. Lewis was in that year well on the way to realizing his preference!

Contrast the situation in Great Britain, where miners have long resisted increases in productivity on the ground that they meant "working yourself or your buddy out of a job" or "merely increasing the bosses' profits." So deeply engrained is this point of view that, after nationalization had ended the bosses' profits and while both coal and the labor to mine it were in extremely short supply, miners continued to resist increases in productivity. In one extreme case, seeking to establish a model mine, the Coal Board spent as much again on re-equipment and modernization as had been paid to the owners when the mine was nationalized; but, as a result of deliberate restriction of production by the workers concerned, *there was no increase whatsoever in output*. Not until the Coal Board appealed to the central office of the union and received permission to shut down the mine and deprive the workers involved of their seniority rights did production and productivity start to reflect the costly mechanization that had taken place. It is possible that such extreme resistance to mechanization is passing; there are observers who believe that the poor performance of the nationalized coal industry is more the result of inadequate management under nationalization than of continuing opposition to improved technology on the part of labor. But whatever the cause, the result is that the Coal Board officially estimates the anticipated increase in productivity over the decade from 1955 to 1965 at 13 per cent, which contrasts with a realized increase of 50 per cent in the United States during the five years from 1950 to 1955!

In short, what unions achieve depends very much on what they seek to achieve. If a union believes that the long-run interests of its members are best served by remaining receptive to changes in technology, the productivity of the industry is likely to rise steadily; but if the union believes that security and the elimination of the possibility of job loss is of primary importance, increases in productivity inevitably will be slower. Again if a union believes that long-run interests of its members are best served by free enterprise, it will attempt to make such a system work; but, if it prefers socialism instead, it can hardly be expected to devote much effort to promoting free enterprise. The implications of this last statement will be elaborated in the section which follows.

Social mobility, socialism, and economic development

Given the closeness of their cultural heritage, the question as to why socialism is so widely accepted in Britain and almost not at all in the United States is of great interest. A full answer is beyond the scope of this chapter, but the matter seems worth raising in order to focus attention on the fact that an economic system must do more than satisfy economic wants; it must be a part of a social organization which provides an acceptable life for its citizens. For there is considerable evidence that it is the character of British society rather than of the British economy which explains the extent of acceptance of socialism and the slowness of British economic development. The subject is worthy of further examination, primarily as an example of the impact of influences other than economic on the performance of an economy.

In Great Britain the prevailing class structure has been far more rigid than in the United States (though the rigidity is, of course, decreasing under the impact of socialism). This rigidity stems from Britain's hereditary aristocracy, based on birth and land ownership. An aristocracy has been defined as a class which has lost its economic *raison d'être*. This has never entirely applied to Britain, as the British aristocrat until recently lived on his estate, was in close touch with his tenants, and played a role in promoting agricultural improvements. Further, though neither he nor his younger brothers—who under primogeniture do not inherit any part of the estate—engage directly in business (which is referred to as "being in trade"), nonetheless, the aristocracy has been able to preserve its position of wealth long after revenue from landed estates declined in importance. In part this was possible because coal was discovered under the estate or the land became urban with the growth of cities, but judicious investments and strategic marriages also played important roles. The result was that, though acceptance into aristocratic circles was always slow, it continued to be the goal of the successful industrialist, who sought to achieve it by sending his sons to proper schools, purchasing estates for the prestige they conveyed, and arranging appropriate marriages between his daughters and aristocrats in need of wherewithal to maintain their position. Hence social prestige continued to depend heavily on the accident of birth, and class lines remained relatively rigid.

This rigidity has been intensified by the character of the English educational system. Even today of the age group between fifteen and eighteen, only about 15 per cent are studying full time, and only about one out of seven of the remainder are engaged in even part-time study. In sharp contrast, over 85 per cent of those between fourteen and seventeen in the United States are enrolled in educational institutions, while in the case of those eighteen and nineteen years old over 30 per cent are enrolled in educational institutions, with 60 per cent of those enrolled, or almost 20 per cent of the age group, attending colleges or universities. Of the 15 per cent between fifteen and eighteen who study full time in Great Britain, by no means all receive a training which makes entrance to a university possible. Further, the decision as to which type of education a child shall receive is normally made at eleven, on the basis of examinations given at that time. Thus, except where parents can afford a private education or the child is so unusually able that he can pass a re-examination when he is fifteen, the decision as to whether a child is even to be prepared for college is made before he is twelve. And these arrangements, which were inaugurated in 1944, represent a *considerable improvement* over those which had previously prevailed.

Of the small minority that continue beyond fifteen on a full-time basis, perhaps four out of five attend a "secondary grammar" school financed with public funds. The famous English "public schools"—actually private schools charging tuition which are "public" in the sense that they are not profit-making—educate relatively few, though they send proportionately more of their graduates to universities, especially Oxford and Cambridge. Hence those who undertake academic work at the university level are drawn from the very small group receiving a private education and the somewhat larger but still surprisingly small group which is selected to be prepared for college at public expense on the basis of intellectual abilities demonstrated at the age of eleven.

At the college level itself England has never had anything comparable to American state universities or municipal colleges. Even today only about 5 per cent of those of college age are enrolled in English universities on a full-time basis, with another 2 per cent attending full time all other institutions of learning, some of which would be called colleges in America. Yet, as Shaw made clear in *Pygmalion*, the British set great store by "accent," which is not easily acquired except by attending college.

As a result, the attractions and prestige offered by the professions and the civil service draw most of the relatively small number of English university graduates, so that there are relatively few available for business. Those who do enter business tend to perform management functions immediately with little or no actual plant experience. There is, furthermore, by American standards, a shortage of technical and staff personnel and junior executives.[1] One result of this is that, in the absence of anyone to whom they can delegate, British businessmen, on being asked why they do not expand their output, often reply: "*I* don't want to work any harder!" A second result is that British business relies for direct supervision on foremen with limited education, who are recruited from the workers' ranks but are not usually considered part of management or candidates for managerial posts. Consequently there is a relatively sharp distinction between management and labor; a British firm, for example, is likely to have a Workers' Club separate from any facilities provided for management—rather like the Army distinction between officers and GI's. In contrast, American firms think twice before providing recreation facilities which are not open to all. In short, on a broad basis, what has been called the "managerial revolution"—under which management is entrusted to those with ability but with little or no stock ownership—has made considerably slower progress in Britain than in the

---

[1] Frederick Harbison, *Quarterly Journal of Economics* (August, 1956), p. 369.

United States—partly because the group from whom managers can be recruited is relatively limited. In consequence, British firms tend to be run by the second and third generation of the founding family to a noticeably greater extent than in the United States—even when the interests of the younger generation have shifted from business and its abilities have declined.

Socialism and social immobility

Why has the British sort of social organization promoted socialism? When Hugh Gaitskell, the present leader of the Labour Party, was recently asked why he became a socialist, his reply was: "I am socialist because I hate and loathe social injustice, because I hate the class structure that disfigures our society, because I hate poverty and squalor. I want to see a society in which rewards go according to merit." [2] Note the emphasis on "class structure": from the viewpoint of a Welsh miner or a London docker the British system has been one under which he and his children seemed endlessly condemned to support a monolithic ruling and owning class to which he had no opportunity whatsoever of belonging. Nothing short of a complete change in the system seemed to offer any hope of getting the bosses off his back and providing his children with an opportunity to realize their potentialities. Of the two perhaps the burden of the bosses was more important. We know from polls that the average man vastly overestimates the importance of profits; without a doubt nothing has been more disappointing to British socialists than to have to recognize after industries had been nationalized how small a contribution the elimination of the private profits involved was able to make to raising the living level of the masses. But now that this has had to be faced, one of the strongest remaining appeals of socialism is that it appears to be the only way that the children of a man with a cockney accent can look forward to the recognition to which their ability entitles them—in short, the only way in which reasonable equality of opportunity can be achieved.

Gaitskell's emphasis on "rewards according to merit" is the reverse side of the same coin. For British socialists are by and large convinced that economic rewards under capitalism reflect not ability, but luck and inheritance. In this they are, of course, backed up by the whole aristocratic emphasis on the "accident of birth"—a matter about which even the ablest man can do nothing once he has chosen his parents. Certainly

[2] More recently, in outlining to the 1958 Labour Party conference the "modern society" which Labour seeks to create, Gaitskell described it as free of "servility and snobbery" and based on "freedom, security, and equality" (*The New York Times,* October 2, 1958, p. 10).

the highly progressive income tax favored by socialists reflects a belief in the undeserved character of large incomes; and equally the highly progressive inheritance tax is an effort to reduce the importance of hereditary wealth. There can be no doubt that there are few aspects of capitalism that are harder to defend than the receipt of large incomes entirely as a result of inheritance. The difficulty is that, as neither gifts nor capital gains are subject to taxation under British laws, a man of inherited wealth willing to invest in growth industries and give his assets to his children five years before his death can relatively easily preserve his family's fortune. And the very progressiveness of the income taxes with which socialists seek to reduce inequality makes it extremely difficult for anyone, no matter how able he may be, to acquire wealth if he starts without it—and the inability to achieve wealth, in turn, diminishes the very social mobility which the socialists are so anxious to promote.

In short, resentment of rigid class lines has been important in explaining the acceptance of socialism and highly progressive taxation, but modification of the existing situation has proved difficult. Systematic taxation of expenditure and capital transfers (rather than income) may well be required if the pattern of consumption is to be made to correspond closely with current contributions to production.

In contrast to Great Britain, the United States has never had an aristocracy. There has, of course, been much discrimination on various grounds—against successive waves of immigrants, against Jews, and against Negroes. But such *class* structure as has existed has been predominantly "plutocratic"—based on the possession of income and wealth rather than birth or land ownership. The lines themselves are not tightly drawn; if there ever was a select group of 400 socialites in New York City as was once alleged, the list has long since been expanded to include anyone with the price of admission to a fashionable café. In fact, there are those who believe that inherited wealth is an obstacle to reaching a top position in management; corporations are said to feel that those with independent means are likely to be lacking in dedication to the interests of the corporation. Many corporations, in fact, have hard and fast rules against nepotism—though a father who is president probably on balance still improves a man's prospects for employment and advancement. In short, social mobility upward—from the masses to the classes—has generally been relatively easy. There was little surprise, for example, when it became known that LeRoy Curtice had retired from General Motors on a pension of $63 a month after serving 28 years as a paint-and-metal inspector in the same year that his brother received $775,000 as president of the company.

Perhaps equally important is the fact that *exit* from the American plutocracy also takes place easily. By and large this is not the result of social policy; inheritance taxes remain at relatively low levels. Yet, despite the fact that the rich provide most of the private saving, this has not lead to the rich getting richer as Marx predicted. In fact, the evidence is on balance in the other direction *even before* allowing for the impact of progressive income taxation. Long-run inflation and restrictions on perpetual trusts have played a role: only in Boston has the professional trustee had some success in preserving for several generations a class where economic *raison d'être* had ceased to exist. Also important has been an environment in which a father's obligation is to provide an education to enable his son to make a living rather than to provide the living. But the flexible, expanding, and dynamic character of American society has undoubtedly been most important of all. There has never been a time when there were not more posts open at the top than could be filled by the sons of those already at the top. In commenting on American social mobility, Professor David McCord Wright has said: "The ideal is a society kept sufficiently decentralized and competitive so that the less able will drop out of the upper income groups while new recruits of the more able appear from below. . . . [While] most Americans have believed in giving men freedom to rise, they have not believed in letting things be too comfortable for the successful *after* they have risen. . . . [With society] kept reasonably flexible and mobile, envy of the more successful has not been very respectable in America. . . . And our relative absence of envy tends to be reflected in greater enterprise and growth." [3] In other words, "fair shares" are much less a problem if it is felt that the shares are received as the result of merit rather than accident—and this in turn tends to stimulate effort and development.

Finally, it may well be that there is an important relationship between the social organization in Britain and the character of competition. Achieving a position in an aristocratic world may well have absorbed only a small part of the energies of the original entrepreneur; but the effect on the second generation, after it had acquired aristocratic values, has certainly been significant. Even when not attracted from business to more "acceptable" occupations, the second generation has found that the world of which it seeks to be a part thinks of business merely as a source of income, so that innovation and the resulting intensification of competition offered at best little prestige and at worst has been open to the devastating charge that it is "ungentlemanly conduct." Under the circumstances a market-sharing agreement—both to provide more income and more time for hunting—may well have been the statesmanlike solution!

[3] *Fortune*, February, 1957.

Some concluding qualifications

It is essential to stress the tentative and illustrative character of the generalizations that have just been presented. They are suggestions offered—by an economist in territory claimed by sociologists—only because purely economic explanations seem inadequate to account in full for either the greater acceptance of socialism or the slower rate of economic development in Great Britain compared with the United States. Although it seems unlikely that any amount of additional work will be able to explain the differences in purely economic terms, further research will certainly bring forward many factors which have not been considered in this brief chapter. For, to repeat what was said in the introductory section, the purpose of the chapter has been to provide some *examples* of the impact on economic development of influences broader than those normally included in the term "economic." Although it obviously would be desirable to be able to cover such influences systematically and completely, as yet we simply do not have either the information or the understanding to do so. Because the discussion has been no more than illustrative and our present knowledge of what is involved is severely limited, it is perfectly possible that the emphasis of this chapter on British deficiencies will turn out to be exaggerated—though the slower rate of British development is a fact which will continue to need explanation. But if this chapter has succeeded in making clear that a full understanding of the factors influencing economic development inevitably reaches beyond economics into other fields, it will have achieved its primary purpose.

PART THREE

DEVELOPMENT
UNDER COMMUNISM

CHAPTER ELEVEN

THE RUSSIAN BACKGROUND

Socialism versus Communism

Both socialism and communism involve government ownership of the "means of production"—in economic terms, government ownership of all capital and natural resources. In the past the main difference between socialism and communism was in regard to the means required to achieve government ownership. The socialist believed that government ownership could be established without violence by existing, predominantly democratic governmental regimes. The communist, on the other hand, while not advocating violence, felt that it would inevitably be used by the property-owning classes to resist efforts to achieve government ownership, so that violent overthrow of existing governments would be necessary. Perhaps the forcible destruction of a democratically elected socialist government in Spain by the military junta under Franco is the best available example of the sort of thing communists consider inevitable.

In recent years these differences have lost much of their meaning. On the one hand, the successful expansion of government ownership in Great Britain by parliamentary means has demonstrated the possibility of peaceful socialization; but so little appears to have been achieved by the mere fact of socialization that the enthusiasm of British socialists for further government ownership has notably waned in favor of other objectives. On the other hand, a communist has come increasingly to mean a person who is prepared to subject himself to the discipline of a communist party controlled by, and for the benefit of, the Soviet Union. It is important to keep this change in mind when attempting to understand the wide acceptance of communism in the thirties. At that time a communist might have been no more than a person who felt that the violent reaction to reform represented by Franco was likely to be widespread. But if he clung on thereafter while the "party line" went through its numerous and violent shifts—believing that Finland attacked Russia in 1939, that World War II was an imperialist war until the day that Germany attacked Russia and a war against fascism thereafter, and that North Korea was the innocent victim of South Korean aggression—he would have become a communist in the present-day meaning of the term. When this is the meaning used in what follows, the term will be capitalized.

Dictatorship and Communism

In communist doctrine there is a different meaning of "socialism." It is a transitional stage during which the victorious dictatorship of the proletariat liquidates the remnants of the bourgeoisie and prepares the way for the classless society of full communism, when the state, which in communist theory is the instrument by which one class suppresses another, will no longer have any function and will, therefore, "wither away." In communist thinking, the Soviet Union is "socialistic" in this sense. The difficulty is that class lines have, if anything, become increasingly marked in the Soviet Union and the state is showing no signs whatsoever of "withering away." Nor is there any clear evidence of any reduction in the degree of dictatorship within the Soviet Union. True in the jockeying for power that followed Stalin's death there was a point at which it was expedient for Khrushchev to attack Stalin's dictatorship and there was a period in which it seemed possible that the satellites would receive greater autonomy. But the difficulties of a partial dictatorship are immense. Recent events suggest that no significant reduction in the dictatorial quality of the Russian regime has in fact occurred.

This raises the question of the extent to which it is possible to examine the Russian economic system without reference to the prevailing political dictatorship. Even though there are no known cases of anything approaching complete government ownership of the means of production unaccompanied by dictatorship, something can be said regarding the general way in which Communism solves the "economizing" problem of allocating scarce means among alternative uses apart from the political system. But when it comes to discussing the economic development with which this volume is primarily concerned—and especially when it comes to discussing the actual achievements of the Soviet

Union—the fact of dictatorship must be kept squarely in mind. For it will be argued in what follows that government ownership in itself by no means guarantees more rapid economic development; it is the actual decisions made that count. Thus, if a dictatorial Communism is able to achieve rapid development by devoting large sums to research and capital formation at the expense of the present generation in a way that would be quite impossible under democracy, the credit belongs, not to the existence of government ownership, but to the existence of dictatorship. Equally, if Russian development has been slowed down by the havoc wrought by Hitler's invasion, the result cannot fairly be blamed on Communism.

To provide a background against which to appraise the Soviet Union's development achievements, the bulk of this chapter will be devoted to a short summary of Russian economic history since the Communist Revolution. Attention will be concentrated entirely on the Soviet Union not only because the achievements of Soviet Communism can only be appraised against the specific difficulties faced by the regime but also because the Soviet Union represents the outstanding example of a Communist regime. Finally, as additional background—though more appropriate, perhaps, to the usual course on comparative economic systems—some of the differences between the way in which the "economizing" problem is solved under Communism and under capitalism will be summarized at the end of this chapter.

Achievement versus cost

In what follows there will appear much that is favorable regarding the economic achievements of the Soviet Union. These achievements have, however, been attained at an immense cost in human suffering. There are three reasons why this human cost will not be stressed. First, to the extent that we are in an economic struggle with the Soviet Union, it is results rather than costs which count. The fact, for example, that Soviet aid to underdeveloped countries is made available by holding down the Russian level of living while American aid has not prevented a rapid rise in our level of living is likely to be of extraordinarily small interest to an Afghan, whose living level is very much lower even than that in the Soviet Union. Second, costs in human suffering which appear utterly prohibitive to one brought up in the Western tradition, with its emphasis on the importance of the individual, have little or no meaning to the considerable majority of humanity who live in countries where human life remains "cheap" and the death rate high as a result of malnutrition and dietary-deficiency diseases—if not outright starvation. Third, human costs will not be stressed to avoid repetition. Let me at this point make it clear, once and for all, that the achievements of the Soviet Union—impressive as they may be—have been won at a cost in human suffering which, in my judgment, has been both unnecessary and staggeringly high. With this over-all judgment firmly in mind, let us now turn to a rapid summary of recent Russian economic history.

War and revolution

Though progress had been made, at the time of World War I Russian economic development had a long way to go. Four fifths of the population were peasant cultivators, perhaps a fifth of whom were so poor that they did not have draft animals but worked their land entirely by hand. While there were a significant number of urban industrial workers, the "middle class" of professionals, businessmen, and technicians was subordinate to an autocratic group of aristocrats, land owners, and bureaucrats which had successfully opposed all efforts at liberalizing the regime politically—so much so that when shortly before the revolution the suggestion was made to the Czar that he should take steps to win the confidence of his people, he could reply: "Surely it is for the people by their conduct to merit my confidence!"

Although the overwhelming proportion of German military strength throughout World War I was deployed on the Western front, after three years of fighting the Russian Army was reduced to a state verging on collapse. Largely for this reason the Czar was overthrown in March, 1917, in a revolution led by moderates and pledged to a continuance of the war. But during 1917 conditions, especially in the cities, continued to deteriorate. As a result the Bolsheviks, a small but well-organized revolutionary group under the leadership of Lenin, who drew their support from the industrial workers and believed with Marx in the necessity for a dictatorship of the proletariat, were able to seize power from numerically larger, but disorganized, moderate elements. The slogan of the Bolsheviks was "Land, Bread, and Peace"—a prophetic slogan because, while they did sue for peace and try to provide bread, the Bolsheviks had no ultimate intention of making land available for peasant ownership. Hence it represented the first, but by no means the last, time the Bolsheviks concealed their ultimate purpose to obtain immediate advantage. Once in power the Bolsheviks ruthlessly but efficiently consolidated their position, so that by the middle of 1918 they were in substantial control of the entire country.

As it became increasingly clear that Germany would be defeated, arms from Allied sources reached various White Russian forces opposed to the revolution, and late in 1918 American, French, and British soldiers landed at Archangel and American and Japanese forces at Vladivostok.

This forced the Communists to concentrate on developing the Red Army, which was done with remarkable efficiency under the leadership of Trotsky. When it became obvious that a major campaign would be required to overthrow the Communists, the Allied forces, which had never clearly formulated what they wished to accomplish, withdrew, and by 1920, all remaining organized opposition had been eliminated. The price paid for the civil war in terms of economic disorganization was, however, immense. Output of large-scale industry is estimated to have fallen to 14 per cent of the 1913 level, and agricultural output declined to the point at which starvation was widespread. It is important to keep in mind that the Communists believe—and to an unfortunate extent believe correctly—that had it not been for direct Allied intervention and indirect aid to the White Russian forces, the major part of the destruction of the revolution would have been avoided and reconstruction started two years sooner.

The New Economic Policy

Not only had production largely collapsed because the Communists had been too busy to develop techniques to implement the nationalization of industry, but the bitterness developed during the civil war had driven a large part of the professional and managerial group into exile. Organizing nationalized industry and replacing the departed technicians could not be done at once. Continuing collapse was averted by a massive strategic retreat called the New Economic Policy. Under it around 40 per cent of Russian industry was returned to private control—especially light industry, distribution, and retailing. At the same time, to reverse the sharp reduction in acreage under cultivation as a result of grain "requisitions" during the civil war, peasants were confirmed in the possession of the land that they held or had seized (though title was technically vested in the state), and were promised unhindered exchange of their products for those of industry. Transport, utilities, and basic industry, however, remained nationalized. On the political side the period was marked by the death of Lenin and the struggle between Trotsky and Stalin to succeed him. An issue in the struggle was whether immediate world revolution was necessary to safeguard the Soviet Union against renewed capitalist aggression. The triumph of Stalin was in part a triumph of the belief that the "building of socialism" was possible within a single country even though the rest of the world remained capitalistic.

During the period of the New Economic Policy, which extended to the inauguration of the First Five-Year Plan in 1928, two main things were accomplished on the economic front: planning techniques were developed to permit the operation of the industry that remained nationalized, and a rapid expansion of education was undertaken to replace the technicians lost during the civil war. In terms of the problems of underdeveloped countries, the length of time required by Russia to develop trained personnel is worth noting. So difficult was the situation that higher education was made available only to the sons of peasants and workers; all others were excluded on the ground that their class background raised questions in regard to their loyalty to the regime. Over-all, during the period of the New Economic Policy the Communist regime was able to consolidate its position, but by 1928 it had made little progress; the level of production was approximately that prevailing before the war in 1913.

The First Five-Year Plan

The First Five-Year Plan had three objectives: nationalization, collectivization, and industrialization. The first represented simply the liquidation of the New Economic Policy. By the end of the period—formally January, 1933—private ownership of the means of production had been completely eliminated. With the exception of collectives in agriculture and producer cooperatives (especially in retailing), ownership was vested directly in the state and formal planning was extended to almost all economic activity.

Elimination of private ownership elsewhere was easy compared to the collectivization of agriculture. Clearly *some* reorganization was necessary. Holdings were so small that the individual farmer by himself could not possibly own and use modern agricultural machinery. In fact, so divided were the individual holdings that the land lying fallow to separate them could, it was estimated in 1928, have grown enough grain to feed Moscow. And we have already noted that the poorer peasants did not even have draft animals. Originally the Plan called for only gradual organization into "collectives"—a sort of cooperative in which land and tools, including livestock and draft animals, are pooled and workers receive a share of the common output based on the value of the work they contribute. But in the enthusiasm generated by the Plan the targets were greatly expanded, provoking violent peasant opposition. Partly this took the form of the slaughter of livestock, including draft animals; but it culminated in a sharp reduction in the acreage seeded in 1932, followed by a partial crop failure. The result was widespread starvation. Although the exact number will never be known, as vital statistics for the period have been suppressed, estimates of deaths from starvation range from 2 to 10 millions—the latter figure equal to half of total Russian casualties in World War II. Even Stalin confessed, in a conversation with Churchill, that the incident was not one of which he was proud. But if the cost appears high—and almost certainly unnecessary—collectivization did serve to reorganize land holdings so as to make the use of modern machinery possible, which in turn permitted a sharp reduction in the percentage of the labor force in agriculture.

To make rapid industrialization possible without a decline in living levels, the First Five-Year Plan counted on sharp increases in productivity in the industrial sector of the economy. These were not in fact realized. Rather than slow the development of the heavy industry provided for in the Plan, production of consumer goods was allowed to decline to the point at which price control and rationing became necessary. By a remarkable coincidence, this decline in Russia came at precisely the same time that Western living levels fell as a result of the Great Depression, but in Russia the decline was the result of emphasis on the production of capital goods rather than waste of productive capacity through unemployment. As the Plan was revised both upward and downward frequently, whether it was "fulfilled" is of little consequence; what it did clearly achieve was to lay the foundation for the Soviet Union's subsequent rapid industrial development.

Hitler and the Second and Third Five-Year Plans

The Second Five-Year Plan, which started in 1933, stressed an expansion of consumption. Peasants were permitted to farm "garden plots" assigned them by the collective and sell freely any surplus they were able to produce. Production of consumer goods was increased, and by 1935 supplies were sufficiently plentiful that rationing and price control were discontinued. More broadly, Russia had by then received widespread diplomatic recognition, the regime felt secure enough to make higher education available even to those whose class background was suspect, the draft of what appeared to be a liberal constitution had been circulated, and there is evidence that the powers of the secret police were being reduced. Among historical speculations few are more fascinating than on what "might have been" if these tendencies had continued. But the threat that Hitler represented had apparently become clear to Stalin by 1936. Evidence that the threat was recognized is provided by the sudden change that occurred in the treatment of abortion, which had been guaranteed as a personal right in the draft of the constitution circulated in 1935 but was suppressed before the constitution was actually enacted in 1936—presumably in recognition of the importance of a high birth rate in offsetting war losses. (Abortion was made legal again in 1955.)

As a result, halfway through the Second Five-Year Plan the emphasis on consumption decreased and the emphasis on capital formation, particularly in the area east of the Urals, and, above all, on production for defense increased greatly. Moreover, the Third Five-Year Plan, which started in 1938, continued this shift in emphasis. Defense, which had absorbed only 3 per cent of the national income in 1928, took 8 per cent in 1937 and 16 per cent in 1940. Even capital formation, which had risen from 15 per cent in 1928 to 21 per cent in 1937, fell back to 14 per cent in 1940.[1] As a consequence the level of living fell appreciably. To the many Communists who believed that socialism would bring rising living levels for the workers, the reversal was a bitter blow. Widespread unrest resulted, especially among old Communists, culminating in the purges of 1937 and the strengthening of the secret police and Stalin's dictatorship. But economically the five years between 1936 and 1941, when Hitler invaded the Soviet Union, were responsible not only for substantial military production, but also for the creation of an industrial base east of the Urals, which to a major extent explains why the Soviet Union was able to maintain military production at a high level during World War II despite Hitler's conquest of so large a part of Russia's original industrial area.

The war achievement

In World War I the Russian Army, after absorbing a minor part of the German war effort, virtually collapsed in three years. Little more than a quarter-century later, after three years of war, the German Army was in full retreat before a Russian Army which had absorbed the major part—perhaps 75 or 80 per cent—of a greatly expanded war effort. There have been few more dramatic reversals in history; yet so little was the change anticipated that, at the start of Hitler's invasion, an outstanding American military expert on Russia was widely quoted as saying: "Only an act of God will allow the Russian Army to hold out for more than six weeks." Note that the German Army was in full retreat in Russia before the Normandy landings and before Allied bombing had achieved any significant impact on the German war effort. While goods supplied Russia under Lend-Lease undoubtedly helped, only in the case of trucks, where perhaps half of those in military use were Lend-Leased, was a military item provided in significant quantity. In fact, it is estimated that Russia produced five times as many mortars, twice as many cannon, and somewhat more tanks than America.[2] Moreover, Russian tanks were considered by the Germans to be the best produced by any

[1] For details, see Table 12-5.

[2] Edward Ames, American Economic Association, *Proceedings* (May, 1951), p. 490.

nation, Germany included. Finally, the military results almost certainly do not accurately reflect the Russian *production* achievement. For the initial German successes appear to have been achieved far more by superior military organization than by superior military matériel.

Russia's military achievement is stressed in this volume devoted to economic development because the statistics measuring Russia's economic achievements are complicated and for many do not carry conviction. But in the competition of actual war, statistical tricks are of no help. We shall see, when we analyze the Russian economy more fully in the next chapter, that Russian military accomplishments were made possible only through considerable "distortion" of the economy and at a heavy price in terms of consumer goods foregone. But the war clearly demonstrated that the planned and nationalized economy of the Soviet Union was capable of organizing its resources to achieve a concrete end such as military strength. This Hitler did not understand—perhaps because his intelligence was no better than ours. It would seem unfortunate to repeat his mistake.

The postwar recovery

Perhaps the most important point to be made about postwar recoveries—both in Russia and elsewhere—is that they are not representative. The destruction of capital by the Germans was immense and production, especially of consumer goods, had by 1945 fallen to a low level. One estimate is that one third of Russian industry was "destroyed" in the course of the War.[3] But the rate of recovery could be expected to be, and was in fact, rapid. For wartime "destruction" is rarely complete: a railroad can be rendered inoperative by blowing its bridges or a power plant by destroying its generators. The economic effort involved, however, in replacing bridges and generators is nowhere near as great as building the railroad or power plant from scratch. The smaller effort shows up in a quite abnormally rapid increase in production, which continues until all the partially destroyed capital is put back into use. The result in the Russian case is that, up to about 1950, rates of increase in production and income are of little significance. Achievements since that date are more important and will be examined more fully in the chapter which follows.

What emerges from this brief outline of Russian economic history? Let us first stress what may appear obvious: the Soviet Union has demonstrated that an economy with practically complete government ownership of the means of production can survive in the face of con-

---

[3] Ellsworth Raymond, *Soviet Economic Progress* (New York: Rinehart, 1957), p. 2.

siderable difficulties and—cost aside—can achieve at least the priority objectives of its leadership. If today this may not seem like much of a conclusion, it should be recalled that numerous economists in the past predicted that planned economies would fall of their own weight. As soon, however, as we try to go further, we run into difficulties. Suppose, for example, we look for a time in which to measure the "normal" rate of development of the Russian economy. At the outside, the thirteen years between 1928 and 1941 and the period since 1950 appear to qualify. But during the first period occurred the perhaps inevitable difficulties involved in the initial efforts at large-scale planning and industrialization and the perhaps quite avoidable waste resulting from the way in which collectivization was achieved. And toward the end of the period there were the difficulties caused by the rapid change during the Second and Third Five-Year Plans from emphasis on consumption and capital formation to heavy stress on military preparations. Only during three or four years of the period—perhaps from 1933 to some time in 1936—was the Communist leadership seriously interested in raising living levels. Obviously under such circumstances the idea of a "normal" rate of development has a rather special meaning. This is not, of course, to deny that the performance of other economies has also been marred by wars, mistaken economic policies, and severe depressions. Rather the point to be stressed is that projections into the future on the basis of past performance, as well as comparisons between economies, are valid only to the extent that underlying conditions are in some sense similar. The outline of Russian economic history just concluded should, therefore, be of help to us when, in the chapter which follows, we consider the future prospects of the Russian economy.

Economizing under Communism

Let us conclude this presentation of the Russian background with a brief contrast between "economizing"—deciding what is to be produced by the scarce means of production—under Communism and under free enterprise. We may distinguish three sets of decisions: those regarding the government, saving and investment, and consumption. In this discussion we shall disregard the dictatorial character of the Russian regime. Undoubtedly the actual decisions taken are different from those that would have been reached in a democracy. But as we are concerned primarily with the mechanism by which decisions are reached, rather than the decisions themselves, such differences may be disregarded.

The government sphere in the narrow sense may be dismissed rapidly. In principle, communism is no different from capitalism. In both cases the government decides to obtain, by taxation or borrowing, control over a certain portion of the economy's output and to use it for purposes believed to be best achieved by government spending rather than in any other way. It is the greater importance of the government's role in connection with saving and investment and consumption which distinguishes communism from capitalism and requires more extended discussion.

Saving and investment under Communism

As we saw in Chapter 8, under free enterprise the government, in general, has provided little of the savings of the economy—perhaps 15 per cent in recent years in the United States. Another quarter of the total has come from the retained earnings of corporations, but the remaining 60 per cent has been provided by individuals. In turn, while the government has absorbed saving by running deficits, especially in wartime, most saving has been invested by private industry. In contrast, while Soviet business organizations save by charging more for their products than it costs to produce them in roughly the same way as American corporations, most Russian saving is provided by the government, which, in the main, raises the money by taxation. Relatively little reliance is placed on individual saving, though such saving is both encouraged and allowed to earn interest.

In apparent contradiction to this statement is the fact that sizable sums were raised in the past by the sale of so-called "mass-subscription" bonds. These can best be thought of, however, as supplementary taxation rather than voluntary saving. The Soviet regime has obviously been operating close to the limits of feasible taxation, having had to cover by taxation not only the provision of most of the economy's saving but, in addition, heavy military spending and extensive "social-security" benefits as well as "normal" government expenditures. Forcing people to make available as much as another 5 per cent of their income against the nominal promise of repayment was undoubtedly easier than raising a similiar amount by additional direct taxation. But the tax element in such bonds has always been large, especially when allowance is made for price inflation. And in 1957 the forced character of the bonds was, in effect, admitted as the Russian regime both discontinued the sale of such bonds and postponed payment of both principal and interest for 20 to 25 years on the 260 billion rubles worth that were outstanding at that time.[4] Hence it seems correct to treat the bonds as a part of the tax structure rather than as a part of the supply of saving.

[4] See F. D. Holzman, *American Economic Review,* June, 1957.

Analytically we may distinguish three problems in connection with saving and investing: (1) who does the saving; (2) who does the investing; and (3) who determines the over-all level of saving and investment? To an important extent the differences between capitalism and communism in regard to the first and third problems are matters of degree; only the second is a matter of principle. Thus, while the Soviet regime has, in fact, relied on taxation to provide the bulk of saving, greater reliance on individual saving is conceivable. The case for doing so is that there are differences among individuals, and for the same individual at different periods of his life, in the ease with which spending can be postponed—differences which are disregarded when saving is provided by general taxation. Where saving is provided by taxation, the "burden" is spread relatively uniformly across the entire population (especially if the tax structure relies heavily on indirect taxation). But if saving is provided voluntarily, it is presumably provided by those who find the "burden" least burdensome. Note that "burden" is quoted. As most people prefer present consumption to consumption in the future, there clearly is a "burden" in the postponement of consumption that saving represents—as the Russian people have found out. But the "burden" may be far less for a rich man who saves $5,000 because he cannot think of anything else to consume than it is for a poor man who with difficulty saves $500 against illness or old age. Provided that the resulting saving is invested in government bonds—which may even be interest-bearing and capable of being inherited—there does not appear to be Communist objection to taking into account such differences in "burden" as may exist by relying more heavily on individual saving. Further, although the Communist regime determines politically as a result of its planning the over-all level of saving of the economy, we have already noted in Chapter 8 that other governments—especially in underdeveloped countries—also have concerned themselves with the over-all rate of saving. Hence in these areas differences are, to an important extent, matters of degree rather than of kind.

On the other hand, it is a basic part of Communist doctrine that means of production cannot be privately owned. Hence private investment, which would lead to privately-owned capital, is inadmissible, and all investment is allocated according to government plan. In contrast, except for a small amount of government investment, investment under free enterprise is by individuals. Suppose we assume that the production objectives established by consumer spending are considered to be "desirable"—a point to which we will return in the section which follows. Under this assumption the essence of the issue between capitalism and communism in regard to investment is *whether the allocation of the funds available for investment by private individuals seeking the largest possible profit is sufficiently superior to allocation according to plan as to justify the compensation that investors receive for their activities.*

Obviously this is not a question to which there is a simple answer. Investment by plan is neither perfect nor costless. A large bureaucracy will be required to do the planning and, like bureaucracies the world over, can be counted on to make many mistakes. On the other hand, investment by individuals seeking profits is also not perfect—and, from the social point of view, misallocation of investment by an individual who misjudges profit prospects is just as wasteful as misallocation by a bureaucrat who misjudges investment needs—even if the individual is wasting money which he himself has saved. One thing is certain: the compensation that is paid for investing, over and above an interest return on saving, is small. While there is no easy way to separate the two, the differential received by corporate investors on the average over and above, say, the interest that the government is paying on its obligations—which is a possible measure of their compensation for investing—is hardly likely to be more than 1 per cent of the national income—certainly less than 2 per cent of total consumption. Hence the choice between private profit-seeking investment and investment according to plan must be made on the basis of the relative efficiency of the alternatives in using available funds so as to realize most effectively "desirable" production objectives.

Consumption under Communism

How can "desirable" production objectives be established? Should we rely on planning, as is done under Communism, or consumer spending, as is done under capitalism? At first sight these appear quite different alternatives; but actually, as before, the difference is largely a matter of degree. All modern capitalist economies prohibit many types of consumption—narcotics, switch-blade knives, reducing pills containing the egg of a tapeworm—and impede the purchase of many others—such as cigarettes and alcoholic beverages. Again many types of consumption are stimulated by being made available free or at less than cost—as, for example, education. Given the influence of advertising and above all of consumer ignorance, it is hard to be certain that the actual production objectives established under capitalism are in any sense "ideal."

Conversely, no Communist economy is likely to plan production without paying at least some attention to what consumers want. But how much attention? In the same speech a leading Communist could say: ". . . the very essence of Soviet trade calls for an all-round study of popular demand and of the diverse requirements of the people" and also "It is the function of Soviet trade to influence demand. . . . It should cultivate the taste of the consumers, bring new goods into use . . . , promote the sale of . . . wholesome food products, and also of useful, well-made and beautiful manufactured goods. . . ."[5] Does the second of these statements involve undue "interference" with consumer choice? Perhaps. But if for the words "Soviet trade" we substitute "advertising," we have a statement that would be heartily supported by the staunchest capitalist on Madison Avenue!

In short, it should be clear that the establishment of "desirable" production objectives even in the case of consumption is not an easy matter. Those who believe in placing most weight on the decisions of consumers as reflected in the way in which they spend their income in the market place are likely to be pleased with the way objectives are established under capitalism; those who believe that most weight should be placed on decisions socially arrived at—which would include many socialists as well as Communists—will place emphasis on planning. In any event, the differences are matters of degree rather than of kind.

[5] A. I. Mikoyan, report delivered at the All-Union Conference of Distributive Workers, October, 1953 (Moscow: Foreign Language Publishing House, 1954), pp. 20 and 39; quoted from A. R. Oxenfeldt, *Economic Systems in Action* (New York: Rinehart, 1957), p. 66.

CHAPTER TWELVE

WHAT RUSSIA HAS ACCOMPLISHED

Introduction

Describing Russian accomplishments is rather like the problem facing the blind men who tried to describe an elephant: what they found depended on the part of the beast they happened to bump into. The problem of description is made even more difficult because the Soviet economy is grossly "distorted" in comparison with a "normal" Western economy. The essence of the matter is that the Communist leadership has shown remarkable ability to achieve its priority objectives: industrialization and military strength. But Communism works no miracles; achievement of these priority objectives has inevitably been paid for by slow development elsewhere. Hence it is easy—by looking at priority areas—to prove that the Soviet Union is doing brilliantly, and equally easy—by looking at areas the Communists consider unimportant—to prove that Russia is doing appallingly badly.

We are dealing with an economy whose over-all industrial production is not much more than a third that of the United States. Yet it is an economy which has produced "not only large, well-equipped conventional military forces, but also nuclear-weapon delivery systems which are at least technologically equal to those of the West, and in some cases possibly superior"; which has "the world's largest submarine fleet, a surface navy second only to the American, and an air force numerically superior to that of the United States"; and which produces half as much steel, 80 per cent as much coal, and 20 per cent more machine tools by value and even more by number than are produced in the United States.[1] And it is equally an economy whose production of consumer durables such as automobiles, refrigerators, and washing machines is miniscule—perhaps 2 to 4 per cent of the American level—and which provides its inhabitants with the worst housing in Europe—even worse than is available in Bulgaria. *Fortune* tried to translate this strange mixture into American terms as follows: "Imagine that the U. S. had an air-nuclear striking power equivalent to what we had, say, two years ago. But imagine U. S. heavy industry where it was thirty years ago. Now imagine that most of the U. S. nonfarm labor force, other than government employees, is working forty-six hours a week in crowded and dirty factories or on heavy construction, for less real pay than it got in 1928, and for a lower standard of housing than it had in 1913. And finally imagine that half of all Americans are still living and working on farms as they were seventy-five years ago, for a living standard even lower than that of the city people." [2] The part of the elephant we happen to bump into obviously does make a difference!

What we shall attempt to do in this chapter is, first, to present some statistical evidence regarding the broad changes that have occurred under Communist planning; second, to attempt some interpretation of the implications of these changes; and finally, to speculate regarding future prospects for the Soviet regime. Because statistics regarding economic accomplishments are of possible military importance, until quite recently the Soviet Union withheld much economic information; even today much less is available than for most other countries. On the other hand, considerable effort has been put into studying Russian accomplishments, and there is general agreement among students of the Soviet economy that the *basic* statistics are not falsified—undoubtedly because to do so would make planning almost impossible. Problems develop when attempts are made to combine individual series into over-all measures to determine the total performance of the economy. For a variety of reasons the combined measures prepared by Soviet statisticians are seriously misleading—perhaps deliberately so. Let us start, therefore, with some basic series measuring physical production and then present some over-all estimates made by Western scholars to shed light on the total performance of the Soviet economy.

[1] Committee for Economic Development, *Soviet Progress vs. American Enterprise* (Garden City, N.Y.: Doubleday, 1958), pp. 83-84; and Ellsworth Raymond, *Soviet Economic Progress* (New York: Rinehart, 1957), p. 43.

[2] *Fortune,* February, 1957, p. 93.

Measures of physical production

The two tables that follow demonstrate forcibly the uneven character of Russian development. Table 12-1 illustrates the sharp expansion of producers' goods as a result of rapid industrialization. Probably coal

TABLE 12-1. PRODUCTION OF PRODUCERS' GOODS

	1913	1928	1932	1937	1940	1945	1950	1955
Coal a	29	35	64	128	166	149	261	391
Oil a	9	12	21	29	31	19	38	71
Steel a	4	4	6	18	18	12	27	45
Electric Power b	2	5	14	36	48	43	91	170

a Millions of metric tons

b Billions of kilowatt hours

SOURCE: *Promyshlennost' USSR* (Moscow, 1957), pp. 40ff. The increase in coal production somewhat overstates the increase in energy achieved because the percentage of lignite, with a lower caloric value, increased from 4 per cent in 1913 and 9 per cent in 1928 to around 30 per cent in 1955.

and steel—the basic fuel and the basic metal—are most important; each increased more than tenfold from 1928 to 1955. It is this sort of performance that makes the Soviet example so obviously attractive to underdeveloped countries and gives weight to the boast that Communism is achieving in one generation what capitalism took a century to accomplish.

The rapid expansion of producers' goods is quite different from the behavior of consumers' goods, summarized in Table 12-2. True between 1928 and 1955 wool fabrics and footwear increased close to threefold; but the quantitatively far more important cotton fabrics little more than doubled. Further, basic agricultural production expanded relatively little. Cattle population, which was slow to recover from the slaughter that accompanied collectivization, was little larger in 1955 than in 1928, and flour production had increased by only one third—the same amount as the increase in population. Only hog population appears to have increased significantly, and an important part of the reported increase was the result of a change in the date on which the count was taken. Over-all it is obvious that consumers' goods—especially agricultural products—have shown no such dramatic increase as occurred in the case of producers' goods.

TABLE 12-2. PRODUCTION OF CONSUMERS' GOODS

	1913	1928	1932	1939	1940	1945	1950	1955
Cotton fabrics [a]	26	27	27	34	40	16	39	59
Wool fabrics [b]	103	87	89	108	120	54	155	252
Footwear [c]	60	(103)	(103)	183	211	63	203	272
Flour [d]	28	24	—[f]	28	29	15	22	32
Cattle population [e]	52[g]	60	38	48	48	48[h]	58	(67)
Hog population [e]	17[g]	22	11	20	23	11[h]	22	(52)

[a] Hundred million meters   [b] Million meters   [c] Million pairs   [d] Million tons   [e] Million head   [f] Not available   [g] Year 1916   [h] Year 1946.

SOURCE: *Promyshlennost' USSR* (Moscow, 1957), pp. 329ff except for cattle and hog population which are from *Narodnoe Khoziaistvo* (Moscow, 1956), p. 118. The 1928 and 1932 total for footwear includes an estimate of the output of small-scale industry taken from the National Bureau of Economic Research's forthcoming *Study of Soviet Economic Growth*, Appendix B, p. B-53. Cattle and especially hog population is undoubtedly exaggerated in 1955, as the date of the count was October 1 before fall slaughtering rather than January 1 as in other years.

Distribution of the labor force

How can we go beyond the production of individual commodities to get at the over-all distribution of the Russian productive effort? One way is to look at the distribution of the labor force. With the rapid industrialization and urbanization that started in 1928, the percentage in the labor force declined but the total number increased by 4 millions. All of this increase, plus 15 millions more released from agriculture in the course of collectivization, were absorbed into nonagricultural employment, which had almost tripled by 1939. This trend was resumed after the war, so that by 1955 another 16 millions had been added to nonagricultural employment, causing the proportion of such employment to the labor force to reach 41 per cent—or three times the 1926 level, as is made clear in Table 12-3. But between 1939 and 1955 there appears to have been no release of labor by agriculture, which instead appears to have absorbed 6 millions of a total increase in the labor force of 22 millions. The estimates for both "agricultural" and "other" employment (which includes the army, forced labor camps, and the like) are subject to a wide margin of error, so that it may be that the absorption by agriculture is overstated. From the long-run point of view, a study which used somewhat different concepts from those just presented concluded that the percentage of nonagricultural employment in relation to the total population was higher in the United States in 1820 than it was in the Soviet Union in 1928; but 22 years later, in 1950, the percentage had risen to the level the United States had attained in 1880.[3]

[3] A. David Redding, *Review of Economics and Statistics*, November, 1954.

TABLE 12-3. DISTRIBUTION OF THE LABOR FORCE
(In Millions Except Percentages)

	1926	1939	1955
Nonagricultural employment	11	30	46
Agricultural employment	70	52	58
Other employment	5	8	8
Total labor force	86	90	112
Population	147	170	198
Nonagricultural employment as percentage of labor force	13	33	41

SOURCE: Estimates for 1926 from Warren W. Eason, "Population and Labor Force," contained in *Soviet Economic Growth*, edited by Abram Bergson (White Plains, N.Y.: Row, Peterson, 1953), Table 3.2 (with the "residual labor force" in 1939 distributed half to Agricultural and half to Other Employment); estimates for 1955 by Harold Wool for the National Bureau of Economic Research.

Two things appear clear: Russia is a long way from being industrialized by the standards of countries such as Great Britain or the United States; but, equally, progress in that direction has been, and continues to be, made at an unusually rapid rate.

TABLE 12-4. DISTRIBUTION OF NONAGRICULTURAL EMPLOYMENT IN THE USSR AND USA
(In Percentages)

	USSR		USA	
	1937	1955	1900	1950
Industry and Construction	55	54	38	39
Transportation and communications	11	10	11	8
Trade	9	9	19	22
Education	8	10	3	4
Other	17	17	29	27

SOURCE: Estimates for the USA from A. David Redding, *op. cit.*; estimates for the USSR computed from data in *Narodnoe Khoziaistvo* (Moscow, 1956), pp. 187 and 190.

The distribution within the nonagricultural total, summarized in Table 12-4, again reflects the Russian emphasis on industry and construction. Even more remarkable is the fact that, on the one hand, twice as large a percentage of the labor force is engaged in trade in the United States as in the Soviet Union, while, on the other hand, the Soviet Union is devoting a percentage to education which is two and a half times larger than ours. By all accounts service in Russian stores is atrocious, and there is no doubt that the multiplication of retail outlets adds much to the convenience of life in the United States. It is, nonetheless, hard not to be concerned about the ultimate impact of the relative distribution of effort.

Behavior of the national income

Further revealing light on the over-all behavior of the Russian economy is provided by information on the way in which the Russian national income has been used, which is summarized in Table 12-5. Social

TABLE 12-5. USES OF THE NATIONAL INCOME
(In Percentages)

	1928	1937	1940	1953
Consumption	73	57	57	48
Social services	6	11	9	8
Administration	3	3	4	4
Defense	3	8	16	16
Net capital formation	15	21	14	24

SOURCE: M. C. Kaser, *Economic Journal*, March, 1957, Table III.

services represent a type of consumption, but even consumption and social services taken together have steadily declined from 79 per cent in 1928 to 56 per cent in 1953. Put the other way round, more and more of the increasing productive capacity of the Soviet Union has been devoted to defense and net capital formation, which have risen from 18 per cent at the start to 40 per cent at the end of the period. The behavior of defense is worth noting. Despite the fact that foreign troops had left Russian soil only eight years previously, defense expenditures in 1928 were quite small, and in 1937, when the menace of Hitler had been recognized, the percentage was still relatively low. Hence the high level that prevailed in 1953 is noteworthy both for the light that it casts on the objectives of the present Russian leadership and as an indication of the increase in net investment that would be possible without lowering consumption standards if military preparations were reduced.

Of even more interest than the uses to which the national income has been put is the rate at which it has been increasing. As the previous chapter made clear, the exact period for which measurement is made has an overriding influence on the results, and even for the same period there is disagreement among foreign scholars. The consensus, however, appears to be that the rate of increase during the two periods running from the start of the First Five-Year Plan in 1928 to 1941 and after 1950, when recovery from the war had been substantially completed, has been between 6 and 7 per cent a year.[4] These estimates are for the total, rather than the per person, increase in income; hence they are influenced by the rate of population growth, which makes comparisons with other countries difficult in view of the fact that the effect of population growth on the increase in output is by no means fully understood. But if we look at the behavior of total income in the United States as reported in Table 3-2, it appears that the Soviet rate of increase in income *for the years involved* was twice the American rate between 1910 and 1930 and a little less than twice the American rate between 1930 and 1950. Finally, if we take the period between 1950 and 1955, when population growth in the two countries was quite similar, the 6 per cent Soviet rate of increase compares with an increase of just over 4 per cent in the United States.[5]

The importance of the time period chosen

Note that the periods chosen for determining the rate of growth of Soviet income just presented were those during which growth was most rapid. Widely different conclusions could follow if less favorable periods were used. For example, a careful study has been made of the extent to which representative industries in the Soviet Union lag behind their American equivalents; this sort of study eliminates problems involved in combining individual series.[6] Table 12-6 presents results for the industries covered in Table 12-1. Thus Russian steel production in 1913 was roughly equal to American steel production in 1892, or 21 years earlier. By 1937 the lag had increased to 32 years and by 1955 it still was 29 years —higher than it had been in 1913. For all 37 industries studied, the median lag was 28 years in 1913, 36 years in 1937, and 35 years in 1955. Moreover, comparisons of production per person are even more unfavorable to the Soviet Union in view of the more rapid Russian population growth.

Which is "correct": the fact that Russian industry was further behind the United States in 1955 than in 1913, or that Russian income has been increasing at least 50 per cent more rapidly than ours? The answer

---

[4] M. C. Kaser, *op. cit.*, Table I summarizes estimates for the earlier period. Only Colin Clark diverges significantly from an estimate in the vicinity of 7 per cent. For the latter period, in addition to the Block estimate cited by Kaser, the 6 per cent figure has come to be widely accepted.

[5] Computed from estimates of Gross National Product in constant dollars contained in Table 7 of the July, 1958, *Survey of Current Business.*

[6] G. Warren Nutter, "Some Observations on Soviet Industrial Growth," *Occasional Paper 55*, National Bureau of Economic Research (New York, 1957).

TABLE 12-6.   LAG OF SOVIET PRODUCTION BEHIND AMERICAN PRODUCTION
(In Years)

	1913	1937	1955
Coal	45	49	47
Oil	14	26	34
Steel	21	32	29
Electric power	13	21	16
Median for all industries studied	28	36	35

SOURCE: G. Warren Nutter, *op. cit.*, Table I.

is that both are "correct"—the one for a 42-year period and the other for a
selected period within the total. But which is relevant when we come to
consider Russia's future prospects? If one anticipates two devastating
wars and a revolution in the next 42 years of Russia's history, the rate of
Soviet development over the longer period is certainly the one to use.
But if one anticipates a continuance of the peacetime conditions which
prevailed during the selected period, then the rate attained during that
period would appear to be more relevant.

Prospects for the future

But even with continuing peace, is it probable that the Soviet
Union will be able to maintain the high rate of development that it has
achieved in selected past periods? Obviously no final answer is possible;
in fact, the answer depends in part upon the factors responsible for the
rapidity of Russian development which are discussed in the chapter
which follows. But certain aspects of the matter can usefully be considered at this point in connection with the character of Russian accomplishments.

Let us start by stressing, first, that the 6 per cent rate of increase in
Russian income is *not* the rate of increase in the priority or favored areas
of the economy; rather it is the rate of increase for the economy as a
whole, *taking the good with the bad*. Second, the Soviet Union did *not*
concentrate on the "easy" areas of the economy and develop them first;
instead Russia concentrated on heavy industry, which is certainly one of
the more difficult areas to expand. The fact that certain areas—such as
agriculture—are behind, in itself proves nothing; to demonstrate that
Russian development must slow down, it is necessary to demonstrate
that, when Russia turns to agriculture, it will be *harder* to develop than
was heavy industry. This is a point to which we will shortly return.
Finally, there is little to be said for the argument that countries always develop most rapidly at the start of their development. Table 3-2 makes

clear that this simply has not been true for the United States. It has been true for individual American industries and it may have been true for the British economy as a whole. But there is no convincing evidence of any slowing down in the over-all growth rate of the American economy —and therefore no basis for assuming that the rate of growth of the Soviet economy will necessarily or automatically slow down.

A second broad consideration to be borne in mind is that rapid growth has certain aspects which make it likely to be self-perpetuating. Suppose we assume that American real income increases at no more than 3 per cent annually starting in 1950; it will then have doubled by 1975. If such growth is accompanied by a continuance of the same distribution between consumption and other uses of income that has prevailed recently, we would achieve the results summarized in Table 12-7. Suppose during the same period that Russian income continued to grow at a 6

TABLE 12-7. ASSUMED RUSSIAN AND AMERICAN DEVELOPMENT

	1950	*1975*
United States	100	200
Consumption	66⅔	133⅓
Other	33⅓	66⅔
Soviet Union	33⅓	133⅓
Consumption	16⅔	33⅓
Other	16⅔	100

per cent rate from a level one third that of the United States. Under such circumstances, despite the fact that Russian income would have doubled twice for a fourfold increase by 1975, it would still be only two thirds of the American level—and even less if American income was to increase at the 4 per cent rate achieved between 1950 and 1955 rather than at the assumed 3 per cent rate. But if we assume that Russian consumption is currently 50 per cent of total production—Table 12-5 suggests that direct consumption, at least, is even less—then consumption in the Soviet Union can double over the next 25 years *and still permit a sixfold expansion in other production!* In other words, it is not enough to show that relatively more research and relatively more capital formation will be required in the future to maintain Russia's rate of growth of income; for Russia will be in a position, if the growth rate is maintained, to devote far more effort to both these items and still provide for an increase in consumption that is rapid by any past standards.

This analysis, the importance of which can hardly be exaggerated, raises two questions: first, will the Soviet leadership be under pressure to permit consumption to more than double during the next 25 years; second, will the more rapid expansion of production other than consumption be sufficient to maintain the 6 per cent rate of increase in total income on which the entire analysis depends? Let us consider each of these questions in turn.

The probable expansion of consumption

The best available evidence is that Soviet real wages in urban areas have only recently approached the level that prevailed in 1928.[7] Because perhaps twice as many people are receiving urban wages as received them in 1928, average real earnings for the country as a whole have risen (as urban earnings are higher than those in agriculture); in addition, as a by-product of the war, the number at work in each family has increased, so that urban *family* income has also increased. But the point to be stressed is that there appears to be no significant urban opposition to the Communist regime despite the slow rate at which real wages have risen. It is hard to believe that the Russian people will not be satisfied with a doubling of their living level over the next 25 years—a rise that may well be as large as that realized in the United States and in all probability rather larger than is likely to be achieved in Great Britain.

Does the fact that Khrushchev has boasted that Russia intends to "overtake and surpass the most highly developed capitalist countries in per capita production" make a more rapid expansion of Russian consumption likely? Not necessarily. For the Khrushchev boast is always confined to selected items—particularly "meat, butter, and milk." These are selections whose consumption increases less rapidly than income, so that American consumption of these items in 1975 might well be equalled within Russia even if Russian consumption as a whole had no more than doubled by that date.

Finally it is not necessary to argue that under *no* circumstances will consumption more than double. All we need stress is that when income is increasing very rapidly, so long as consumption increases significantly less rapidly, increasing relative amounts can be devoted to such crucial items as research and capital formation. Actually much depends on an item not previously mentioned—military expenditure. If such expenditure were to decline relatively, a more than doubling of consumption and a more than sixfold expansion of nonmilitary other production would *both* be possible; in fact, in strict logic both would be possible so long as the military share of total production remains constant. Over-all, it seems fair to conclude that the share of total production devoted to consumption may, without raising serious problems for the Soviet leadership, de-

[7] Janet G. Chapman, *Review of Economics and Statistics,* May, 1954.

cline in the future as it has in the past, so that the portion of total productive effort that can be devoted to other production may well rise significantly.

The role of borrowed technology in Russian development

The mere fact that the Soviet Union is likely to be in a position to devote relatively larger amounts to research and capital formation by no means guarantees that the past rate of development will be maintained in the future. Let us examine some of the arguments that have been put forward suggesting that a retardation in the rate of Soviet growth is likely. One such argument is that Russia will in the future no longer be able to borrow technology developed by the West. As wartime experience made clear, however, borrowing is not always easy. Not only are screw threads and gauges likely to be different but conditions of manufacture and use are likely to vary sufficiently to make substantial redesigning necessary. For example, the modern complicated American automobile engine designed to be manufactured to close tolerances and to burn high-octane gasoline has almost no relevance to Russian needs, which are for a low-compression engine that is simple in manufacture and reliable in operation.

There is no doubt that the Soviet regime has been quite willing to borrow Western technology when it seemed desirable to do so. But it is the impression of students of Russia that the borrowing has reflected not so much inability to develop their own technology when urgently needed, as an inability to develop separate technology in all areas at the same time. In priority areas, such as atomic energy, military equipment, and rocketry, Soviet technology is clearly not only their own but first-rate. True German scientists were of some help in the latter case; but it is doubtful whether they did not on balance help America more than Russia. In fact, the contrast between Russia and the "West" is misleading. For the rate of American development itself reflects substantial borrowing from the rest of the "West."

In short, particularly during the period from 1928 to the war, when Russia was extremely short of technicians, borrowing from the West permitted those that were available to concentrate on priority areas and to this extent undoubtedly speeded up the growth of Russian income. But the acute shortage of technicians that marked the thirties has been substantially eliminated by the subsequent massive Soviet investment in education and research (described more fully in the chapter which follows). The problem, therefore, becomes an essentially economic one: how much more will it cost the Soviet Union to develop its own technology in the future (borrowing, say, no more than we borrow from other nations) compared with what it cost to adapt borrowed technology in the past? Undoubtedly it will cost more. In the light of both the relatively small cost of research in general and the relatively small amount of technology that Russia borrowed, however, the increasing cost involved is one which Russia, in my judgment, will have no difficulty in meeting. Hence I do not believe that the rate of growth of Russian income will on this account be slowed down—though the Soviet Union will undoubtedly have to devote more resources to research as technology which was previously borrowed is in the future developed independently.

Possible increases in capital requirements

Because capital formation is so much more costly than research and development, the possibility that capital requirements may increase in the future in relation to output is considerably more serious. The difficulty is that we know very little about the behavior of capital-output ratios, and much of what we do know applies to periods when rates of capital formation were relatively low. When rates are low, capital formation can be a serious problem. As was pointed out in Chapter 8 in discussing the role of saving, in the United States the value of capital is today roughly three times the national income. When 5 per cent of the national income is devoted to net capital formation (which is of course the same thing as net saving or net investment), the ratio of capital stock to net capital formation is 60, and when 10 per cent is saved, the ratio is 30. But when net capital formation reaches 25 per cent—the rate currently prevailing in the Soviet Union—the ratio falls to 12, and at a 40 per cent rate—admittedly unlikely but not inconceivable in the Soviet Union by 1975—the ratio falls to a mere 7½. In short, where the capital stock is large to start with or the rate of saving high, the entire importance of capital formation is far less than in an underdeveloped country starting from scratch. In fact, there is a certain "benefit of backwardness" involved. When capital formation is rapid—nine tenths of Russian industry is estimated to have been built since 1928— the average age of capital equipment is lower and the average quality of the capital stock higher than when accumulation has proceeded at a slower pace. This is a factor from which Russia has benefited in the past and will continue to benefit in the future if the pace of development is maintained.

Moreover, there is no general reason to believe that capital requirements may increase more rapidly than output in the future. In the United States, output has been increasing *faster* than capital requirements, especially since about 1910, so that the capital-output ratio has been *falling.* In fact, in 1950 output per unit of capital was a third *higher* than it had been in 1875.[8] One argument suggesting why the opposite is likely to occur in Russia is that "social overhead capital" has been neglected there. In capitalist countries part of the problem of "social overhead capital" is statistical. When we discussed the measurement of output in Chapter 1, we noted that no way has been discovered to measure the contribution to current production of government capital; hence increased spending for schools and roads absorbs capital without bringing about any measurable increase in current output. And it may also be true that the contribution of investment undertaken primarily to improve the quality rather than the quantity of output is not adequately reflected in our national income estimates.

In the Soviet case we really have two problems: is investment going to become increasingly necessary in areas whose contribution to current production cannot be measured or can only be measured inadequately; and is investment going to become increasingly necessary in areas with a high capital-output ratio? Obviously Russia is going to have to invest increasing sums on roads and other forms of "social overhead capital." But during the periods in which the 6 per cent rate of increase in income was realized, starting when Russian income was very much lower than it is today, very large investment was made in education—one of the most costly of all types of "social overhead capital." As a result a high level of literacy has been achieved. It is, therefore, by no means obvious that future investment in "social overhead capital" will have to increase *on a relative basis*—though perhaps some relative expansion may turn out to be necessary.

The problem of Soviet agriculture

Is it likely that Soviet investment in areas with a high capital-output ratio will be increasingly necessary in the future? One area often mentioned in this connection is agriculture. There is no doubt that Russia is going to have to invest increasing sums in agriculture, partly to provide a better diet but also because expansion of the labor force for the next decade or so will depend mainly on releases from agriculture, as the number entering the labor force as a result of population increase is severely limited for the immediate future by the low levels to which birth rates fell during World War II. The backwardness of Russian agriculture is hard to believe. With somewhat less fertile land but rather more under cultivation than in the United States, perhaps half of the Russian labor force succeeds in growing little more than half as much

[8] Moses Abramovitz, "Resource and Output Trends in the United States Since 1870," *Occasional Paper 52,* National Bureau of Economic Research (New York, 1956).

food as is grown by the 10 per cent of the American labor force that remains in agriculture. How are we to interpret this sad state of affairs?
Russia is currently feeding her population—even if rather badly by our
standards. To feed them better would certainly have absorbed scarce resources that have been utilized to speed industrialization and increase
Russia's military power. Are we, therefore, to say that Russian agriculture
is a clear example of the failure of planning to provide the Soviet people
with a desirable diet or a tribute to the success of Soviet planning in
carrying out the objectives of the Soviet leadership?

It seems to me that, given the objectives of the Soviet leadership,
the second alternative is closer to the mark. Only if the Soviet regime
had tried to expand agricultural output in the past and failed—so that
massive investment in the future would be needed to bring about an expansion of output—would Russian agriculture be likely to present a serious future problem. But Soviet agriculture, broadly, has provided enough
food so that food shortages have not interfered with the expansion of
industrial output and released about as many workers as the industrialized area could effectively cope with. Under these circumstances there
has been little reason for any serious effort to be made to increase agricultural production and productivity. In fact, the very backwardness of
Russian agriculture should make expansion relatively easy, now that improvement has become desirable to provide incentives for industrial
workers and to expand the industrial labor supply.

Moreover, what would appear to be most urgently needed is
additional agricultural research; that we have by no means exhausted possible agricultural improvements is shown by the fact that American agricultural productivity since World War II has been increasing more rapidly than ever before—even more rapidly than productivity in industry.
But public expenditures for agricultural research in the United States
since the war have been running at perhaps one thirtieth of 1 per cent of
national income! Clearly research alone will not solve the situation; large
amounts of capital will have to be invested in Russian agriculture as well.
But it is by no means certain that the capital-output ratio in agriculture
will turn out to be higher than it has been in the area of heavy industry on
which Russia thus far has concentrated—and even less certain that
agriculture will present a problem in view of the rapidly expanding productive effort that the Soviet leadership will have at its disposal to devote to research and investment. And, to the extent that rapid increases
in agricultural production and productivity are achieved, the resulting
release of labor will go far to offset any labor shortage that may develop
in industry.

Housing and capital requirements

The one area where substantial investment involving a high capital-output ratio will clearly be required is in housing—where the ratio is perhaps 10 to 1 as compared with 3 to 1 in the economy as a whole. Russia's rapid urbanization has brought about an appalling housing shortage. Space per person fell from 6 square meters in 1928 to just over 4 in 1937 and less than 4 in 1950. This means that each urban Russian has for his own use less than 50 square feet of space, which is perhaps one tenth the American level—about enough to hold two large beds! But, in a somewhat different sense than before, this is another example of the "benefit of backwardness." So low is the level from which Russia starts that a relatively small investment in housing—perhaps one third the American amount—can nonetheless bring significant reductions in the housing shortage. In fact, housing production in 1957, though small by American standards, appears to have been large enough to increase average urban space available by perhaps 10 per cent even after allowing for population growth. Hence, though housing will clearly absorb increasing amounts of investment, it is by no means certain the sums involved will put a serious strain on the economy in view of the increasing amounts that will be available.

Conclusions

It should be stressed again that this entire discussion of the prospects for Russian development is highly speculative. Also it should in fairness be stressed that the opinion of most Russian experts is rather more pessimistic than the discussion just concluded; most believe that Russia will not in the future be able to maintain the rate of growth recently achieved. But in the past Russian experts have shown a notable bias in the direction of pessimism. To the question "Will the rate of Russian development slow down in the future" perhaps the fairest over-all answer is the famous Scotch verdict: "Not proven."

CHAPTER THIRTEEN

FACTORS EXPLAINING
RUSSIAN DEVELOPMENT

Introduction

Perhaps the most important thing to be stressed about Russian economic development is that the factors responsible for it are substantially the same as those that are responsible for development anywhere else: encouragement of basic and applied research to provide new and improved technology; introduction of the better technology by rapid innovation; provision of additional capital through high saving and investment; discovery and utilization of the country's natural resources; and, in general, the fostering of a climate which favors economic development. When we consider each of these factors in the discussion which follows, we will find that there are obvious differences between the Soviet Union and the United States: the process of innovation is, for example, organized rather differently under capitalism than under Communism. But over-all, we will find that the similarities far outweigh the differences.

Research in the Soviet Union

If the Russians have any single "secret weapon" explaining their rapid economic development, it is the emphasis that they have placed on research and technology. As we have seen, this was to a considerable extent forced on the Communists by Russia's loss of technicians during the civil war. Their response was a massive investment in education to replace those who had been lost. Up to World War II the Soviet Union's rapidly expanding technological needs could only be met in priority areas; it was during this period that Russia borrowed—and greatly benefited from borrowing—Western technology. But after 1945 the situation changed drastically as the Soviet regime felt itself in a position to expand significantly its scientific activities. It is the situation that has prevailed since 1945 on which we shall concentrate.

How has it been possible to develop science rapidly—especially under a dictatorship? First, Russia has had a long tradition of scientific achievement, especially on the theoretical side. But of six outstanding Russian scientists recently listed by *Fortune,* the oldest was twenty-one at the time of the Communist revolution and four were thirteen or younger. While some of today's scientists received a part of their training in the West, the present status of Russian science represents, to an important extent, a return on the educational investment of the twenties and thirties. Second, no area of Russian society has enjoyed greater freedom than the physical scientists—so much so that the greater relative freedom has been a factor in inducing able students to choose science and especially basic science. True Stalin's espousal of Lysenko's mistaken ideas set back Soviet genetics a generation; but nothing comparable occurred in other areas and Communist doctrine now urges Russian scientists to make use of Western scientific discoveries even though the discoverers suffer from an "erroneous philosophical outlook."

Communist support of scientific research

Soviet support of science has been lavish—in terms of the educational system, facilities for research, and the living level of scientists. Let us consider each of these. Emphasis on science starts at the secondary school level. While average and inferior students are apparently increasingly being trained on a vocational basis to take their place in industry, brighter students are admitted to "ten-year schools," where they devote 40 per cent of their time to mathematics and science, with four years of chemistry, five of physics, and mathematics through trigonometry compulsory. The schools operate on a six-day week, ten months in the year. Thereafter, each student is paid by the government while he continues his studies, with those in technical schools receiving half as much and those in graduate schools as much as the average industrial worker. It is obvious that able students in the Soviet Union are not lost to science because they lack resources to finance their education.

Numerous examples could be given of the lavishness of the facilities for scientific research that have been provided; one will suffice. Russia today has the world's largest atom smasher—almost twice the size of the largest machine operating in the United States. Plans have been developed for larger American units, but Congress has been loath to provide funds as the cost is in the order of $100 millions and further improvements in design may be possible. Russia did not wait for design improvements; instead she built her smasher with 36,000 tons of iron in its magnets when very much less would now suffice. The result, however, is that the Russians have in actual operation a machine characterized by a group of American scientists as capable of discoveries that "could at any time create a furor similar to that caused by the launching of the satellites."[1]

Even more impressive than physical facilities, which are hard to sum up on any over-all basis, is the unique Institute of Scientific Information. Founded only in 1953, the Institute systematically abstracts—and circulates throughout the Soviet Union—the articles contained in 8,000 professional journals, including 1,400 from the United States, 800 from Great Britain—and 3 from Madagascar! In contrast, of the 1,200 Russian scientific journals received by the Library of Congress, only 30 are regularly translated into English. This explains why a group of American laboratories recently spent five years and $200,000 to solve a research problem—only to find that the results had long since been published in Russia! One can understand the British biologist who declared: "In general biology [the Institute is] publishing 100,000 abstracts a year. No other agency in the world is doing this job. I wish to God I could read Russian."[2]

In addition to the unusual degree of political freedom, an important factor in recruiting scientists is the paucity of alternative opportunities. Little Soviet talent is wasted on distribution—advertising, salesmanship, marketing—and less in settling legal matters. Even practicing physicians, most of whom are women, are not highly regarded and rank only slightly above factory foremen. Yet salaries paid Soviet scientists are large even by American standards and by Soviet standards are immense. An outstanding scientist may earn from twenty to fifty times as much as a factory worker. "Soviet scientists, almost alone among Russians, may equip their homes with refrigerators, TV sets and record players. They may maintain weekend cottages in the country and spend their vacations on the Black Sea Riviera. They are, except the topmost political and industrial brass, the most favored class in the Soviet Union. 'Class distinctions are greater than anything I had ever imagined,' reported a

[1] *Life* (December 16, 1957), p. 110.
[2] *Fortune* (February, 1957), p. 119.

British chemist [in 1956]. 'Scientists and professors always seem to have a host of servants, maids and chauffeurs.' "[3] As we shall also see in connection with innovation, a regime with the theoretical objective of "From each according to his abilities, to each according to his needs" is today, in all probability, readier than any other economy to provide material rewards to those who help in fulfilling its objectives.

The state of Soviet science

What sort of science has been achieved by all this effort? Dr. Lee DuBridge, president of the California Institute of Technology, has made the following over-all appraisal: "The Russians were in the position after World War II that we were in in the 1920's. They woke up, and they've been going like mad. Whenever that happens, you'll find that progress is greater in some directions than in others. . . . It's not like a race between two horses but more like a race between two fleets of 100 yachts. Some of their yachts are ahead and some are 'way back. But their whole fleet is moving faster, and all their yachts could pull ahead." [4]

Perhaps in some ways even more remarkable than the over-all achievement is the emphasis on basic research. A recent report of the National Science Foundation, while noting that by American standards Russia is still technologically underdeveloped, stresses that the balance between basic research and applied research is more favorable in the Soviet Union.[5] "In the purely theoretical fields, Soviet scientists are as good as any in the world, and in fact a pronounced emphasis on theory dominates all of Soviet science." [6] For a country starting from behind and very much interested in immediate practical results, this is a remarkably foresighted distribution of effort.

In short, the Soviet leadership—to a degree that appears greater than in the case of any other country—seems convinced that nothing is more important for economic development in the long run than a high and effective level of scientific research. Having come to this conclusion, the Soviet regime has created an institutional framework which is "exceedingly well contrived to assure, first, that the largest fraction of the most able people goes into science and engineering as professional fields and, second, that the energies of those able people are directed toward the attainment of those production goals Mr. Khrushchev and his col-

---

[3] *Life* (December 16, 1957), p. 118.

[4] *Life* (December 16, 1957), p. 109.

[5] *Basic Research: A National Resource* (Washington: Government Printing Office, 1957), p. 45.

[6] *Fortune* (February, 1957), p. 117.

leagues consider most vital."[7] And, one may add, that conditions have
been created such that scientific research is "being pursued with an
urgency . . . reminiscent of a wartime operation" and has as its objective nothing less than "to overtake American science in its great diversity,
its high quality, and its magnificent sweep." [8]

It is the basic emphasis of this entire volume that nothing is more
important in explaining economic development than effective programs
of basic and applied research. It follows that no aspect of the Soviet
Union represents more of a challenge to free enterprise in general and
the United States in particular than the program of scientific development that the Soviet regime has been able to create.

Innovation under Communism

In any dynamic economy such as the Soviet Union the distinction
made by the economist between the entrepreneur—who combines land,
labor, and capital using *existing* techniques of production—and the innovator—who introduces *new* techniques—loses much of its meaning.
With nine tenths of Russian industry developed since 1928 and technological improvements heavily emphasized it is obvious that Russian
management has actually been devoting a major part of its energies to
innovation. We can tell, therefore, much about innovation by examining
how business is managed in the Soviet Union.

First, under the Soviet regime the powers of management have
been steadily strengthened and those of labor unions steadily weakened.
It is not too great an exaggeration to say that the basic function of a
Russian union today is to get more work out of its workers. While some
of the powers of management—such as the right to refuse permission for
a worker to transfer to another job—were of wartime origin, similar to
Britain's "labor direction," and have recently been reduced in scope, the
prerogatives of Russian management remain in many regards sufficient
to make envious an American capitalist of even the old school. Second,
as in the case of the living level of scientists, the Soviet Union, since the
First Five-Year Plan, has shown increasing willingness to provide large
material rewards for superior industrial performance. This has been true
at all levels: the famous Stakhanovich, who became the symbol of efforts
to increase productivity, was a coal miner richly rewarded for innovations in mining technique. But it has been most systematically true for
managers, who receive large bonuses every time they overfulfill the
quotas set by the Plan.

---

[7] Harry Schwartz, *New York Times Book Review* (December 22, 1957), p. 1.
[8] Robert E. Marshal, *Bulletin of the Atomic Scientists* (February, 1958), p. 83.

Why is a manager important in a planned economy? Does he have to do anything except execute routine objectives given him by the Plan? It is true that a manager under capitalism, who starts out limited only by a quantity of money, has a wider range of choice than his Soviet counterpart, who will have his raw materials, his labor supply, and even the additions to his capital equipment fixed by the Plan. But the lack of worker organizations may well mean that a Soviet manager has even greater latitude in the way in which he utilizes the labor and materials given him so as to maximize output; and it is larger output in relation to input that is involved in increases in productivity. Moreover, to the extent that the Plan is faulty, it is the manager who must improvise. Actually he has considerable room for maneuver, being able to barter surplus supplies for those which are short and to use the "manager's fund"—technically allocated to improvements in the living conditions of the plant's workers but often capable of being diverted to other purposes—to facilitate such exchanges. In fact, successful managers consistently maintain reserves—both of money and materials—for emergencies, and there have developed a group of "expediters" who live well by arranging "deals." Most of this sort of thing is illegal and often wasteful; but is tolerated so long as managers are enabled thereby to achieve increased production.

This is not the place to attempt an appraisal of the effectiveness of planning. There is considerable evidence that Russian plants do for themselves many things—like producing screws with slow-speed machinery—which could be better done by others—in this case, specialized screw manufacturers using high-speed equipment. But this desire to be independent of others, in part at least, grows out of the Soviet effort to operate its plant capacity at a pace rarely achieved under capitalism except in wartime. In fact, the sort of barter deals just discussed are not too different from those which take place in a capitalist economy under the impact of wartime shortages. One also gets the impression that the number of those inspecting and checking up on the operation of the Plan is unnecessarily large. Certainly both the establishment of production objectives under planning and checking on their achievement is complicated; there is no doubt that judging results by profits is a remarkably effective way of gauging productive efficiency.

But the point with which we are concerned is not the relative productive efficiency of the two alternatives in "economizing" resources in a "static" sense; rather we are concerned with the extent to which they are likely to lead to a "dynamic" expansion of productivity over time. What the Soviet authorities have done is to recognize the importance of management, strengthen its powers, and reward it liberally when it achieves results—without too much concern over the means used. Moreover, the results that have been sought have been overwhelmingly the rapidest possible expansion of output. The essence of the conventional case for capitalism is that existing quantities of the productive factors, utilizing existing techniques of production, will be most effectively used under a profit system. But in Russia not only is the capital supply rapidly changing—a point to which we shall return in the following section—but technology is also in a state of flux.

In such circumstances the pressure on a Soviet manager to innovate —to try new ways of doing things—may possibly be greater than on his capitalist opposite number. Under capitalism, unless a firm is large enough to risk experimentation, "proof" that a new technique is unlikely to "pay off" is an adequate defense for not innovating. If the "proof" is valid, it should of course also rule out the use of the new technique under communism; for "unprofitability" merely means that there is some other way of achieving the same result with a smaller use of scarce resources. But, viewed dynamically, the whole process of developing new techniques is not a matter which lends itself to precise calculations. A certain "irrationality" which prefers output to profits may well "pay off" over a somewhat longer period of time by making profitable techniques which appear at the start to be unjustified. But the relative speed of innovation under capitalism and communism is a speculative matter likely to depend on particular circumstances. What does appear certain is that Russia has succeeded in creating a system which stresses and encourages rapid innovation.

Capital formation in the Soviet Union

In the preceding chapter we pointed out that net capital formation (the same thing as net saving and net investment) has not only been increasing but at 25 per cent of income is at one of the highest levels ever recorded for any economy in peacetime. Whether this represents "exploitation" of the present generation for the benefit of future generations need not concern us. What needs to be stressed is that Russia's rapid capital formation is clearly an important factor helping to explain the rapidity of Russian development.

The high rate of net capital formation in the Soviet Union has had a number of effects. Compared with most underdeveloped countries capital has of course become relatively plentiful. The comparison with a developed country such as the United States is more complicated because of the extent to which increases in productivity can be achieved in our case without net capital formation by the embodiment of advanced technology in capital replaced through reinvestment of depreciation allowances. But to keep the average age of capital as low as the age achieved by net capital formation at the Russian rate would require extremely rapid rates of depreciation; it is likely, therefore, that Russian capital equipment is, on the average, younger than in any other country.

Also significant is the extent to which net capital formation at the Russian rate changes the whole character of capital use. In the preceding chapter we saw that, if a capital stock worth three times national income is taken as typical of a developed country, countries saving 5 per cent of their national income would have a ratio of capital stock to net capital formation of 60 to 1 in contrast to a present Russian rate of perhaps 12 to 1. In the former case the emphasis on economizing capital that has appeared in most discussions of investment criteria for underdeveloped countries undoubtedly makes sense. But in the Russian situation capital availability is going to change radically, unprecedentedly, and to an unknown extent during the lifetime of capital goods that are currently being produced. Under such circumstances the whole process of deciding how capital can best be used becomes at once more complicated and less important than in the case where continued extreme capital scarcity is likely to continue.

Natural resources and Russian development

Starting in the early twenties, the Soviet Union embarked on a systematic and thorough exploration of its available natural resources as a result of a government policy to map out all reserves of any metal that could conceivably have some use. One by-product of this effort was the discovery of uranium in Siberia in 1931—long before any thought of its usefulness as a nuclear fuel had arisen. A second by-product has been the development of excellent prospecting methods and a large corps of men competent in the earth sciences. In fact, Russian knowledge of the polar regions is unexcelled.

In general, the Soviet Union is well supplied with natural resources, though their availability in the case of minerals and fertility in the case of agricultural land is on the average less than in the United States. Only a few items are scarce, and these can in most cases be obtained from satellite countries. Thus even in the absence of trade between the Soviet and Western blocs, Soviet economic development would not be held back to any important extent by shortages of natural resources.

The general climate and Russian development

Early in the thirties the famous British cartoonist Low captioned a drawing of what he considered a typical factory scene: "Peasant girl, just off the farm, absent-mindedly trying to milk a steam hammer." Hugh

Cooper, the American engineer responsible for the Dnieperstroy dam, when asked to comment on an even larger hydroelectric development, simply returned the plans with the note: "The elevator in my apartment house does not work." The whole idea of a nation recently defeated in war, 80 per cent peasant, without any tradition of mechanical ingenuity, attempting rapid industrialization appeared humorous in the extreme. Little more than a decade later Low's peasant girl could have been turning out some of the best tanks the world has ever seen and 25 years later she could have worked on the rocket that put Sputnik in orbit. Perhaps her "take-home pay" from development has thus far been small, but she is convinced, as few are in any other nation, that rapid development is possible.

Further, to an extent probably approached only in the United States, she is convinced that development is not a matter of rubles and kopeks —or of profits—but an end in itself. Partly this is a matter of defense. The local "Palace of Culture and Rest" during the thirties had an illuminated map with arrows which lit up at Archangel and Vladivostok in response to the question as to where the Allies had invaded Russia; and the memory of Hitler remains fresh. But partly it grows out of a spirit of competition. For while capitalist competition is considered rotten and bourgeois, "socialist" competition against the production norm—or against another factory—is taken to be wholly desirable.

Now a new competition is offered: "to overtake and surpass the most highly developed capitalist countries in per capita output." The appeal is wide. To the scientist, there is the challenge of "overtaking American science in its great diversity, its high quality, and its magnificent sweep." To the man in the street, there is the prospect of equalling —even surpassing—the American consumption of "meat, butter, and milk." Undoubtedly this will not be as easy as Khrushchev makes it sound. But the climate that has been created in the Soviet Union will certainly help to promote the development effort that Russia makes.

PART FOUR

UNDERDEVELOPED AREAS

CHAPTER FOURTEEN

THE ROLE OF POPULATION

The Malthusian analysis

Toward the end of the eighteenth century Thomas R. Malthus, an Anglican cleric, got into an argument with his father regarding the usefulness of reform. From the argument, in order to show that reform was futile, came Malthus' famous *Essay on the Principles of Population,* which contended that population tended to increase approximately at a geometric ratio while food production increased at no more than a roughly arithmetic ratio. As a result population could be expected to increase faster than production until living standards fell to the subsistence level, at which point the "positive checks" of war, famine, and disease could be counted upon to bring to an end the excessive increase in population. Hence living levels could exceed the subsistence level for no more than brief periods, and any attempt to improve man's lot was clearly a waste of time. Since Malthus wrote, the population of the United States has increased from perhaps 4 to 175 millions and our level of living has risen immensely; to a lesser degree the same thing has happened in the whole of Europe. Thus it would certainly seem as if history has proved Malthus spectacularly wrong for western Europe and the United States.

How could he have been so wrong? From the start he recognized the possibility of "preventive checks," which include infanticide, abortion, birth control, postponed marriage, and continence within marriage. As a good Anglican cleric he understandably did not place much stress on abortion and infanticide—and birth control as we now know it did not then exist. Thus Malthus' conclusion that the positive checks would inevitably operate stemmed from his scepticism regarding the possibilities of postponed marriage and continence within marriage—which he called "moral restraint." Taken by itself, his pessimism regarding "moral restraint" seems justified by experience. There is little evidence that continence has been a significant factor in holding down birth rates, while systematic postponement of marriage seems to have been of broad historical significance only in the case of Ireland. The Irish tradition of postponement grew out of the Potato Famine that started in 1845, which was so drastic that the population was cut almost in half in a decade. It is doubtful, therefore, if the Irish solution can be applied generally. Hence Malthus' pessimism made considerable sense for the world he knew. If the preventive checks were likely to be either ineffective or unacceptable, it appeared inevitable that population would continue to increase until living levels had been forced down to the subsistence level, when a further expansion would be prevented by the operation of the positive checks of war, famine, and disease.

What has changed since he wrote? First, birth rates have declined drastically. The *extent* of the decline can be properly attributed, I believe, to the increasing availability of modern birth control. This statement should not be misunderstood. Mere availability of birth control will not reduce birth rates if people do not want small families, while the desire for small families may reduce birth rates, by increasing abortion and moral restraint, even if birth control is not available. But it seems quite unlikely that the decline would have been as drastic as it has been in the absence of modern birth control. And the decline has been drastic. Had the rate of increase of population realized in the United States from 1800 to the Civil War been maintained to the present time, our population would be three times larger than it now is—or more than 500 millions. So effective has population limitation become that there has been doubt whether some nations would maintain their numbers. In the case of Great Britain, the latest estimate, which takes into account the increase in birth rates since World War II, is that the population will increase little more than 2 millions before at least becoming stationary and perhaps starting to decline. Malthus' first error, therefore, was his failure to foresee modern birth control.

In addition, Malthus buttressed his pessimism by arguing that production could increase approximately at an arithmetic ratio while population would increase roughly geometrically. For this he has been roundly criticized on the ground that production can and has increased faster. This is certainly correct if the arithmetic ratio is taken literally. Such merit as the ratio has is in emphasizing the "diminishing returns" that result when increasing quantities of labor are applied to a given quantity of capital and natural resources with an unchanged technology. In company with the other economists of his day, Malthus underestimated the extent to which technology could be improved and capital increased. And he also made the mistake of worrying about "diminishing returns" at a time when the opening of the almost empty areas of the Americas, South Africa, Australia, and Siberia made available, to those people whose living levels have been rising since he wrote, an increase in natural resources on a scale that can never again be duplicated. The result of all three—improved technology, additional capital, and expanded natural resources—has been a vast increase in production which has made possible a drastic and unprecedented decline in death rates. Had it not been for the accompanying—but usually delayed—decline in birth rates, the increase in population would have been even larger than it was.

In short, Malthus made three errors: he failed to foresee the development of modern birth control, the improvement of technology and the increase in capital that have taken place, and the vast and unique expansion of the natural resources available to the Western World that has also occurred since he wrote. As a result, his predictions have been spectacularly wrong. But let us not lose perspective: rising living levels are the exception rather than the rule. Over most of the world even today—and even more certainly over the whole period since Malthus' time —population is, and has been, so large that periodic famines and dietary-deficiency diseases remain of significant importance in the death rate. As a result, much of the human race remains at, or close to, the subsistence level.

The possible increase in population

So much for the past; as a prophet Malthus could hardly have been worse in respect to the Western World. But what of the future? The first thing we need to understand is that appreciable population growth is *physically* impossible for any considerable period of time. All living species have the ability to multiply at a rate more rapid than the environment can eventually support. In the case of the more elementary forms of life, the potential increase is immense. The amoeba, for example, is capable of dividing—which means doubling—every hour. As a result, if the environment were to continue favorable, a single amoeba could produce *in less than a week* progeny which weighed more than the world. In a couple of decades, if they all survived, the progeny would fill the known universe and be propagating at the rate of one known universe an hour!

Compared to the amoeba, humans reproduce quite sluggishly. It is, however, well within our capacity to double every 25 years. Apart from immigration, this is the rate at which our own population increased from 1800 to 1860. Even at half this rate, which is the rate of increase that has prevailed in the United States since the end of World War II, the geometric progression of population growth rises remarkably rapidly, as the following table shows. In short, if the rate of growth we achieved

TABLE 14-1. POSSIBLE WORLD POPULATION [a]
(In Billions)

Year	50-year doubling	Year	25-year doubling
2350	1,526	2150	1,526
2550	59,605	2250	59,605
2750	2,328,306	2350	2,328,306

[a] The 1950 world population has been taken as 2.5 billion.

during the first 60 years of the nineteenth century were to prevail for the world as a whole, in 400 years the human race would number 2 quadrillions. Even if only our present rate of increase were to continue, the same number would be reached in 800 years.

What would this involve in terms of human density? Including deserts and Antarctica, the total land area of the world is estimated at between 36 and 37 billion acres, which works out at around 1 quadrillion, 600 trillion square feet. At present there is for each living person an average of about 15 acres—or perhaps 650,000 square feet. Even at the slower rate of increase the land available per person would be reduced to about 1,000 square feet by the year 2350, to almost 25 square feet by 2550, and to less than 1 square foot by 2750. At the faster rate reduction to 1,000 square feet would take place by 2150, to 25 square feet by 2250, and to less than 1 square foot by 2350. Carrying the projection to its logical conclusion, all the matter of the world would have to be transformed into human beings before 3000 if the faster rate of increase were maintained and before 4000 at the slower rate. Clearly a geometric progression is an impressive thing! Under the circumstances it seems only fair to concede to Mr. Malthus that an appreciable rate of population growth cannot be maintained indefinitely—or even for periods that, after all, are relatively short when measured against the span of human history.

The immediacy of the problem

The virtue of carrying our geometric progression to its logical conclusion is that it demonstrates that nothing science can do, even in an atomic age, to increase the productivity of our resources—short perhaps of exporting people to other planets, which by present accounts do not appear particularly hospitable—will eliminate the necessity for a cessation of population growth. But the vice of carrying the progression to its logical conclusion is that it gives the impression that the whole matter will only become important in some dim distant future. Most of us do not easily think in terms of quadrillions—or even a thousand years. But the practical problem is much more immediate. To illustrate: we have just seen that land area per person over the world as a whole works out at about 650,000 square feet. The average for the United States is over 500,-000 square feet, for India 100,000 square feet, and for Japan 50,000 square feet. Only about 15 per cent of Japan can be cultivated, so that food produced domestically, which meets only about 75 per cent of Japanese dietary needs, is raised on 7,500 square feet of land per person—a plot less than 90 feet square—by what is probably the most intensive agriculture prevailing anywhere. Let us assume, rather optimistically, that science by various means (some of which are considered in Chapter 16) will be able to make the whole world 100 per cent more productive than the present arable area of Japan, so that every 5,000 square feet of land—every plot 70 feet square—the world over (Greenland, Antarctica, and the Sahara desert included) will, on the average, be able to support a person. Maintenance of a 1.5 per cent annual rate of population increase—which is approximately that presently prevailing for the world as a whole as well as for the United States—would reduce the square feet available per person to 5,000 well before 2250—or in less than 300 years. World population would then number over 300 billions, and world-wide population density would be seven times the present density of England and one quarter the present density of New York City!

There is of course nothing definitive in the figure of 5,000 square feet per person. If we wish to live in cells like hens in a hen bank and be fed protein gruel piped in from culture tanks on the roof, it is quite possible that far more than 300 billion human beings will be able to survive, so that the present rate of increase can continue for considerably more than 300 years. But if there are to be steaks in the future of the human race, the time during which population can continue to increase at its present rate appears relatively short. And if we raise our sights still higher and think in terms of providing the whole world a few centuries hence with something approaching the present American standard of living, it may well be that the world already has altogether too many people.

The inevitability of preventive checks

In other words, the length of time during which population can continue to increase depends predominantly on the sort of world we want when growth ceases—a conclusion we will explore more fully in the discussion which follows. But even if we are content to end up at a subsistence level, appreciable population growth must cease within a few centuries. This is not a matter of choice but a physical necessity. Further, if we want growth to stop with a level of living above the subsistence level, preventive checks will have to bring about an even more rapid cessation of growth. Though this last statement appears controversial, it is actually almost a tautology—true by definition. For famine and widespread disease are clearly inconsistent with a level of living above the subsistence level. True there is the theoretical possibility that high birth rates could be just offset by an appropriate level of warfare so as to maintain living levels above subsistence without resort to preventive checks; the possibility, however, does not seem of much practical importance in a world where warfare has become atomic. But if all positive checks—famine, disease, and war—are ruled out, then the cessation of population growth can only be brought about by the operation of the preventive checks.

Among the preventive checks there appears little to be said for infanticide, and neither a general increase in continence within marriage nor a general rise in the age of marriage seem likely to make a major contribution. For the influence of rising educational standards and increasing urbanization on the average age of marriage has been more than offset, at least thus far in the case of the United States, by the greater speed with which high earnings are attained in an era when it is no longer necessary to learn elaborate craft skills. Thus, while later marriage may be of some help in particular cases, especially where the age of marriage is now quite low, the basic choice among preventive checks would appear to be between abortion and birth control. Particularly in countries with well-developed medical facilities, abortion may, for a time at least, play an important role. In Japan, where population pressure is perhaps more intense than in any other country, probably over 50 per cent of pregnancies are currently being terminated by abortion. In fact, if all pregnancies currently terminated by abortion instead resulted in births, the Japanese birth rate would show only a small decline from its postwar peak; hence it seems clear that birth control has been of little importance in the sharp decline of birth rates that has in fact taken place. Though the latter is more difficult to introduce and requires more foresight, it seems likely that, in the long run, main reliance will come to be placed on birth control. Even Russia, which has traditionally relied on abortion, has in the last year or so shown increasing interest in making birth control generally available. Recently discovered techniques appear capable of being used under the conditions which prevail in underdeveloped countries, and have been estimated to be capable of halting population growth for an annual cost—excluding the cost of introducing the techniques—of as little as a half of 1 per cent of the national income of a country like India.[1]

Some faiths, notably Roman Catholicism, object to the use of mechanical birth control devices and prefer a modified form of continence in which intercourse is confined to the "safe" period during which pregnancy is impossible. But all religions appear to accept the need for relating the number of children to social and economic circumstances, and their acceptance of this need will undoubtedly become more complete as population increases. Religions seem, therefore, to be mainly concerned with the methods to be employed in limiting population growth and, in general, do not oppose population limitation as such, provided that the method utilized is acceptable. It may well be that new contraceptive methods will be developed in the relatively near future which will both be highly effective and be sanctioned by all religious faiths.

Finally, it is important to stress that, while preventive checks are inevitable if living levels are to remain above the subsistence level, there is *no automatic process by which growth is halted.* What has been called the "theory of demographic transition" seemed to imply otherwise. The suggestion was that, starting from an equilibrium marked by high birth and death rates, the effect of development was first to reduce death rates and then, after a lag during which population grew rapidly, birth rates also, as birth control became available and urbanization made small families desirable. However well this description may have fitted the Western World up to World War II, when birth rates had fallen to low levels under the world-wide impact of the Great Depression, it no longer applies to areas like the United States, Canada, Australia, or New Zealand. For these countries have *higher* rates of population increase than the world as a whole—and higher rates than applied to the "area of Western settlement" during most of the period of Western development. Yet these four countries are *among the top five in per capita incomes in the entire world.* It seems quite clear, therefore, that development, even to the highest living levels the world has ever seen, gives no guarantee whatsoever that it will bring with it any cessation of population growth.

[1] Details are presented in the *Review of Economics and Statistics* (February, 1958), pp. 78-79.

Population size and resource use

What we have done thus far is to demonstrate by taking a long-term point of view—perhaps a disconcertingly long-term point of view—that cessation of population growth is inevitable. Our primary reason is that we must ultimately run out of resources—or, even more basically, matter. This conclusion, therefore, is in sharp contrast to the conclusion of Chapter 9 that thus far natural resources have not been either very costly in individual countries or very important in explaining differences in Western living levels. But the emphasis of Chapter 9 was on the present situation, which reflects the fact that very little of the world thus far has been industrialized. If we look to the future—and particularly if we contemplate world-wide economic development—the picture that emerges is quite different. The matter is worth examining in some detail.

Resources are of two types: those which are continually renewed by nature, as in the case of water power, and those which get used up as they are utilized, as in the case of coal and oil. Let us concentrate on resources which get used up. Suppose, to illustrate the matter, we analyze the implications of raising the level of living of the world to two thirds of the American level by the year 2100; let us assume that this would involve world-wide resource consumption at two thirds the present rate in this country. As total world population is today perhaps fifteen times ours, it follows that world-wide resource consumption under the circumstances would be ten times the present American rate if no increase in population took place in the meantime. On the other hand, if world population over the period continues to increase at the present 1.5 per cent rate, then by 2100 world resource use would be 80 times our present rate. What this would mean in relation to presently known supplies of some of our leading wasting resources is summarized in Table 14-2.

In view of our experience with past predictions of exhaustion of our petroleum reserves, comparisons of this sort are suspect; but clearly the supplies of these materials are in fact limited. Although subject to a wide margin of error, the maximum figures presented may well be on the high side. The estimate for coal assumes that all coal found in seams more than a foot thick down to 4,000 feet and in seams more than two feet thick between 4,000 and 6,000 feet will be utilized, and in the case of oil the estimate assumes that fourteen times as much petroleum will be produced in the future as has so far been recovered, that natural gas will provide an additional amount equivalent to 40 per cent of the liquid petroleum total, and that petroleum extracted from shale will provide as much again as liquid petroleum.

If these estimates are broadly correct, they indicate that raising living levels for the world as a whole to something approximating those now prevailing in the Western World will throw a severe strain on available resources. Even without population increase and without making any allowance for use during the period required to raise living levels, our estimates indicate that a rise to the level suggested would leave coal alone with a supply likely to last more than 100 years. But if meanwhile population increased eightfold, as it will if the present rate of increase continues, then nothing except coal would be likely to last much more than a decade.

TABLE 14-2.   RESOURCE USE WITH VARIOUS POPULATIONS

| Material | Use | | | Reserves | | Years Available | | | |
	Present U.S. use	Tenfold increase	Eighty-fold increase	Mini-mum esti-mate	Maxi-mum esti-mate	Tenfold increase Min.	Max.	Eightyfold increase Min.	Max.
Coal (billion tons)	.5	5	40	730	7300	146	1460	18¼	182½
Petroleum products ᵃ (billion barrels)	3	30	240	260	2400	8⅔	80	1½₂	10
Steel (billion tons)	.1	1	8	100	——	100	——	12½	——
Copper (million tons)	1	10	80	100	——	10	——	1¼	——

ᵃ Includes petroleum equivalent of natural gas.

SOURCE: Estimates from Harrison Brown, *The Challenge of Man's Future* (New York: Viking, 1954), Chaps. V and VI.

The most obvious implication of these comparisons is least important. For they do not mean that the world is ever likely to run out of energy or metal. There was a time in the nineteenth century when people worried as to whether the reduction in the numbers of sperm whales meant that no one in the twentieth century would be able to read at night! It is already quite clear that it will be possible for us to replace the fossil fuels with either atomic or solar energy, while steel and copper can also be replaced, probably by aluminum and magnesium. The problem of meeting *specific shortages* of natural resources can certainly be solved.

What then are the significant implications? Let us first repeat the conclusions of Chapter 9: thus far shortages of natural resources have not raised, and in the immediate future are not likely to raise, problems of any importance; but this is because only a small part of the world uses resources at rates even distantly approaching American usage. At the other extreme we may repeat the conclusion of the earlier part of this chapter: ultimately it is resources—or, if you will, matter—which limit both population growth and living levels. What we have just been dealing with is the intermediate situation. In it, even if (as has just been suggested) specific shortages of fuels such as coal and metals such as steel *can* be handled, the shift to other energy sources or other metals will not be *easy*. Much of our present stock of capital goods has been developed to exploit fossil fuels, and steel remains our outstandingly important metal. The loss of inherited capital involved in the shift to alternative metals and energy sources in any event will retard significantly the increase in income that would otherwise have been possible—and *the retardation will be greater, the greater the interim increase in population.*

Though rather less important, a second conclusion is perhaps worth mentioning. Atomic energy, the most immediately available substitute for fossil fuels, did not—and almost certainly could not have—become available as the result of the operation of free enterprise. For the sums expended on atomic research were well beyond the capacity of any private company. It may well be that the major changes in energy sources and materials that world-wide economic development entails will require a substantial increase in government "interference" with free enterprise to promote the development of substitute techniques and materials. Certainly the magnitude of the job involved in world-wide economic development, which these comparisons have suggested, is little understood— which is perhaps inevitable, as we have as yet no more than scratched the surface.

CHAPTER FIFTEEN

POPULATION AND LIVING LEVELS

Introduction

This chapter is concerned with the relationship between population and living levels. The first question to be considered is whether there is an "optimum" population size which will maximize real income per person. Once it is recognized that population must in any event be limited by preventive checks to maintain living levels above subsistence, the possibility of limiting numbers so as to achieve the largest possible real income per person obviously arises. We shall find, however, that no very precise definition of "optimum" can be provided.

The problem of optimum population is relatively remote. The second half of the chapter deals with the more immediate problem of the relationship between the growth of population and the growth of real income. First, we will want to examine the effect of population growth on the growth of real income—both total and per person—but we will also want to examine the effect of growth of real income on the growth of population, as it is obvious that causation works in both directions. Recall that "real income" summarizes the goods and services produced valued at constant prices and is, therefore, a measure of total production. To simplify, we shall use "income" in this sense in the discussion which follows.

Diminishing returns and optimum population

To what extent does the principle of diminishing returns, which was outlined in Chapter 9, aid us in determining optimum population? Suppose we take labor—which we can consider as equivalent to population (disregarding changes in the percentage of the population in the labor force)—as the variable factor. The principle suggests that there is a point at which output per unit of the variable factor is at a maximum and a second point at which total output is at a maximum—beyond which any additional labor does more harm than good. Is not the first of these the point at which income per person would be at the highest possible level and the second the point beyond which additional population would make no contribution whatsoever to production? The answer is "yes"— but, as we saw in connection with the discussion of Malthus in the preceding chapter, only for *a given quantity of resources and capital and a given technology.* Even if there is something to be said for treating resources—or ultimately matter—as fixed, obviously the same does not apply to capital and technology.

There is, moreover, a further difficulty. Because the principle was first formulated in connection with land, it was easy to suggest that output would never take place under *increasing returns*—where *a given increase in labor leads to a more than proportional increase in output.* Under such circumstances labor is being applied to "too much" land and output would be higher if the available labor was used with less and less land until the optimum combination was reached. Unfortunately this reasoning does not apply to the economy as a whole; outside agriculture output frequently has to be undertaken *before* the optimum combination can be achieved. Farmers can leave idle any excess quantity of land; but in the case of a railroad between any two points one cannot leave idle those sections which give rise to little traffic and still have a railroad between the points involved! This means that railroads—and much of industry—may well be producing under conditions of increasing returns. The same thing would happen in agriculture if excess land could not be left idle; if one man was compelled to spread his labor evenly over, say, 10,000 acres, he would be able to achieve very little indeed, so that up to the point of optimum output additional labor applied to the 10,000 acres would lead to a more than proportional increase in output. Thus, for any economy taken as a whole, we are likely to find at any time some areas where diminishing returns have already set in, some which are producing at the optimum level, and some which are operating in the range of increasing returns.

Can any over-all balance be struck for the entire economy which would offset the areas of increasing returns against those with diminishing returns and so give some indication of where the over-all optimum might lie? The only answer is that we certainly do not as yet have sufficient information to strike such a balance with any precision. Moreover, if we are interested in the population that is *ultimately* optimum, it is a balance which would have to be struck, not in terms of existing capital supply and technology, but in terms of the capital supply and technology that might exist at some ultimate future time. Finally, optimum population is obviously not a matter that is going to be settled entirely in economic terms.

Because the problem is difficult and not entirely economic, there has been a tendency in economics to state the difficulties and let the matter drop. This is unfortunate. Ultimately—as the previous chapter demonstrated—it is obvious that there is a point beyond which additional numbers must reduce living levels despite increases in capital or improvements in technology. The decision as to whether the future holds protein gruel piped in from a culture tank on the roof, an occasional steak, or an approximation of the largest possible income per person is a decision which the human race is going to make—either consciously or by default. It would seem undesirable to have it made by default simply because precise information on optimum population was lacking. We shall feel free, therefore, to venture some guesses on the subject in the discussion which follows.

Population growth and living levels

Let us turn from the ultimate relationship of population and living levels to the immediate problem of the effect of population growth on the growth of income. At first sight it might seem that, short of the point of maximum total output as given by the principle of diminishing returns, any increase in population, by adding to the labor supply, would add *something* to production and income. But this is not true even in the short run if the possibility of increases in capital and improvements in technology are not ruled out (as they are in connection with the principle of diminishing returns). The reason is that additional population, besides offering additional labor, requires additional maintenance, which may be at the expense of capital formation and technological improvements. In an economy such as India, which is at a low level of living but is interested in the general welfare of its people, slower population growth may well *speed up* the increase in even *total* income (and not merely income per person)—though it is possible that in a developed economy subject to business cycles, slower population growth may possibly intensify such cycles and so *retard* the rise in income.

A careful study of prospects for India, which we will shortly exam-

ine in detail, suggests that in the Indian case a rapid rate of population
growth is in fact likely to slow down the growth of total income. But let
us start with the more general—and, at least for India, more favorable—
assumption that the increase in total income will not be affected by population growth. To the extent that this assumption is correct it follows
directly that the rise in living levels depends on the extent to which total
income increases faster than population. Suppose we assume that the
average annual income per person in an underdeveloped country is $50—
as it was in 1952-1954 in the case of Burma.[1] The following table indicates
the income per person that will prevail in the year 2000 in such a country if the increase in total income exceeds the increase in population by

TABLE 15-1. INCOME IN 2000 GIVEN VARIOUS EXCESSES OF INCOME INCREASES OVER
POPULATION INCREASES STARTING WITH A 1950 INCOME OF $50 PER PERSON

Percentage excess	0	½	1	1½	2	2½	3	3½	4	4½	5
Resulting income	$50	64	82	105	135	172	219	279	355	452	574

varying amounts. This table means that, if the growth of income exceeds
the growth of population by 1 per cent, income in 2000 will be $82 per
person, while if income growth exceeds population growth by 2 per cent,
income in 2000 will be $135. The effect of various possible combinations
on income in 2000 are set forth in Table 15-2.

TABLE 15-2. INCOME IN 2000 UNDER VARIOUS CONDITIONS STARTING WITH A 1950
INCOME OF $50 PER PERSON

Annual percentage increase in population	Annual Percentage Increase in Income				
	2	3	3½	4	5
0	$135	$219	$279	$355	$574
1	82	135	172	219	355
1½	64	105	135	172	279
2	50	82	105	135	219
3	31	50	64	82	135

The actual increases in total income that may be possible will be
considered in the chapter which follows, but for preliminary purposes
we may note that since the Civil War the annual increase in total Ameri-

[1] The qualifications discussed in Chapter 1 regarding the direct comparability of such
an estimate should be recalled.

can income has averaged about 3.5 per cent. If this rate were to be realized in a country such as Burma over the next 50 years, Table 15-2 shows that income per person would rise to perhaps $280 if there were no population increase during the period, to perhaps $135 if the present rate of world population increase were to prevail, and to only $64—or by $14—if population were to increase at a 3 per cent rate. Note again that these results depend directly on our conclusion that increases in total income and population can be treated as independent. If this is correct, it follows inevitably that rapid population growth involves a proportionate reduction in the rate at which income per person will rise.

The case of India

Can we go beyond this assumed independence of the growth of income and population? In the case of India it appears from a careful study by Coale and Hoover that rapid population growth will retard the growth of total income.[2] One reason is that, over the next 30 years on which the study concentrates, rapid population growth would add relatively little to the labor force (most of even the 1986 labor force having already been born).[3] On the other hand, rapid growth greatly increases the sums required for education, housing, and general welfare—at the expense of investment designed to expand production and income. It is worth stressing that the estimates that follow are *not* a prediction regarding India's future development; rather they are designed to show the effect of differences in the rate of growth of population on an *assumed* pattern of growth of income—which is exactly what we are interested in. Three estimates of fertility (which for our purposes can be taken as equivalent to birth rates) are used: "high fertility" assumes a continuance of present fertility; "medium fertility" unchanged fertility until 1966, and a 50 per cent decline between then and 1981; and "low fertility" a 50 per cent decline by 1981 starting at once. Finally, a sharp decline in death rates as a result of development is assumed—a point to which we shall shortly return.

The first set of figures in Table 15-3 deals with *total income*, while the last two sets deal with income per "consumer" (which can be taken for our purposes as approximating income per person). The first set of estimates suggests that not only will total income increase more rapidly as fertility declines, but that no significant rise in the rate of increase

[2] Ansley J. Coale and Edgar M. Hoover, *Population Growth and Economic Development in Low-Income Countries: A Case Study of India's Prospects* (Princeton: Princeton University Press, 1958).

[3] The authors are convinced that extending the analysis over a longer period would not significantly alter their over-all conclusions.

in income is likely until fertility declines. The second set of estimates gives an indication of the impact on living levels that is involved. The difference between high and low fertility is the difference between a 38 per cent and a 95 per cent increase in average living levels in the next 30 years. Finally, note that under the impact of high fertility the rate at which the average living level improves slows down over the period— from 1.4 per cent to a mere 0.9 per cent—while under low fertility the rate of improvement more than doubles—from 1.5 to 3.4 per cent. The case for an immediate decline in fertility in a country such as India is hard to deny.

TABLE 15-3. INDIAN INCOME GROWTH WITH DIFFERENT RATES OF POPULATION GROWTH

	1961	1966	1971	1976	1981	1986
Total Income	(Annual percentage increase)					
High fertility	3.3	3.3	3.4	3.4	3.5	3.5
Medium fertility	3.3	3.3	3.4	3.5	3.7	4.0
Low fertility	3.3	3.5	3.7	3.9	4.2	4.5
Income per consumer	(Indices, 1956 = 100)					
High fertility	107	114	120	126	132	138
Medium fertility	107	114	121	131	148	170
Low fertility	108	117	128	143	165	195
Income per consumer	(Annual percentage increase)					
High fertility	1.4	1.2	1.0	1.0	0.9	0.9
Medium fertility	1.4	1.2	1.2	1.6	2.1	2.8
Low fertility	1.5	1.6	1.8	2.3	2.9	3.4

SOURCE: Coale and Hoover, *op. cit.*, Tables 37 and 38.

Death rates and development

We have just considered the impact of population growth on the rate of development; now let us consider the impact of development on population growth, starting first with death rates and then covering birth rates in the section which follows. In any year the difference between the actual birth rate and the actual death rate gives the rate of population growth. In the United States, for example, our birth rate is roughly 25 per thousand and our death rate roughly 10 per thousand; the difference between them gives the rate at which our population is increasing—15 per thousand or 1.5 per cent. At the present time death rates in different countries vary from less than 8 to 25 or 30 per thousand—or even more. Where the rate is below perhaps 14 per thousand it is the result of rapid population increase in the immediate past and could not be maintained if population became stable. This is so because the people who were seventy in 1950 were born in 1880, when our population totaled 50 millions. The

number who are seventy today, therefore, is far smaller than the number
who would reach seventy if our population were to remain stable at 175
millions. This means that the number of people in the age groups where
death rates are highest is today small compared with what it would be
if population were stationary. More specifically, while our actual death
rate today is around 9.5 per thousand, which implies an expectancy of
over one hundred years, in fact our actual life expectancy is only about
seventy years. Thus very low death rates reflect not only the degree of
development of a country but also the speed with which its population
has been increasing. The Japanese rate at 7.7 per thousand, for example,
is significantly lower than our own—not because their life expectancy
is higher but because their rate of population growth has been more
rapid. Hence all developed countries can look forward to *rising* death
rates as the rate of increase in population slows down in the future.

Exactly the opposite prospect is faced by underdeveloped countries.
For both the high death rates and the frequently low observed rate of
population increase in such countries—despite high birth rates—reflect
the continuing operation of the positive checks. Specifically, this means
that people—at least until very recently—have starved to death in countries such as China and India whenever there was a crop failure, and they
are undoubtedly still dying from diseases which would be prevented by a
more adequate diet. But, in addition, many underdeveloped countries
suffer from diseases not resulting from dietary deficiencies which can be
eliminated at extremely low cost by modern public health measures. For
example, in the case of Ceylon an antimalaria campaign using DDT
costing 15 cents per person was able to reduce the death rate in districts
infected with malaria by more than 11 per thousand, which contributed
heavily to an over-all decline in the death rate from 20 in 1946 to less
than 11 in 1954. Because the cost is so small relative to the results
achieved, public health measures of this sort are among the very first
things undertaken by any development program. In the Indian case it is
estimated that over half the population live in districts infected with malaria. If the antimalaria program, which is already under way and is expected to be completed by 1961, is as effective as it was in Ceylon, it
would by itself reduce the over-all Indian death rate by more than 5 per
thousand.

Moreover, rising production resulting from development also means
that there will be a reduction in the importance of dietary deficiency
diseases. Even in the case of Ceylon, which has a substantially higher
level of living than either India or China, a quarter to a half of hospital
admissions are for malnutrition, and the effect of higher incomes on
children's chances of living results in the rich having appreciably more
surviving children than the poor, despite the fact that the number born

to the rich is significantly lower.[4] In the case of India the study by Coale and Hoover estimates that the death rate, which has already declined from over 30 per thousand in 1951 to perhaps 25 at the present time, will be as low as 21 by 1966 and 15 by about 1975. In short, if development is effective, it cannot help being accompanied by sharp declines in prevailing death rates in underdeveloped areas.

Birth rates and development

What effect is development likely to have on birth rates? There seems to be a wide-spread feeling that the *mere effort* to raise living levels will automatically and immediately reduce birth rates. But if there is a connection between living levels and birth rates, it would appear to be with living levels which have *actually risen*. Countries such as China and India, for example, have experienced substantial development, in the sense of increases in production, in the past. China's population is believed to have increased fourfold since 1700—which if correct would be appreciably faster than the population of France and not so very much slower than that of the United Kingdom—while India's is believed to have increased from 150 millions to more than 350 millions since 1800. Both improvements in technology and utilization of previously uncultivated land made these expansions possible. But the vast increases in output involved led neither to a significant improvement in average living levels nor a significant reduction in birth rates: all that has happened is that vastly more people live on the verge of starvation.

It is of course true that, in general, countries with high living levels have lower birth rates than underdeveloped areas. In the absence of any restraints birth rates ranging between 40 and 50 per thousand are quite possible. This is the range within which the Indian rate is believed to have fluctuated since 1880; students believe that the rate remains above 40, though the reported rate (which suffers from serious underreporting) is considerably lower. An unrestrained rate of 40 per thousand is, therefore, by no means extreme. In contrast, developed countries rarely have rates higher than 25 to 30 per thousand. But countries with wide differences in living levels may have similar birth rates, suggesting that major increases in living levels may occur without birth rates being affected. In Puerto Rico, for example, the birth rate has until very recently been substantially higher than the reported Indian rate and may even have been higher than the actual Indian rate (corrected for underreporting). But the Puerto Rican level of living is much higher than the Indian—ten times as high on the basis of a comparison of average incomes. Higher

---

[4] Theodore Morgan, *Economic Journal*, December, 1953.

living levels may facilitate the introduction of birth control techniques or may increase the extent of abortion and, conceivably, continence. But, unless birth control devices actually become available as a part of the higher living levels, it is by no means certain the birth rates will be significantly reduced. In fact, it could well be that, until birth control devices become available, the effect of development will be to *raise* birth rates by improving maternal health and increasing the frequency of intercourse.

Population growth and development

In estimating the probable rate of population growth in countries subject to development, it follows that we cannot project current rates of increase, as these are heavily influenced by the positive checks which successful development will eliminate. What rate of population growth is likely if development eliminates the positive checks but does not make birth control available? A rate of 3 per cent—or a difference of 30 per thousand in birth and death rates—would be probable in such circumstances. There are, in fact, exceptional cases where even higher rates of increase have been realized. Mexico, for example, has a higher rate, and the Hutterites, a religious sect living in the Dakotas, Montana, and Canada, have a birth rate of about 46, a death rate of less than 5, and a rate of increase of over 4 per cent—which involves doubling in 16 years and may be the most rapid rate of expansion in the world! But a 3 per cent rate has prevailed in many different countries and at many different times. To cite some widely different examples, population increased at a 3 per cent rate in the United States from 1800 to 1860, in Puerto Rico after its recent rapid economic development, and among the Arabs of Algeria and Palestine (before the establishment of Israel), when development was expedited by a rapid inflow of French and Jewish capital. It is increasing almost that rapidly in Ceylon, where the rate of increase has more than doubled since 1946 to 2.9 per cent. And the Coale-Hoover study estimates that a rate of 2.6 per cent will be realized in India if fertility remains unchanged—lower than 3 per cent only because it is believed that development will not succeed in lowering the death rate below 15 per thousand.

In short, to expect a rate lower than 3 per cent is almost certainly to anticipate either that the development program will not fully succeed, leaving positive checks in operation, or that birth control or abortion will be available to a significant extent. In the case of Japan, which is sometimes cited as a country which succeeded in raising its living level without restricting population growth, it is worth recalling that the death rate during most of the period of her modernization was 20 per thousand or higher and that abortion and infanticide (not fully reflected in the death rate) appear to have persisted, so that Japanese population increase was, in fact, restricted to a rate substantially below that which is possible under modern conditions.

Wastefulness of high birth and death rates

One final point regarding population and living levels is worth making. High birth rates, even when balanced by high death rates so that population is not increasing, are an extremely inefficient way of maintaining a population. For high birth and death rates involve substantial waste through investment in children who do not live to become productive. In the case of India only a little more than half of the children born in any year live to be fifteen. It has been estimated that 3 per cent of the Indian national income is devoted to maintaining those who die before reaching the age of 15, contrasted with 0.1 per cent in the case of England.[5] If the production which thus is allocated to unproductive investment, over and above that allocated in England, could instead be added to productive investment, the rate of Indian capital formation would be increased by close to 50 per cent. To this extent it is not low saving but wasted investment in children that is responsible for India's shortage of capital!

Some conclusions

Although the assumption is probably unduly favorable for countries such as India (where rapid population growth will probably retard the growth of total income), the discussion just concluded suggests that, to the extent that the increase in total income can be assumed to be independent of the increase in population, improvement in average living levels will depend entirely on the extent to which total income increases more rapidly than population. But we have also just seen that the growth of population is likely to speed up, as development brings a sharp decline in death rates, to as much as 3 per cent annually unless birth rates decline. Let us next discuss, before considering the over-all prospects for underdeveloped areas, the increases in production and total income that may be possible.

[5] W. Lee Hansen, *Journal of Political Economy* (June, 1957), p. 260.

CHAPTER SIXTEEN

PRODUCTION IN
UNDERDEVELOPED AREAS

Possible increases in food production

The basic requirement in underdeveloped areas is food. One way of obtaining more food is to grow more within the given country; another is to industrialize and obtain food in exchange for industrial products. For underdeveloped areas as a whole, the latter possibility appears to be of quite limited importance. True, countries such as Belgium, Holland, and Great Britain attained both high population densities and high living levels by becoming specialized manufacturing areas and depending on the rest of the world for food. Japan has been, and may continue to be, a manufacturing center for Asia in a somewhat similar fashion. But imported food depends on food surpluses elsewhere; hence specializing in mining or manufacturing, although it may aid a few countries, does not offer a general solution for underdeveloped areas unless the production of food can be greatly increased in such areas taken as a whole.

What are the prospects for increasing food production? The answer depends in part on what we mean by food. It is, for example, possible that use of land to produce algae known as *Chlorella* will prove to be the most efficient way of converting solar energy and the carbon dioxide of the air into edible material. The technique involves spreading plastic coverings over flat land areas to form shallow pools of water to which appropriate mineral nutrients are added. The resulting crop can then be harvested continuously and mechanically by extracting the *Chlorella* with filters and replacing the nutrients as they are consumed. Harrison Brown has estimated that if three times the cultivated area of the United States could be devoted to algae culture, world food production might be increased roughly twentyfold.[1]

Intriguing as this sort of calculation may be, it is important to remember that not only has the technique still to be demonstrated but also that it is of a sort difficult to apply in underdeveloped areas. For the level of agricultural yields in such areas is already higher than one might think. As the following table shows, yields *per acre* in Asia are as high as in Oceania (predominantly Australia and New Zealand) and 80 per cent as high as in North and Central America. But Asian yields *per person* in agriculture are only 8 or 9 per cent of the American and Oceanian levels. Specifically, in the United States 8 million farmers cultivate 360 million acres, an average of 45 acres apiece, while in India 75 millions work 320 million acres, or rather less than one tenth as much per person. Thus techniques now in use in developed countries generally do not grow appreciably more per acre but rather grow roughly the same amount with vastly less labor. Although algae culture would theoretically permit much more to be obtained from a given land area, it would require little labor and great amounts of capital. As a result it seems much better adapted to the needs of developed countries, where labor is relatively scarce and capital relatively plentiful, than to underdeveloped countries, where the situation is reversed.

TABLE 16-1.   AGRICULTURAL YIELDS IN 1947-1948 [a]

(In Metric Tons)

	Yield per hectare	Yield per person in agriculture
World Average	1.30	0.42
North and Central America	1.50	2.57
South America	1.39	0.48
Europe	1.34	0.88
Oceania	1.20	2.38
Asia	1.20	0.22
Africa	0.73	0.12

[a] Excluding the Union of Soviet Socialist Republics.

SOURCE: Food and Agriculture Organization of the United Nations, *Monthly Bulletin of Food and Agricultural Statistics* (Vol. 2, No. 9, September, 1949); quoted from A. R. Oxenfeldt, *Economics for the Citizen* (New York: Rinehart, 1953), p. 86.

[1] Harrison Brown, *The Challenge of Man's Future* (New York: Viking, 1954), Chap. IV.

Apart from algae, Brown's estimates of possible increases in world-wide food production are considerably less striking. He estimates that supplementary irrigation of 40 to 50 per cent of the land presently under cultivation might double its yield, that an increase equivalent to present production might also be brought about through extension of the area under cultivation (largely in the tropics), and that foreseeable improvements in agricultural techniques, including improved plant breeding and selection, might bring about a further doubling in all areas, or a sixfold increase from all sources. Such a program would obviously require large capital expenditures: Brown estimates that merely doubling food production would require an investment of $100 billions. For perspective keep in mind that, at a 1.5 per cent annual rate of increase, population will expand sixfold in 125 years.

The possible increase in Indian food production

Suppose we turn from the general problem to the specific possibilities for increasing food production in a typical underdeveloped country such as India. There is no doubt whatsoever that much more can be raised than is now being grown, as Indian yields for rice and wheat are only about one third those achieved in Japan. There is, of course, no area of the world which is so intensively cultivated as Japan, with only 7,500 square feet per person under cultivation compared with 40,000 square feet, or more than five times as much, in India. Further, although only 15 per cent of Japan is cultivated in comparison to 40 per cent of India, extension of the cultivated area will probably be easier in India than in Japan—though relatively little reliance is being placed on extensions of cultivation in Indian development planning. If the area under cultivation could be increased and the level of Japanese yields attained, India would appear to be able to support a vast increase in population.

Several qualifications are in order. Only about 75 per cent of Japanese dietary needs are supplied by domestic production, so that, even at Japanese yields, 10,000 square feet would be needed to support a person solely by domestic production. Nor is India in a position to draw upon the fisheries which have been important for Japan. Further, almost half of the cultivated Japanese land is irrigated, making use of the runoff from the nonarable 85 per cent of the total land area. While considerable expansion of irrigation in India is certainly possible to something ultimately approaching the Japanese percentage, the more land that is cultivated the less water from uncultivated lands will there be for irrigation. Finally, it is by no means certain that India will be able to achieve Japanese yields on the much larger area under cultivation in India—but neither is it impossible. In short, a 50 per cent expansion in the area under cultivation and a tripling of yields would appear to be about the maximum increase likely on any presently foreseeable basis. This would mean that food production would be four and a half times larger. Such an expansion is certainly conceivable *in time* even without resort to algae culture, but equally it will not be easy to achieve.

The probable increase in Indian production

Thus far we have been discussing what is possible. What is probable—as to both food and total production? In the case of agriculture, India starts from such a low level that impressive immediate progress seems likely, particularly if rainfall is plentiful. But although Japan underwent one of the fastest rates of development in history, Japanese food production, even optimistically estimated, increased less than 300 per cent between 1850 and 1950, which works out at a little better than 2 per cent a year allowing for compounding. In fact, a more detailed study of the period from 1885 to 1915, when Japanese growth was highly impressive, concludes that the increase averaged 1.9 per cent per year for agricultural output and 1.3 per cent per year for agricultural output per acre.[2] True the Second Indian Five-Year Plan projects rates between 3 and 4 per cent for the period from 1956 to 1961. But, on the other hand, R. A. Gopalaswami, the Indian Census Commissioner, estimated in 1953 that the best that could be hoped for over-all would be a one third increase in Indian food production in the next 15 years, and that an increase of this magnitude—2.2 per cent a year—would require a stepped up development program beyond anything then planned.

Over-all, it seems fair to conclude that the achievement of a 3 per cent annual rate of expansion of agricultural output for a sufficient number of years to cancel out variations in rainfall would be a substantial accomplishment. This is the rate that Coale and Hoover, after an extended examination of Indian agricultural prospects, believe is likely to prevail over the 25 years from 1956 to 1981. It is a rate which will certainly be exceeded in years of plentiful rainfall, but it is rather unlikely to be exceeded for any extended period.

Agriculture and production as a whole

In almost all developed countries the importance of agriculture has steadily declined. Predominantly this reflects the fact that as people become increasingly well off, they spend a declining percentage of their income on food. There have been cases in underdeveloped countries

[2] B. F. Johnson, *Journal of Political Economy,* December, 1951.

where agriculture increased in importance; it is believed, for example, that the rural population of India *rose* from 50 to 70 per cent of the total between 1850 and the present time. The increase was apparently caused by a relatively rapid improvement of productivity in the non-agricultural area, as factories replaced village industries, combined with an increase in population that was as rapid as the increase in *total* output. In such circumstances, if food is to remain constant as a percentage of total production—which is what one would expect in the absence of any increase in average living levels—then *more* effort must be devoted to agriculture to offset the *slower* rate of increase in the productivity of agriculture. The essence of the matter is that during the last century the increase in total Indian production only achieved an increase in numbers—thereby requiring food to remain a constant percentage of total production—rather than a rise in living levels—which would have led to a decline in the relative importance of food. As is to be expected, most development plans, which assume that living levels are going to be raised, provide for a more rapid expansion of total than of agricultural output.

Is there any reason to believe that total output is likely to be easier to increase than agricultural output? We can establish a basis for answering this question by seeing how the broad factors responsible for the development of developed countries under free enterprise and under Communism apply in the case of underdeveloped areas. That such factors continue to be of vital importance seems basically correct. The student should note, however, that underdeveloped areas have many unique problems, and that a substantial literature dealing, often in considerable detail, with such problems has become available. The system of land ownership, for example, often makes it legally difficult, if not impossible, to consolidate into a single economic unit the numerous small parcels that one farmer may own. In general, these specific problems of underdeveloped areas tend to make development even more difficult than would appear from the discussion which follows, so that the estimates to be presented are probably, if anything, somewhat on the optimistic side. But even if our conclusions are unlikely to be seriously affected, it remains important to keep in mind that the discussion in no sense represents a full consideration of all the manifold problems that are faced by underdeveloped areas.

Technology and underdeveloped areas

A major advantage of underdeveloped areas is said to be that they can draw upon the technology of developed areas. In the main this is true. But, as already noted in connection with the Soviet Union, even among developed areas there are limits to technological exchange; differences in the system of measurement alone may necessitate substantial redesign if the borrowing country is to use available standardized parts and tools. Thus screw threads vary significantly from country to country, and an engine designed in inches cannot easily be manufactured by a machine tool calibrated in centimeters. Even more important, most research in developed areas is undertaken to save labor—a goal frequently achieved by using much additional capital. But in underdeveloped areas labor is plentiful and capital scarce. The implications of this state of affairs are much debated. There is one group who believe that, just because they are available, the latest machines should be utilized even if they require large capital investment. There is no doubt that there is much to be said for this point of view if rapid development is sought or likely to be achieved: for it permits the underdeveloped country to "benefit from backwardness" in acquiring industry which is up to date. The fact that Japanese equipment was consistently more modern than British machinery greatly intensified the difficulties faced by Britain's textile industry and helped explain how Japan was able to develop into a position where it could undertake to exchange textiles for food on a large scale. Certainly, where capital availability has reached the Russian level, only the latest technology makes sense.

But there are those who feel that, where capital shortage remains as acute as it is in most underdeveloped countries, available knowledge should be used to design equipment requiring less capital investment and meeting, in general, the special needs of underdeveloped areas. This is, however, by no means always easy. An underdeveloped country, with abundant coal but lacking the capacity to export goods in exchange for oil, needs for its railroads a simplified steam locomotive. But no company in the United States produces steam locomotives, and it is doubtful if very much research has been done on such locomotives anywhere in the Western World in recent years. This at least is a product used in the West. When it comes to a solar stove, which would permit India to utilize as fertilizer the cattle dung now serving as fuel, it is quite obvious that the West has no developed technology whatsoever to contribute.

It is by no means impossible that a country such as India will attempt the worst of both alternatives. There is immense pressure on a newly independent country to develop, for reasons of national prestige, a certain number of industries which require large capital investment—such as steel and petroleum refining. Yet, faced with an acute shortage of capital and the immediate need to expand employment opportunities for those underemployed in rural areas, India is also placing emphasis on the redevelopment of village industries. If such industries can compete with factory production, the case for them may be good; but in India they are to be encouraged by taxing competing factory products—which presumably means that village industries will be more costly than factory production and to this extent will lead to a lower total production than would otherwise be possible. The issue, moreover, is complicated by a noneconomic preference for village industries. Their previous decline was blamed on the British, so that fostering them—as Gandhi did when he wore homespun cloth—represented a form of resistance to British rule.

Several conclusions emerge. First, applying the technology of developed countries to underdeveloped areas will not be as easy as it might first appear. Second, determination of the appropriate technology in any particular case is also not going to be easy. And, finally, there is an urgent need for effort—both within and without underdeveloped areas—to be devoted to the creation of technology appropriate to such areas.

Capital shortage and economic development

Because it is closely related to technology, let us consider the role of capital formation next. There is perhaps more general agreement regarding the need for additional saving and capital formation to expand production in underdeveloped areas than in regard to anything else. But the very fact that the income of such areas is low means that the needed increases are difficult to achieve. This is another classic case of "For whosoever hath, to him shall be given . . . ; but whosoever hath not, from him shall be taken away. . . ." In underdeveloped countries saving rarely amounts to more than 4 to 6 per cent of the national income—contrasted with three or four times as much in countries such as the United States, Canada, and Japan and five or perhaps even six times as much in Russia.

Where countries actively seek development, there is little doubt that this percentage can be raised. But the difficulties are real. In India, for example, half way through the Second Five-Year Plan the rate of monetary saving is estimated to have reached 7 per cent, with perhaps another 1.5 per cent of nonmonetary investment, predominantly in rural improvements. Perhaps 3 per cent of the 7 is the result of government development outlays and 1 per cent is provided by retained corporate earnings. But the level of living is so low that even India's somewhat socialistically inclined government feels itself unable to raise by taxation for all government purposes more than 10 per cent of the national income; and of the roughly 90 per cent of income left at the disposal of individuals, only in the order of 3 per cent is saved. Moreover, the present Indian regime is committed both to an expansion of consumption as development progresses and also to a reduction of income inequality, so that only to a limited extent can the provision of saving by upper-income groups play the role it has in the development of other areas.

Under these circumstances can the rate of saving be increased? Almost certainly it can. Indian plans call for a steady rise to 12 per cent or more a couple of decades hence. But planning, in the nature of the case, tends to be circular: a planned increase in saving gives rise to a planned increase in income which makes the planned increase in saving possible! It is hard to go beyond this. There has been considerable interest in recent years in capital-output ratios—especially the marginal ratio relating the increase in capital to the increase in output. We have noted already that the ratio has been in the order of 3 to 1 in the case of developed countries such as the United States, and it does not appear to have been much different thus far in the case of the Soviet Union. An over-all ratio of this sort should be used with care. If the emphasis of this volume on the importance of technology is correct, then the stability of the ratio reflects, more than anything else, the stability of the rate of technological improvement. Obviously changes in the rate of improvement will affect the ratio, as technological improvements may make an expansion of output possible without any expansion whatsoever in capital. For what they are worth, studies in the Indian case, looking particularly to the character of necessary capital investment, have come to the conclusion that the ratio may be somewhat lower than usual—perhaps 2½ to 1. On this basis the present level of monetary saving would be related to a roughly 3 per cent increase in income, while total saving might relate to perhaps a 3.5 per cent increase.

Innovation and the general social environment

In developed countries we took for granted the fact that there would be innovators and concentrated on such things as the effectiveness of competition and the extent of social mobility—to name but two among many. In underdeveloped countries, the question of who is to innovate is vital. In many such countries there have been only two important social groups —peasants who worked the land and aristocrats who derived their income from land ownership and whose function, if any, was to govern. Those in between—entrepreneurs in our terminology—were looked down on as either middlemen or money lenders performing no useful function. Add to this the fact that the democratic leaders of such countries frequently have advanced concepts of welfare, derived from their education in developed countries, which make unacceptable large rewards like those received by entrepreneurs during our own period of development, and the difficulties involved in relying on private enterprise should be clear.

On the other hand, able government administrators in underdeveloped countries are a scarce commodity. It is a major virtue of free enterprise that it recruits for positions of economic importance people of ability whose talents might otherwise be wasted because of their inability to pass the civil service examinations likely to be required of government administrators. We have seen that it took Russia an all-out educational effort for a decade to replace people of ability who were killed or who migrated during the Russian Revolution, and that during that decade reliance was placed on free enterprise under the New Economic Policy. Particularly for countries which have just become self-governing, a shortage of trained administrators is likely to severely limit the effectiveness of the government as an innovator.

It may well be that the compromise between the two alternatives is likely, from the development point of view at least, to be worse than a forthright adoption of either. At the very least it is inevitable that government will concern itself with the course of development and that its concern will have repercussions on private innovation. In the case of India, for example, the government has both reserved for itself the development of certain areas such as railroads, iron and steel production, and the mining of coal, iron ore, and copper, and also established a second category—including nonferrous metals, machine tools, essential drugs, commercial fertilizers, synthetic rubber, and road and sea transportation—which is to be "progressively state-owned" in that expansion is to be permitted only in the government sector. Looking at incentives, a ceiling on individual incomes in India has been officially proposed; the emphasis is certainly quite different from the Russian willingness to use material rewards lavishly to achieve its ends. Most important of all, the production of a considerable variety of consumer goods by village industries is to be encouraged by restraints on large-scale production, which include differential excise taxes, direct prohibition of the production of certain items, and prevention of the further expansion of the capacity of large-scale firms. The extent to which arrangements of this sort reduce the incentive for innovation by private firms seems obvious; yet India continues to rely heavily on private enterprise over a wide area of the economy.

Prospective increases in total production

The emphasis of the discussion just concluded may be unduly pessimistic; it may be that the difficulties will not be as severe as they appear. But effective technological adaptation and development, significant saving, and conditions favorable for innovation are essential if development is to take place and will not be easy to achieve in underdeveloped areas. The low level of living makes it hard to take resources from consumption for either research or saving, and the conflict between an approach relying primarily on government and one relying primarily on free enterprise, by promoting uncertainty as to which course will be followed, adds to the difficulty. Certainly *rapid* increases in production are not likely.

Can we say more than this? Recently total Indian income has been increasing at perhaps 3.5 per cent each year, and the study by Coale and Hoover concludes that a rate in this vicinity—faster than the increase in food production—can probably be maintained. The rate of increase called for by the various Five-Year Plans is in the order of 4.5 per cent annually. But India has so far benefited from two temporary advantages: a rapid expansion of agricultural production as a result of unusually favorable rainfall and a rapid expansion of industrial production as a result of the considerable excess industrial capacity that existed at the start of the planning period, so that maintenance of the recent 3.5 per cent rate of increase is by no means assured. For perspective let us recall that, since the Civil War, total American production has increased at a 3.5 per cent annual rate. True we have seen that the Russian rate has run as high as 6 per cent or more and that it is possible that Russia may be able to maintain a rate this high in the future. But it should be obvious from our discussion of the factors responsible for Russian development that similar rates elsewhere are unlikely. Over-all it seems fair to conclude that maintenance by a country such as India of a rate of increase in over-all production in the range of 3 to 4 per cent for any extended period will be a considerable achievement. In fact, a recent United Nations Report, which was perhaps unduly pessimistic, was unwilling to estimate the possible rate of increase for underdeveloped areas as a whole at higher than 2.5 per cent.[3]

The role of foreign aid

Thus far we have considered development predominantly as if it were a domestic problem. Does the possibility of foreign aid alter the picture? The basic answer is that it could but is unlikely to do so at levels of aid which appear politically probable. Foreign aid can take many forms, but two are perhaps most important: technical assistance and capital contributions. Technical aid can be made available at small cost to ourselves and with highly productive consequences for the countries receiving help. We have discussed in some detail, however, the difficulties that are involved in adapting the technology of developed countries to the needs of underdeveloped areas; technical assistance should not be expected to work miracles.

As a contribution to crucial initial increases in investment, foreign

[3] *Measures for the Economic Development of Underdeveloped Countries* (New York: United Nations, 1957).

capital contributions can be of real significance. But the sums required for rapid development of underdeveloped areas as a whole are very large indeed. The United Nations Report just mentioned estimated that, of the 2.5 per cent annual increase in production believed to be possible, only 1 per cent is likely to come from unaided domestic development efforts. This may well underestimate what is possible locally, as the Report was interested in making the strongest possible case for foreign aid. But to bring about the remaining 1.5 per cent increase in production, the report estimated that underdeveloped areas as a whole would have to receive more than $10 billions of foreign funds each year. Even if we accepted only half the estimate of the report, it would still be perhaps four times more than is currently being received by underdeveloped countries from all foreign sources. In fact, it has been estimated that to raise the Indian rate of investment alone to the present Japanese level would require almost $2 billions of foreign aid annually—close to twice the amount currently available to *all* underdeveloped countries.

In short, as "seed corn" the role of foreign aid is of real importance. But if a major contribution is to be made by foreign aid, a vastly larger expansion of such aid than now appears probable will be necessary.

CHAPTER SEVENTEEN

PROSPECTS FOR
UNDERDEVELOPED AREAS

Prospects without preventive checks

As is by now obvious, in my judgment the prospects for the development of underdeveloped areas depend to a major extent on the prospects for population limitation. So far the attempt has been made—perhaps not wholly successfully—to discuss the issues involved reasonably objectively. The present chapter represents, to a considerably greater extent, the statement of a point of view. It is, therefore, only fair to stress that the entire emphasis of this presentation on population problems is unusual. Most literature on underdeveloped areas has concentrated on discussing what is needed to increase production. Even then the emphasis has been on saving and capital formation, with resources and technology receiving relatively little attention.

Because of this unusual emphasis on population, it is important that the case should not be overstated. *Limited progress* may well be possible *in the near future* with *no greater population limitation than in the recent past.* M. K. Bennett, for example, an authority on food production, has concluded: "If, now, I am obliged to face the question: *can* the world's population possibly grow between 1950 and 2000 at its rate of growth from 1900 to 1950, implying an addition of 1,200 million people to the count, I will say it *can,* and it *can* do so with rising consumption

208

levels."[1] *It is important to stress that this may well be true.* Nothing in what has been said denies the possibility that, if we are content with a rise—any rise—in consumption levels over the next 50 years, such a rise may well be possible with no greater limitation of population than took place between 1900 and 1950. But it is important that the implications of the three qualifications with which Dr. Bennett hedged his statement should be clearly understood.

First, the rate of increase is specified as that which took place between 1900 and 1950. But during this period, as a result of the operation of the positive checks, the rate of increase—less than 1 per cent for the world as a whole—was not only less than that which presently prevails but much less than is likely under modern development programs unaccompanied by the use of preventive checks. Specifically, recall that during most of the period of her development the Japanese death rate was 20 or more per thousand, but Ceylon is undertaking development with a death rate of 11 per thousand. It is for this reason that the over-all behavior of the world's population has not been presented; for past increases are far slower than are likely in the future. Take the case of India: from 1891 to 1921 the annual growth of population averaged ⅙ of 1 per cent; from 1921 to 1951 it averaged 1 per cent; it is now running at 1.5 per cent; and the Coale-Hoover study estimates that, with present fertility, it will soon reach 2.5 per cent even if the death rate (at present perhaps 25 per thousand) does not fall below 15 per thousand—one third *higher* than the *present* rate in Ceylon! In short, successful development efforts can be expected to bring about rates of population increase which approach 3 per cent in the absence of preventive checks. But at a 3 per cent rate the total increase in population by 2000 would be vastly larger than the figure Dr. Bennett mentions.

Second, the amount of the rise in consumption levels is unspecified by Dr. Bennett. A question to which developed countries need to give serious consideration is how long "just any rise" in consumption in underdeveloped areas will remain an acceptable objective to such areas. This is a matter to which we will return shortly.

Finally, Dr. Bennett confines himself to the next 50 years. After what already has been said it is necessary only to mention that the need for population limitation becomes increasingly urgent the longer the time period with which we are concerned.

[1] M. K. Bennett, *The World's Food—a Study of the Interrelations of World Populations, National Diets, and Food Potentials* (New York: Harper, 1954).

The immediate case for preventive checks

Let us illustrate the immediate case for preventive checks by reference to India. We have, in the case of India, the unique study by Coale and Hoover estimating the differences in average income which are likely to result, *with the development effort in each case otherwise unchanged,* if present fertility continues or if it is cut in half by 1986. Their conclusion is that, with unchanged fertility, income by 1986 may have increased by 38 per cent to perhaps $85 per person, but if fertility is cut in half, the rise may be 95 per cent to almost $120. Thus their study confirms Dr. Bennett at least until 1986: *some* improvement of living levels is clearly possible with unchanged fertility. But it equally confirms the emphasis of this volume: a *significant* improvement of living levels is possible only with reduced fertility, which of course can only be achieved through the use of preventive checks.

What lies back of these differences is fundamentally very simple. Recall the estimate that the *direct* cost of making birth control devices available on a scale sufficient to halt population increase in a country such as India may be as little as a half of 1 per cent of Indian income. This does not include the cost of introducing such devices, but this may, in some cases at least, add relatively little to the expense of introducing the health measures which are likely to be a part of any development program. In contrast, assuming a capital-output ratio of only 2½ to 1, to provide for even a 1.5 per cent increase in population would require net capital formation equal to over 4 per cent of income; while, if the population increase were 2.5 per cent, net capital formation would have to be over 6 per cent. Nor is this all. So long as any rate of population growth is based on birth and death rates which are higher than necessary, there is the further waste of the resources used to support children who die unnecessarily before reaching the age at which they became economically useful—a waste which may amount to perhaps 3 per cent of income in a country such as India. In short, the basic immediate issue is simply whether the very limited capital formation of underdeveloped areas should be used predominantly to increase numbers or to raise the living level of the present population.

The narrow margin on which the whole fabric of Indian development rests so long as fertility is unchanged is worth stressing. True the best present guess is that income may be increasing at 3.5 per cent, while population is not immediately likely to increase at more than 2.5 per cent. But a decline in the growth of income to 3 per cent and a rise in the rate of population growth to 3 per cent—which is the rate that would result with present fertility and a death rate equal to that of Ceylon—

would be *enough to bring the rise in average living levels to a halt*. It seems obvious that population limitation is essential if there is to be any *certainty* of development.

Finally, population limitation is going to become *increasingly difficult in the future*. As development and health measures bring about a decline in death rates, without limitation population growth will speed up. But this in turn will bring an increase in the percentage of women of child-bearing age, which will make future limitation increasingly difficult. We may illustrate what is involved by pointing out that, given the present estimated death rate, the Indian population would be static with the birth rate prevailing in the United States. But if the death rate falls from the present level of perhaps 25 to 15 per thousand, stability will require a birth rate which is 60 per cent of our level; and if the present Japanese death rate and age distribution were to emerge, immediate population stability would require a birth rate which is less than *a third* of our level!

Another way of putting this point is to state it in terms of death rates. We noted earlier that a death rate of 13 or 14 per thousand is consistent with our present life expectancy of seventy or so years. Hence, to achieve population stability, birth rates must ultimately fall to 13 or 14 per thousand. Where birth and death rates are now *higher* than this, stability could be achieved with birth and death rates at the level of 13 or 14 per thousand. But where death rates are now *lower*—as they are in most developed countries—*immediate* stability would require birth rates even lower than 13 to 14 per thousand. Realistically this means that for Japan and developed countries generally, immediate population stabilization requires such low birth rates as to be in effect impossible. Underdeveloped countries are not yet generally in this situation. But they will be if they do not undertake population limitation before health measures and development cause death rates to fall below 13 or 14 per thousand.

The ultimate case for preventive checks

Thus far we have concentrated on immediate issues. But while the immediate case for the use of preventive checks is a strong one, the ultimate case is far stronger. Admittedly it involves concerning ourselves with the shape of a world which we shall not live to see; but it is a shape which will be *immensely influenced by the decisions which we make*. To illustrate the matter, let us set forth in extreme form the alternatives which India faces in the longer-range future. In the last chapter we estimated that eventually India might well be able to grow 4½ times as much food as she now produces. Hence one alternative open to India is to utilize this potential increase to support 4½ times her present population at the living levels which now prevail. Population would then number over 1½ billions and population density would be more than twice that of Japan at the present time. As food production may well be capable of increasing at a rate close to 3 per cent a year, under this alternative population could expand at its 1.5 per cent present rate until perhaps 2050 or even at a 3 per cent rate until the end of this century.

But suppose, on the other hand, we examine the sort of expansion in food consumption per person that might be possible if there were no further increase whatsoever in Indian population. Under such circumstances would it be possible to provide the present Indian population with a diet not necessarily the same as that currently available to Americans but of *equal complexity and variety?* The average American consumes over four pounds of food (or drink) each day, containing perhaps 3,100 calories, while the average Indian consumes perhaps one pound with perhaps 1,700 calories.[2] To provide this quantity of food there is under cultivation in the United States 100,000 square feet of land per person, with an additional 215,000 square feet in farms but not under cultivation.[3] In contrast, the total land area works out at 100,000 square feet per head in India, with about 40,000 square feet under cultivation. The part of American farms not under cultivation is, of course, of major importance in providing the dairy products, meat, and poultry which are so important in our diet; but if India were to produce these products, it would have to be done, not by using land for grazing, but by cultivating it so as to raise feed. To strike a rough equivalence, let us assume that the 215,000 square feet of uncultivated land incorporated in American farms is the equivalent of 80,000 square feet of cultivated land, which would mean that America cultivates the equivalent of 180,000 square feet per person to obtain our present diet. But if our previous assumptions about India are correct—that she will be able to expand her cultivated area by 50 per cent to 60,000 square feet per person and raise her yields three-fold to roughly the Japanese level—then it also follows that India will ultimately be able to provide her present population with a diet as complex and varied as that of the average American.

Thus, as we look to the relatively distant future, India may use her development potential to achieve one of two extreme alternatives: a vast mass of humanity living at, or close to, the subsistence level, or her present population achieving some approach to the living levels of the West. Clearly, if the latter objective is sought, population growth cannot

[2] In these comparisons no allowance has been made for (1) differences in the average weight of Indians and Americans; (2) differences in climate; or (3) the rather remote possibility that India could become a permanent net importer of foodstuffs.

[3] No adjustment has been made for land used to grow exported agricultural products, as in recent years agricultural imports for consumption have somewhat exceeded total agricultural exports.

continue for long. To achieve a diet comparable to ours, during every 50-year period in the future that population continues to increase at the present rate, India will have to achieve a further doubling of her agricultural yields—to 6 times ours by 2000, 12 times by 2050, and 24 times by 2100. And if population growth were to rise to 3 per cent, the increase in yields would have to be achieved twice as fast.

Further, if we look to total production rather than food alone, it still seems likely that immediate population limitation will be needed if average living levels are either to be maximized or to approach Western levels. Conclusions on this score must remain tentative until we know more than we now do regarding optimum population. It is true that the benefits of mass production—or "increasing returns" in the technical sense —are most likely outside agriculture. But, since mass production has been achieved in America with a population less than half that of India, it is hard to resist the conclusion that the present Indian population is as large as, if not larger than, that which will maximize average living levels even in the relatively distant future. Obviously this judgment may be wrong if only because the future is inevitably uncertain. But to the extent that it is correct, it means that any further increase in population will reduce more or less permanently the living level that India can hope to achieve.

Hence, from both the immediate and the longer-run points of view, the case for immediate use of preventive checks seems, to me at least, clear-cut. It has, in fact, been necessary to argue this matter so carefully only because we approach it from a Western point of view. Mr. Nehru, head of the Indian government, was prepared to put the matter much more simply when he said: "We should be a far more advanced nation if our population were about half what it is."

Preventive checks and Chinese Communism

A primary reason why we as a nation are interested in development is to make sure that the underdeveloped areas not now under Communist control remain a part of the free world. There is no doubt that it is the prospect of rapid development that gives Communism its appeal for underdeveloped areas: to follow in Russia's footsteps and "achieve in a generation what it took capitalism a century to accomplish" is an enticing prospect. In determining which alternative is taken by underdeveloped areas as a whole, nothing is likely to have greater influence than the relative success of the development programs of India and China. Let us, therefore, briefly examine this rivalry.

From our discussion of the Soviet Union we know that countries under Communist domination, in general, are likely to be relatively willing to sacrifice the immediate welfare of their people in order to accomplish ultimate objectives. Clearly Russia continues to devote a percentage of her income to research, capital formation, and military preparations that would be difficult to defend politically in a democracy. Chinese plans indicate that a similar effort will be made to achieve a high rate of capital formation with emphasis on those industries essential for military strength. Mere attainment of a high savings rate of course does not assure development; if the savings are badly used, no more may be achieved than is possible with a lower rate and proper use. But there seems little reason to count on misallocation of savings in China. Hence, the higher probable rate of saving, together with the willingness to suppress ruthlessly opposition to the changes which are an inevitable part of development, means that China has certain important advantages. On the other hand, China's population density is now twice India's, so that long-range improvement in agriculture will undoubtedly be more difficult to achieve in China than in India. On balance, although it is possible that Indian income will grow faster than China's, it appears rather more likely that the higher probable rate of saving in China will not be offset by other factors. In any event the *differences on the production side will almost certainly be small.*[4]

To the extent that this is correct it follows that significant differences in the behavior of living levels are likely only if there are significant differences in the rate of population growth. What are the prospects in this regard? Until recently China followed Russia's lead in arguing that population problems were impossible under Communism. But since 1955 there has been a sharp reversal of policy, so that birth control is today both legal and actively encouraged, and attempts are also being made to raise the age of marriage. It is too soon to judge how effective these efforts to limit population growth will be; but if the full force of the Communist organization were put behind birth control, birth rates might well decline significantly.[5]

In India, although there is widespread recognition of the problems caused by excessive population and sums have been appropriated by the government to encourage birth control, the first method tried, involving continence during fertile periods, turned out to be substantially ineffective. Currently experiments are being conducted with alternative devices and the results are said to be encouraging, but the matter remains on an

[4] This conclusion was reached before China's recent widespread establishment of communes. The extent to which this drastic and costly effort will speed up the increase in production cannot yet be determined.

[5] During 1958 evidence of a considerable reduction in Chinese enthusiasm for birth control accumulated, leaving Chinese population prospects quite uncertain. This *uncertainty* does not alter the *importance* of population limitation in deciding the rivalry between China and India.

experimental basis and no real effort has yet been made to reach the mass of the people. As a result, demographers do not believe that there has been any noticeable decline in actual birth rates, though the reported rate, which suffers from serious underreporting, does show a decrease.

To summarize: we have suggested that the decision as to whether living levels first rise significantly in China or in India is likely to depend more on the behavior of population than on the behavior of production. To the extent that this is correct, it follows that the country which first introduces preventive checks on a substantial scale is the one which will win the present contest—and thereby influence to a major extent the future development of underdeveloped areas.

Our concern with underdeveloped areas

Why should we concern ourselves with underdeveloped areas? Is there any reason why we should not continue to enjoy our unprecedented affluence without worrying about the rest of the world? Obviously a full answer to these questions transcends economics. We have already given an important reason for concerning ourselves with development: to preserve the free world as we now know it. But there are economic reasons for being concerned with development that are worth pointing out. With 7 or 8 per cent of the world's population, we today account for perhaps half the world's consumption of scarce materials, and the Report of the President's Materials Policy Commission in 1952 made it clear that in the future we will become increasingly dependent on the rest of the world to provide us with the materials that we will need.

From a longer-range point of view, it is worth keeping in mind that developed areas are progressing appreciably more rapidly than underdeveloped areas, so that the differences in living levels between developed and underdeveloped areas are increasing and will almost certainly continue to increase. Just how long are increasing differences in living levels likely to remain acceptable to areas on which the developed world will increasingly depend for its raw materials? If the United States could not exist half free and half slave, can the world as a whole continue indefinitely half developed and half underdeveloped?

Our role in economic development

How can the United States best contribute to the economic development of underdeveloped areas? One obvious—and obviously controversial—contribution would be for the United States to incur the research costs of finding and developing simpler and more effective contraceptives. The sums now being spent on contraceptive research are trivial; a tiny part of what has been spent to develop the atomic bomb would in all probability achieve vastly improved techniques in the relatively near future. To the extent that our emphasis on the preventive checks is justified, it is obvious that there is no more important—or more economically effective—contribution that we can make.

Looking beyond the immediate future perhaps what is most required is an understanding of the magnitude of the problem in order that the measures we undertake are related to what is required. There is reason to hope that, once reasonable restraint on population increase has been achieved, our increasing scientific knowledge will enable us to offset the heavy drain on our wasting resources that world-wide development entails. Then we could look forward to a wide and steady rise in general living levels—which we now take for granted but which actually has thus far been realized in only a small part of the world. It would be a serious mistake, however, to underestimate the difficulties that will have to be overcome.

It is also an equally serious mistake not to recognize the uniqueness of the opportunity that we now have, which may never be offered us again. The decision as to whether the world is to be populated by many billions living at or close to the subsistence level or by far fewer living at appreciably higher and rising levels is going to be made, consciously or otherwise, in the next century. At the very least, failure to achieve significant increases in living levels in underdeveloped countries may well result in the loss of our struggle with Communism, whose appeal is great in such areas precisely because it promises to do something effective about living levels. But even if we avoid this danger, the sheer magnitude of the effort required to raise living levels in underdeveloped areas may make the job next to impossible if world population reaches tens of billions before expansion is effectively restricted. Yet it is by no means certain that the world can exist indefinitely half developed and half underdeveloped; it may well be that achievement of world-wide economic development is essential if Western civilization as we know it is to survive.

INDEX

INDEX

Abortion, 182
Abramovitz, Moses, 51, 74n., 103, 163n.
Advertising, 4, 30
Affluence, economic development and, 8-10
Agriculture, 5
    research in, 52, 65-66, 69-70
    in Soviet Union, 163-164
    in underdeveloped areas, 197-201
Agriculture Department, United States, 52, 69, 89
Algae, production of, 197-198
Allocation, resource, 2
Allowances, capital consumption, 20
    depreciation, 20, 98
Ames, Edward, 144n.
Atomic Energy Commission, 59
Automobile industry, innovation in the, 83-87

Bennett, M. K., 32, 208-210
Birth control, 182-183, 210, 214
Birth rates, economic development and, 194-195
    high, wastefulness of, 196
Bituminous Coal Act (1937), 87
Bituminous coal industry, research and, 66-67
Brown, Harrison, 185, 198, 199

Capital, defined, 1n.
    economic development and, 103

Capital—*Continued*
  foreign, 206-207
  formation, 98
    saving and, 98-99
    in Soviet Union, 172-173
  government, 24
  shortage, economic development and, 203-204
    in Soviet Union, 162-165, 172-173
Capital consumption allowances, 20
Cartels, 95
Chapman, Janet G., 160*n.*
Chlorella, 197-198
Clark, Colin, 46*n.*, 157*n.*
Coal industry, bituminous, research and, 66-67
Coal Mines Act (Great Britain, 1930), 87
Coale, Ansley J., 191*n.*, 192, 194, 200, 210
Commerce Department, United States, 19, 20, 22-23, 24, 39
Communism, 10
  Chinese, preventive checks on population and, 213-215
  consumption under, 149-150
  dictatorship and, 138-139
  economic development under, 137-174
  economizing under, 146-147
  innovation under, 170-172
  investment under, 147-149
  saving under, 147-149
  socialism vs., 137-138
  See also Soviet Union
Competition, innovation and, 88-92, 97
  research and, 64-65, 79-80
Consumption, under communism, 149-150
Cooper, Hugh, 173-174
Cotton industry, research and, 65-66
Council of Economic Advisers, 77

Death rates, economic development and, 192-194
  high, wastefulness of, 196
Defense Department, United States, 59
Depreciation allowances, 20, 98
Deterioration, of capital equipment, 19-20
Developed countries, compared with underdeveloped countries, 28-30
  economic development in (*see* Economic development, in developed areas)
Development, defined, 15
  See also Economic development
Dictatorship, communism and, 138-139
Diminishing returns, principle of, and optimum population, 188-189

Distribution, 2-3, 4, 5
   adapting, to the changing character of American life, 92
"Do-it-yourself" movement, 23

Economic development, affluence and, 8-10
   birth rates and, 194-195
   British achievements in, 42-44
   capital and, 103
   capital shortage and, 203-204
   communism and, 137-174
   death rates and, 192-194
   in developed areas, 35-134
   factors influencing, 46-47, 49-134
      innovation, 82-97
      natural resources, 111-123
      research, 49-81
      saving, 98-110
   foreign aid and, 206-207
   importance of, 6-8
   income measures of (United States), 39-41
   labor unions and, 126-128
   materialism and, 125-126
   meaning of, 15-16
   measuring, 16
   population growth and, 195-196
   relationship between usual subject matter of economics and, 3-4
   social mobility and, 128-131
   socialism and, 128-133
   Soviet Union achievements in, 139-174
   in underdeveloped areas, 177-216
      United States role in, 215-216
   United States achievements in, 35-41
   in world perspective, 10
Economic performance, possible improvements in, 4-6
   vs. economic understanding, 4
Economic rent (*see* Rent, economic)
Economic understanding, economic performance vs., 4
Economics, subject matter of, 1-3
   relationship between economic development and, 3-4
   value judgments in, 10-12
Economizing, 2, 5
   under communism, 146-147
Effort, involved in work, 15, 16-18
England (*see* Great Britain)
Exchange, 47, 48
Exchange rates, 26-28

Expenditures, military, 22-23, 39
    research, 52-55, 58, 59, 60
Exports, 5

"Feather-bedding," 126
Food and Agriculture Organization, 31, 198
Food production, in underdeveloped areas, 197-201
Foreign aid, economic development and, 206-207
Foreign capital, 206-207
Franco, Francisco, 138
Free enterprise, research and, 55-57

Gaitskell, Hugh, 131
Galbraith, John Kenneth, 8n.
George, Henry, 112, 118
Gilbert, Milton, 27n.
GNP (see Gross national product)
Government, capital, 24
    contribution to research, 52, 58, 59, 60, 76-77, 80-81
    cost of, 20, 21, 22-23
    rate of saving and the, 107-109
Great Britain, economic development in, 42-44
    industrial development retarded in, 94
Gross national product, 5, 6, 20, 21, 23, 27, 28
    obtaining the, 19

Hansen, W. Lee, 196n.
Harberger, Arnold C., 73n.
Harbison, Frederick, 130n.
Hitler, Adolf, 139, 143, 144, 145, 174
Holzman, F. D., 147n.
Hoover, Edgar M., 191n., 192, 194, 200, 210
Hours of work, 45-46, 46n.
    in Great Britain, 44
    in United States, 38
Housing, in Soviet Union, 165

Income, equality of, 22
    national (see National income)
    personal, 24n.
Income accounts, usefulness of the system of, 24
"Index number problem," 27, 51

India, effect of population growth on income in, 189-192
    production in, possible increase in, 199-200
Industrialization, impact of, on estimates, 23-24
Industry, contribution to research, 52-54, 58, 59, 61-76
    innovation in (*see* Innovation)
    nationalization of, 95
    small-scale, research and, 65-67
Infanticide, 182
Innovation, 50, 82-97
    in the auto industry, 83-87
    cartels and, 95
    communism and, 170-172
    competition and, 88-92, 97
    conditions favoring, 82-83
    defined, 49, 84
    importance of, 50-52
    labor unions and, 126
    meaning of, 83-84
    nationalized industry and, 95
    oligopolies and, 93
    by public utilities, 96-97
    rapid, example of, 83-87
    slow, example of, 87-88
    in underdeveloped areas, 204-205
Institutes, productivity (*see* Productivity institutes)
Inventions, 49, 63
Investment, 98-110
    under communism, 147-149
    See also Saving

Jeffreys, James B., 43
Johnson, B. F., 200*n.*

Kaser, M. C., 156, 157*n.*
Keynes, John Maynard, 46, 102
Khrushchev, Nikita, 160, 169, 174
Klein, Burton, 60*n.*, 64*n.*
Kravis, Irving B., 27*n.*
Kuznets, Simon, 37, 40, 45, 101, 104, 105*n.*, 106

Labor force, expansion (United States), 38
    in the Soviet Union, 154-156
Labor unions, economic development and, 126-128
    innovation and, 126

Land, defined, 111
Langmuir, Irving, 57
Lend-Lease, 144
Lenin, Nikolai, 140, 141
Levels of living (*see* Living, levels of)
Lewis, John L., 127
Liu, Ta Chung, 30*n*.
Living, levels of, 18
    comparisons between developed and underdeveloped countries, 28-30
    comparisons in physical terms, 30-32
    differences in, 25-32
    measurement of, 15-24
    population and, 187-196
    range of, probable, 32
    transportation costs and, 118-119
  standard of, 18
Lysenko, Trofim, 167

Macroeconomics, 3
  defined, 3
  waste in area of, 5-6
"Make-work," 126
Malthus, Thomas R., 177-180, 188
Market prices, 2, 21
Marshal, Robert E., 170*n*.
Marx, Karl, 102, 140
Materialism, economic development and, 125-126
Microeconomics, 3
  defined, 3
  possible improvements in area of, 5, 8
Mikoyan, A. I., 150*n*.
Military expenditures, 22-23, 39
Monopolies, 4, 53
  defined, 53*n*.
Morgan, Theodore, 194*n*.

National income, 20, 21, 24
  differences in, 25, 26
    significance of estimates, 26-28
  level of, 3
  population growth and, 189-192
  in the Soviet Union, 156-157
National product (*see* Gross national product; Net national product)
National Science Foundation, 53*n*., 54, 54*n*., 58, 58*n*., 60, 77, 169
Nationalization, of industry, 95

Natural resources, 111-123
  inferior, 119-122
  paying for, 119-120
  process of development and, 122-123
  in Soviet Union, 173
  superior, 119-120, 122
  types of, 184
  use of, population size and, 184-186
Net national product, 20, 21, 23
Nutter, G. Warren, 157*n.*, 158

Oligopolies, 53
  defined, 53*n.*, 72
  innovation and, 93
  objections to, 73, 73*n.*
  research and, 72, 73-78, 80-81
Oxenfeldt, A. R., 150*n.*, 198

Patent system, practical research and the, 68
Performance, economic (*see* Economic performance)
Personal income, 24*n.*
Population, death rates and economic development, 192-194
  growth, effect on income, 189-192
  increase in, Great Britain, 42
    possible, 179-180
    United States, 28
  living levels and, 187-196
  natural resources and, 184-186
  optimum, diminishing returns and, 188-189
  preventive checks on, 208-215
    inevitability of, 182-183
  problem, immediacy of the, 180-181
Price fixing, innovation and, 87
Prices, market, 2, 21
Product, gross national (*see* Gross national product)
  net national (*see* Net national product)
Production, factors of, 21, 111
  flow of, 18-19
    measurement of, 19
  large-scale, encouragement of, 74-76
    research and, 72, 80-81
  in Soviet Union, 153-154
  in underdeveloped areas, 197-207
  value of, 22

Productivity institutes, 77-81
  basic applied research and, 78-79
  proposal for, 77-78
Profits, defined, 22
  monopoly, 4
  negative, 22
  research and, 79-80
Public utilities, innovation by, 96-97
Purchasing power, 26, 28

Quantity, as a measure of wealth, 18

Raymond, Ellsworth, 145*n.*
Redding, A. David, 154*n.*
Rent, 22
  economic, as a surplus, 114-115
    defined, 112
    importance of, quantitative, 115-118
    meaning of, 112-114
Research, in agriculture, 52, 65-66, 69-70
  background of, 52-53
  basic applied, 61-65
    competition and, 64-65
    importance of, 61-62
    rewards from, 63-64
  competition and, 79-80
  defined, 49
  environment favorable to, importance of, 81
  expenditures for, 52-55, 58, 59, 60
  free enterprise and, 55-57
  fundamental, 49-60
    need for, 57-58
    program for, 58-60
  government's contribution to, 52, 58, 59, 60, 76-77, 80-81
  importance of, 50-52
  industry's contribution to, 52-54, 58, 59, 71-76
  large-scale production and, 72, 80-81
  oligopolies and, 72, 73-76, 80-81
  practical, 61-81
    in the United States, 61
    patent system and, 68
    problems, 71-72
  present pattern of, 53-55
  productivity institutes and, 77-79
  profits and, 79-80

small-scale industry and, 65-67
  in the Soviet Union, 166-170
Resource allocation, 2
Resources (*see* Natural resources)
Ricardo, David, 112, 115
Robertson, D. H., 109n.
Russia (*see* Soviet Union)
Ruttan, Vernon W., 70n.

Sacrifice, involved in work, 15, 16-18
Saving, 105-107
  behavior of, 104-105
  capital formation and, 98-99
  under communism, 147-149
  contribution to economic development, 109-110
  defined, 98
  economic development and, 103-104
  importance of, 101-103, 104
  rate of, government and the, 107-109
  rates of, comparative, 105-107
  sources of, 99-101
  in underdeveloped countries, 203-204
  uses of, 99-101
  See also Investment
Schultz, Theodore W., 69, 89n., 116n.
Schwartz, Harry, 170n.
Securities and Exchange Commission, 89, 90
Shaw, George Bernard, 130
Sheahan, John, 96n.
Sherman Act, 87, 93
Smith, Adam, 47
Social immobility, 131-133
Social mobility, economic development and, 128-131
Socialism, communism vs., 137-138
  economic development and, 128-133
Soviet Union, 48, 137-174
  agriculture, problem of, 163-164
  capital formation in the, 172-173
  capital in the, 162-165, 172-173
  consumption, probable expansion of, 160-161
  economic development in, 139-174
  economic history of, since Communist Revolution, 139-150
  First Five-Year Plan, 142-143
  future prospects, 158-160
  housing in, 165
  labor force distribution in, 154-156

Soviet Union—*Continued*
  national income, 156-157
  natural resources, 173
  New Economic Policy, 141-142
  postwar recovery, 145-146
  production in, 153-154
  research in, 166-170
  science in, 169-170
  Second Five-Year Plan, 143-144, 146
  technology in, 161-162
  Third Five-Year Plan, 144, 146
  World War I and, 144-145
  See also Communism
Specialization, 47, 48
Stalin, Joseph, 141, 142, 143, 144, 167
Standard of living, 18

Tariffs, 5
Taxes, indirect business, 20, 21
Technical assistance, 206
Technology, changes in, defined, 49
  in Soviet Union, 161-162
  underdeveloped areas and, 201-203
"Transfer payments," 24n.
Transportation costs, living levels and, 118-119
Trotsky, Leon, 141

Underdeveloped countries, comparisons with developed countries, 28-30
  economic development of, 177-216
    United States role in, 215-216
  innovation in, 204-205
  preventive checks on population in, 208-215
  production in, 197-207
    food, 197-201
  prospects for, 208-216
  saving in, 203-204
  technology and, 201-203
  United States concern with, 215
Understanding, economic (*see* Economic understanding)
Unemployment, 39
Unions (*see* Labor unions)
United Nations, 25, 26, 28, 29, 30, 32, 206, 207
United States, Agriculture Department, 52, 69, 89
  Commerce Department, 19, 20, 22-23, 24, 39
  Defense Department, 59

economic development in, 35-41
    margin of error in estimates of, 36, 38
hours of work in, 38
labor force, 38
population increase, 38
Utilities (*see* Public utilities)

Value judgments, role of, in economics, 10-12

Walters, Dorothy, 43
Wealth, quantity as a measure of, 18
    stock of, 18
Wilson, Charles, 57
Women, in the labor force, 38